In the series *Politics, History, and Social Change*,
edited by JOHN C. TORPEY

ALSO IN THIS SERIES:

NICHOLAS TOLOUDIS

TEACHING MARIANNE AND UNCLE SAM

✳ ✳ ✳

*Public Education, State Centralization,
and Teacher Unionism in France and the United States*

 TEMPLE UNIVERSITY PRESS
Philadelphia

TEMPLE UNIVERSITY PRESS
Philadelphia, Pennsylvania 19122
www.temple.edu/tempress

Copyright © 2012 by Temple University
All rights reserved
Published 2012

Portions of Chapters 2 and 3 were originally published in Nicholas Toloudis, "*Instituteur*
Identities: Explaining the Nineteenth Century French Teachers' Movement," *Social
Movement Studies* 7, no. 1 (May 2008): 61–76, and Nicholas Toloudis, "Pedagogical
Conferences and Stillborn Professionalism among 19th Century *Instituteurs*, 1830–1848,"
Paedagogica Historica 46, no. 5 (October 2010): 585–599.

Library of Congress Cataloging-in-Publication Data

Toloudis, Nicholas, 1977–
    Teaching Marianne and Uncle Sam : public education, state centralization, and teacher
unionism in France and the United States / Nicholas Toloudis.
        pages cm. — (Politics, history, and social change)
    Includes bibliographical references and index.
    ISBN 978-1-4399-0906-5 (cloth : alk. paper) — ISBN 978-1-4399-0908-9 (e-book)
1. Teachers' unions—France—History.   2. Teachers' unions—New York (State)—New
York—History.   3. Education and state—France—History.   4. Education and state—
New York (State)—New York—History.   I. Title.
    LB2844.53.F8T65 2012
    331.88′113711—dc23

                                                                                2012003236

♾ The paper used in this publication meets the requirements of the American National
Standard for Information Sciences—Permanence of Paper for Printed Library Materials,
ANSI Z39.48-1992

Printed in the United States of America

2 4 6 8 9 7 5 3 1

To Mark Kesselman, my own greatest teacher

To Chuck Tilly, no longer my reader, still my audience

*And to all teachers, past and present, who have sought—both
in the classroom and out of it—to nurture the values and practices
in their students that are so vital to our collective existence:
community, justice, and art*

Much of the underlying comparative institutional history of education remains to be written.

—PETER LINDERT, *Growing Public: Social Spending and Economic Growth since the Eighteenth Century*

CONTENTS

PREFACE

The cover of this book depicts two iconic images, one representing France and the other representing the United States. The smiling Marianne sits with one hand on her spear, the other hand leaning against her shield. The eagle's wings are spread, and it peers at Marianne with interest and perhaps a touch of ferocity. So it has been for France and the United States for two hundred years, and so it is today. The French and American dispositions on all things political continue to generate reciprocal intensity, curiosity, and, at times, animosity. The eighteenth-century revolutions for which these two countries are so widely known have yielded such different polities and economies that their distinct methods of administering public services might seem a foregone conclusion.

The separate historical trajectories that these two countries have followed with regard to public education, state centralization, and teacher unionism are, in a sense, no surprise. When it comes to education politics and what the role of organized teachers is and ought to be, we might well speak of the Chinese curse "May you live in interesting times" as going hand in hand with the ruler's answer to the question about whether the French Revolution was a good thing: "It's too soon to tell." The jury is out on precisely how "interesting" the current age is with respect to such matters as collective bargaining in education and the appropriate role for the central government in schooling the masses. Uncle Sam, in particular, has spent the past quarter century embroiled in soul searching and, increasingly, in public politicking about the role of organized teachers in education politics. Events in Wisconsin, Rhode Island, and Washington, D.C., over the past few years seem to suggest that it is precisely the eagerness to come to a political decision on this point that makes our time so interesting.

But for the entrenched power of teachers' unions, education reform would be a relative cakewalk, and a viable path forward for educating our children in an accountable, efficient, cost-effective manner would materialize. Or so the story goes. But while the U.S. government is more heavily involved in public education today than at any other time in our nation's history, its involvement pales in comparison with the highly centralized interventionism of France. Marianne's hand in the realm of public education has been firmer for longer, for reasons that this book explores in some depth. But the political conflicts that spurred the drive to centralize public education in France have been replaced by others, concerns over the threat posed by an overly powerful Catholic Church having long since evaporated. The dilemmas of an education system that is too highly centralized, meanwhile, have been part of public understandings of public schooling in France since the tumultuous protests of 1968. The iconic images displayed on the cover of this book represent different aspects of national archetypes that bear on our understanding of these countries' educational systems, past and present.

Just as these representations convey different meanings, so, too, does the title *Teaching Marianne and Uncle Sam*. From one standpoint, this is a book about how, over a period of a hundred years or so, two different states have changed the ways they have projected power in a very particular setting: the public school classroom. Marianne and Uncle Sam, in this respect, represent states that have taken very different approaches to regulating public education and, in particular, the men and women who work as teachers. In France, the Revolution of 1789 initiated a long-term conflict over the role of the Catholic Church in primary schooling, a role that had previously gone unchallenged. The elementary schools became a battleground for the conflict over the role the Catholic Church should play in French society. The culmination of this battle in the opening decade of the twentieth century yielded the version of secularism that the French call *laïcité*. The politics and implementation of secular primary schooling generated their own sources of conflict, independent of but powerfully shaped by the conflict over secularism—that is, the question of the appropriate political role for organized teachers in the republic. In the United States, meanwhile, public education became a political concern as a result of a set of social demands and political circumstances quite different from those in France. Rural school consolidation and urban school reform occurred at different paces, in response to different sorts of pressures, and as a consequence of a different kind of politics. But the effect on teachers was quite similar—their political power was reduced. And their response to the reduction in influence in the classroom was collective (although, as later chapters demonstrate, it was not unified).

From another standpoint, the title *Teaching Marianne and Uncle Sam* refers to the teachers themselves. In both countries, governments have periodically politicized teachers' corps for the purpose of inculcating loyalty and renewed commitment to a nationalizing agenda. The word *instituteurs*, which the revolutionaries of 1789 ascribed to primary educators in France, refers to this task: they who will institute—in essence, bring into being—the nation. Although public education has never been as firmly embedded in national politics in the United States as in France, even American teachers found themselves thrust into this role. The Americanization movement described in Chapter 4 was not simply a movement to reshape immigrants according to a particular notion of what it meant to be an American. It was also an effort to reshape public school teachers' corps from the top down. In this sense, Marianne and Uncle Sam are themselves the objects of an inculcation process—agents of the state, being shaped by legitimating authorities. To paraphrase Karl Marx, the teacher himself must be taught—or herself, since the feminization of teaching, particularly in primary education, occurred coterminously with the other changes documented in this book, and that is an important part of the story.

As the debate over the role of teachers' unions in education politics roils around us, more than a decade into the twenty-first century, a look back at the late nineteenth and early twentieth centuries provides much-needed perspective. The current debate over accountability in education, in which teachers' unions find themselves under the public magnifying glass, is only the latest version of an old question: Who should have power to control the public schools? And, relatedly, how should that power be used? During the time period covered in this book, teachers have struggled to respond collectively to changes in the polities, societies, and administrative structures in which they work. They have never been silent, and—for better or for worse—there is no reason to expect them to be silent during the current round of education reform. The lesson is that, when it comes to the role of teachers in education politics, it is always too soon to tell.

ACKNOWLEDGMENTS

And so a long journey comes to an end. This project began with a dissertation idea in the fall of 2000 in a seminar hall at Columbia University. The thesis that emerged from it, though well received by my advisers and colleagues, left me with a sinking feeling about errors of omission and interpretation and lapses into long-windedness and thickheadedness. Beyond my motivations of professional advancement and genuine passion for the topic, I was determined to write this book to correct the flaws of my dissertation. Perhaps I was being overly self-critical, but soon enough the sinking feeling turned into exhilaration and enthusiasm, and back to work I went.

Some of the work that went into this book is derived from the research I did while I was still a graduate student. The fruits of my labor in the Bibliothèque Nationale in the fall of 2003 and the Archives Nationales in the spring of 2004 continue to propel my writing. I extend my thanks to everyone, in and out of the academy, who made that year in France as exciting and personally rewarding as it was educational, especially Michael Mayer, Ousmane Traore, and Rebecca Scales, as well as Christine Musselin of CEVIPOF (Centre d'Étude de la Vie Politique Française). In addition, I tip my hat to the members of the staff at the Tamiment Library of New York University—home of the Wagner Labor Archives—who have helped me on my occasional visits to that wonderful room on the tenth floor of the Bobst Library since the spring of 2005.

Between then and now, I have changed institutional affiliations four times. Rutgers University's Political Science Department, Bowdoin College's Government Department, Mount Holyoke College's Politics Department, and now Bowdoin College's Government Department once again have all been so supportive of me that I cannot believe my good fortune to have been affiliated with even one of them, much less all. To my past and current department chairs—Dennis Bathory, Jean Yarbrough, Chris Pyle, Joan Cocks, and Allen Springer—I offer my heartfelt thanks for providing a young scholar with such hospitable environments for developing his professional resume. My thanks, in addition, go to my students, who have done so much to enrich my professional existence over the past five years.

Much to my good fortune, a June 16, 2009, *New York Times* article alerted me to the existence of *Dreamers and Fighters*, a documentary about the Communist teacher purges in New York City during the 1950s. The website devoted to the film included contact information that led to an e-mail exchange and then a trip to the city to meet Lori Styler, one of the documentary's chief architects; Lisa Harbatkin, whose ongoing mission to learn more about the role of the New York City Teachers' Union in the lives of her mother and her colleagues has driven her to do an enormous amount of research on the history of the union; and Clarence Taylor, who had recently put the finishing touches on his own book about the union, *Reds at the Blackboard*, which has since been published by Columbia University Press. I learned a lot at my first (nearly three-hour) meeting with them, and I am particularly grateful to Clarence Taylor for letting me see the draft of a book chapter that dealt with the repression of the union. Lori put me in touch with Henry Foner and Paul Becker, both former teacher unionists, and a subsequent meeting with Henry yielded a ninety-minute conversation that opened new pathways for my research. Lisa proved to be a wonderful research mate at the Municipal Archives, and in early August 2009 we spent a couple of days at 31 Chambers Street, excitedly sharing our insights and our archival discoveries with each other as we progressed. These individuals deserve much of the credit for the final product that is Chapter 6.

A number of colleagues and friends have been instrumental in helping me through, both personally and professionally. The Politics Department of Mount Holyoke College was my intellectual home for three years, and I could hardly imagine a more pleasant environment to work in. It helped to have an office on the second floor of Shattuck Hall, where Chris Pyle and Joe Ellis—a couple of American history experts—were on hand for good chats and good advice on all things professional and I could avail myself of Preston Smith's take on progressive politics in urban America and the friendliness of English professors Nigel Alderman, Chris Benfey, Bill Quillian, and Liz Young. The folks who rounded out the Politics Department were all stellar colleagues, but I owe special thanks and acknowledgment to Calvin Chen, Luis Jiménez, and Liz Markovitz, a trio of younger colleagues who gave me a lot of good advice and companionship; Penny Gill, who lent me her office (her "real estate") and always made time for me; and Tim Delaune, office mate extraordinaire. Dan Czitrom of Mount Holyoke College's History Department read my work on New York City and helped correct some inaccuracies about New York City in the Progressive Era. He also gently counseled me not to ignore religious and ethnic cleavages within the teachers' corps, a lacuna in my analysis of education politics in New York that I addressed, though perhaps not as fully as he would have liked. Meanwhile, Jeff Selinger of Bowdoin College and Jason Opal of McGill University and their families have graced me with their intellectual acuity and warm companionship. Stacey Hunt and Carolyn Craig did the same during my year at Rutgers University. At the very end of the writing process, Meghan Roberts, also at Bowdoin College, offered some helpful advice about the material on nineteenth-century France, and Laleh Khalili, of the School of Oriental and African Studies in London, gave me some pointers on how to liven up the first couple of chapters of the book. Shelley Deane and Seth Jaffe at Bowdoin College and Catherine Paden at Simmons College have kept me thinking and smiling. And to all my other colleagues, past and present, at Rutgers University, Mount Holyoke College, and Bowdoin College, I offer thanks and applause for their friendliness, encouragement, and (though my readers may tire of the word by the end of this book) professionalism.

The network of scholars that I encountered as a graduate student at Columbia University has become a professional support mechanism and a source of warm friendships—a gift that keeps on giving. In particular, I thank Stacie Goddard, Nicole Hala, Laleh Khalili, Mona Lena Krook, Adrienne LeBas, Patrick Leblond, Paul Macdonald, Cecilia Martinez, Denise Milstein, Tom Mullaney, Joe Parent, Eleonora Pasotti, Graeme Robertson, Roger Schoenman, Cecelia Walsh-Russo, Alex Weisiger, and Matt Winters, each of whom has supported me, at various times over the past decade, as a colleague and as a friend.

As I think back over my intellectual trajectory, I remember how important some of my college professors were to me. They demonstrated what it means to be a responsible, professional intellectual. Mark Blyth and Kirstie McClure, in particular, have continued to be a part of my journey. I thank them both for their good humor and wise words and the time they continue to take to keep me in their respective orbits.

At Temple University Press, my thanks go to Alex Holzman, Micah Kleit, and John Torpey. When Alex first heard my book idea, he encouraged me to include a discussion of the significance of 1968; his advice helped shape the concluding chapter of the book. Micah guided me through the entire publication process, from manuscript submission to book production, with patience and care. And John has shown faith in this project since he first saw my proposal.

Outside the academy, a host of individuals have been a source of lasting emotional support. I cannot imagine a list complete enough to preclude fear of exclusion, but I would be truly remiss if I did not mention Hillary Bouchard, Danielle Carriveau, Julie Danho, John Gallucci, Emily Harting, Annie Kelley, Joanna Michelson, Freya Recksiek, Sean Smith, and Anthony Spano, as well as Damien Newton and his family and all of our friends who convene in North Carolina every Memorial Day weekend. In ways in which they may not be aware, each has made me feel like a more important part of the world. My parents, for their part, brought me *into* the world and with the help of my brother have taught me to work hard and think for myself as I make my way through life.

I count myself lucky not only to have known Charles Tilly, however slightly, but also to have had the opportunity to be counted among his students and advisees. Until his death in the spring of 2008, he advised, guided, and inspired me—directly, in his office and via e-mail, and indirectly, through his example as a scholar and teacher. I continue to read his work, remember his voice, and consult the notes I took while in his office, in his classroom, and in the magnificent Contentious Politics workshop, which gathered together such formidable thinkers every Monday afternoon during my years at Columbia University. I cannot conceive of a single scholar whose work and whose professional demeanor have had so profound an impact on the way that I think and the way that I carry myself as a college professor. I miss him, and I can only hope that this book does at least some justice to the example set by his extraordinary scholarship.

And finally, I must acknowledge Mark Kesselman, without whom I would not be where I am and could not have accomplished what I have. My relationship with him has deepened enough over the past twelve years to make a sustained reflection feel too personal for me to set to page; suffice it to say that as an adviser, critic, cheerleader, counselor, teacher, and friend, he is *sans pareil*.

1

✳ ✳ ✳

The Puzzle of
Turn-of-the-Century
Teachers' Politics

I

✳

Teachers, Politics, and the State

In August 1900, the first national meeting of locally organized primary school-teachers' associations took place in Paris. Thirteen years earlier, the education minister Eugène Spuller had legally forbidden the teachers (*instituteurs*) from organizing their own trade union. Over the decade that followed, they made no concerted effort to form a national association, but throughout provincial France, small groups of teachers quietly formed their own associations of "pedagogical improvement."[1] Then, in 1898, half a dozen *instituteurs* from different parts of the country proposed, in their respective associations and provincial pedagogical pamphlets, to organize a meeting of teachers in the town of Laon, in the *département* of Aisne.[2] The occasion was to inaugurate a monument being erected in honor of three of their Aisnian comrades—Leroy, Debordeaux, and Poulette—who had been killed in the Franco-Prussian War. Some 120 teachers representing fifty-two locally organized associations attended that meeting. The charismatic and persuasive Achille Deum, a teacher from the town of Asnières, near Paris, chaired the meeting and called for a national meeting of teachers' associations to be held in Paris the following year. Between August 6 and 8, nearly 400 French schoolteachers congregated in the city, representing eighty local groups. The education minister, Georges Leygues, attended the meeting and gave his blessing to the corporate body, thus making him the first education minister to break with his post-1887 predecessors who had been hostile to the *instituteurs'* associations. The congregated teachers discussed pedagogical issues, but they also discussed the organization of the teachers' "friendly societies" (*amicales*) and the possibility of an even larger congress the following year. The teachers' 1901 congress was so large that the education minister forbade the teachers from meeting in 1902, fearing that teachers would, in imitation of their public-sector comrades in the post offices, phone companies, and tax offices, take advantage of a loosening of the state's association laws.[3] Nevertheless, the congress of August 1900 was part of a long, unsteady path toward the acceptance of teachers' collective political existence.

While French teachers were fighting for the very right to hold collective meetings in 1900, American teachers were, that same year, deeply and openly embroiled in city politics. On March 27, Robert Van Wyck, the first mayor of the newly consolidated New York City and a Tammany Hall stalwart,[4] held a hearing at City Hall to discuss the Davis Bill, which would provide increases in teachers' salaries, tax hikes to finance them, and a reform in the city's auditing system.[5] By the time the meeting opened at four o'clock, nearly two thousand teachers, most of them women, had already crowded into City Hall. They filled the corridor leading to the mayor's office, crammed themselves into the ante-room of the office, and even stood on radiators and windowsills to get a better view of the proceedings. For the next two hours, the mayor discussed the Davis Bill with representatives of the teachers' and principals' associations while the assembled teachers listened and made their feelings known; after someone spoke, the teachers applauded, cheered, laughed, booed, or hissed. The president of the New York City Teachers' Association, William Ettinger, was the teachers' hero that afternoon; one of the school commissioners, John Harrigan, was the villain of the piece. Ettinger complained that the teachers hardly benefited from the previous salary bill, while Harrigan charged that the new bill, if signed into law, would place an unfair tax burden on city residents. Several days later, the mayor officially handed down his veto of the Davis Bill, but even though he had the support of many city administrators, Tammany Hall was out of favor in state government. The state senate and assembly, both controlled by the Republican Party, overrode the mayor's veto.[6] When the Republican governor, Theodore Roosevelt, held a hearing to discuss the Davis Bill, a large contingent of city teachers made the trip to Albany to be heard.[7] Roosevelt spoke favorably of the bill, mentioning in passing a defect that would later be addressed: its discrimination between the salaries of men and women teachers. Early in May, the governor signed the bill into law.[8]

French and American teachers found themselves in very different situations with regard to their capacity to make collective public demands at the end of the nineteenth century. While the *instituteurs* were still fighting to make legitimate public claims on state authorities in 1900, teachers in New York City (even then, the country's largest school district) contended against the city administration with relative freedom. French teachers were legally barred from unionizing, and even their efforts at forming relatively quiescent associations attracted disciplinary attention; collective public claim making was nearly nonexistent. New York City teachers, although not formally unionized, suffered no administrative sanctions for their collective claim making.

But a quarter of a century later, teachers' political circumstances in both places had changed. By 1925, the vast majority of French teachers—both the male *instituteurs* and the female *institutrices*—were affiliated with one of the two national teachers' unions: the socialist Syndicat National des Instituteurs (SNI) and the more radical, Communist Party–affiliated Fédération des Membres de l'Enseignement Laïque (FMEL). Both organizations maintained alliances with the labor unions of blue-collar workers, collectively and publicly supported the politicians they favored, and repeatedly made public statements and participated in public demonstrations in favor of the secular republic and against the resurgent Catholic Church. Although the unionization of state employees was still in a legal twilight zone, state authorities' willingness to suppress the radicalization of the teaching force had largely evaporated.

In the United States, meanwhile, city teachers were on the defensive. The National Education Association (NEA), then as now, was the country's largest association of educators. But the NEA of the 1920s discouraged teachers from political action. The more militant American Federation of Teachers (AFT), meanwhile, remained a loose-knit collection of locals, and it was losing the battle for membership with the NEA. In 1925, about one thousand New York City teachers were part of the city's AFT local, the Teachers' Union (TU), a small percentage of the city's teaching force. This organization attracted accusations of disloyalty to the country and official restriction from conducting meetings in public schools. The New York state legislature had, over the governor's veto, commissioned Senator Clayton Lusk to investigate Bolshevism in the schools and, from 1919 to 1924, his committee worked to eliminate radicalism from the state's political establishment. The Lusk Committee "called every teacher who had been accused of unpatriotic behavior during the war to Albany to testify before a widely publicized set of hearings."[9] Even members of the other teachers' associations in the city, collectively constituting (as of 1924) the Joint Committee of Teachers Organizations (JCTO), found themselves assailed by the Board of Education for their participation in city politics, on account of such activity being "unprofessional."

After twenty-five years, teachers' relationships with state authorities had changed in both places but in different ways. The *instituteurs* and *institutrices* had fought to gain recognition for their claim making and their very right to maintain a collective presence without official molestation. By 1925, that battle had very nearly been won. The American teachers, however, found an encroaching city government and an unwelcome state presence placing their political associations in jeopardy. By 1925, American teachers' public claim-making activities, while far from being eliminated, had become stigmatized.

What explains this shift in the political orthodoxy of teachers' involvement in collective claim making? And how does the answer to that question vary across cases? In the twenty-first century, these questions could scarcely be more relevant. Today, teachers constitute one of the largest bodies of workers in the advanced industrialized world, much greater than the industrial workers who are usually studied by scholars of labor activism and contentious politics. The size of teachers' corps and education budgets is displayed in Table 1.1. States

TABLE 1.1　PUBLIC SCHOOLTEACHERS AND EDUCATION IN THE ADVANCED
INDUSTRIALIZED DEMOCRACIES

Country	No. of school teachers (2005)	Teachers as percentage of labor force age 25–64 (1999)	Percentage of budget expenditure on education (2005)
Belgium	100,346	NA	12.1
Canada	451,300*	3.5	NA
Denmark	NA	NA	15.5
Finland	91,288	4.3	12.5
France	828,334	4.5	10.6
Germany	1,120,493	3.9	9.7
Greece	183,782	NA	9.2
Iceland	7,128	7.8	18.0
Ireland	64,621	4.7	13.9
Italy	827,669	4.7	9.2
Japan	1,020,470	3.0	9.5
Luxembourg	NA	3.7	NA
Netherlands	NA	NA	11.5
Norway	107,517†	5.2	16.7
Portugal	179,964	NA	11.3
Spain	537,427	5.2	11.0
Sweden	195,346	4.2	12.6†
Switzerland	127,416	3.9	16.3†
United Kingdom	577,596	3.8	12.5
United States	4,020,988	4.2	13.7

Sources: Data gathered from Organisation for Economic Co-operation and Development (OECD),
Teachers for Tomorrow's Schools (Paris: OECD, 2001); United Nations Educational, Scientific and Cultural
Organization (UNESCO), "Table 19: Finance Indicators by ISCED Level," available at http://stats.uis
.unesco.org/unesco/TableViewer/tableView.aspx?Reportid=172.
* 2004 data.
† 2006 data.

spend an enormous amount of money on financing their education systems, and teachers' salaries and benefits constitute a sizable proportion of their education budgets. Teachers themselves constitute a huge proportion of these countries' workforces. One might imagine that the sheer size of this constituency would merit study, but there has been very little systemic analysis done comparing the political power of organized teachers across cases, and none at all examining this power over time.

The size of teachers' corps is matched by the influence of their unions in national politics. Across the United States, Western Europe, and Japan, teachers' unions have become important players in national education politics. Their associations have fought not only for the higher salaries and better working

conditions that are the "bread and butter" of trade unionism but also for education reform and funding, improved school safety and infrastructure, human
and trade union rights, gender equality, and economic justice. At a time when
organized labor has been reeling under the combined pressures of falling trade
barriers, deregulated labor markets, changing workplace technologies, and
neoliberal ideology, teachers' organizations have retained influence and some
cohesiveness in public politics. In addition to the voice of unions in national
politics, Education International, a coalition of 402 teachers' organizations
spanning 173 countries, campaigns for better schools and social justice issues
more generally, holds regional conferences around the world, and publishes
a series of bulletins and magazines about its activities and educational issues
worldwide.[10]

But, as I have suggested, it was not always so. How did teachers' collective
claim making acquire its political legitimacy? And how can we explain the differences in teachers' experiences across countries?

In this book, I seek to answer these questions by examining the politics
and effects of state elites' efforts to consolidate central authority over schooling
the masses. I demonstrate that, during critical periods in the history of public
education, the expansion of state control changed teachers' political opportunity structure and capacity for political action in unprecedented ways. *Centralization of education* challenged long-established relations between teachers,
educational administrators, and political regimes. The variable, dynamic histories of centralization politics, teachers' contention, and the political legitimacy of teachers' associations shaped the interactions between teachers and
the state during these crucial periods. The centralization of education precipitated a long-term struggle between previously docile teachers and state agents
who needed teachers to do their work quietly, cheaply, and "professionally." The
struggle was fought in public through a combination of contained politics in
state capitals and contentious politics in the streets, while smaller-scale, but no
less consequential, conflicts were fought further from the public eye by those in
charge of training prospective teachers. The outcome was unexpected: Teachers' associations eventually became institutional actors, embedded in the state,
bargaining with their bosses over a set of issues that teachers had not expected to
find themselves dealing with. Teachers' collective action was then and remains
now a reflection of ongoing battles over teachers' proper role as state actors.

The centralization of education systems required teachers to be mobilized
and gave state authorities the tools to prescribe proper behavior among teachers, creating an apolitical identity for them. When teachers resisted these efforts to categorize them as passive tools of the state, state elites responded by
reinforcing the social boundaries that distinguished teachers from others and
exploiting the differences within teachers' corps, pitting men against women,
primary school teachers against secondary school teachers, and political radicals against moderates. These tactics generated conflict within teachers' corps,
but contrary to the intentions of state authorities, they also stoked the flames

of teachers' contentiousness, as associations of teachers now petitioned the state not only for better salaries and working conditions but also for recognition as teachers' legitimate political voice. Governments' efforts to mobilize teachers to enact centralized education and politick in its favor, in other words, bred a parallel process of mobilization by which teachers resisted these efforts.

The very efforts of state administrators to consolidate authority at key moments in the late nineteenth and early twentieth centuries produced a politics of *selective engagement* between state authorities and associations of politically assertive, but internally divided, teachers. Selective engagement politics responds to collective claim making that seeks to exploit latent (or blatant) divisions within the teachers' corps, divisions often created or reinforced by the centralization process itself. However, I also argue that such a politics has the unintended consequence of recognizing the legitimacy of some teachers' collective claim making at the expense of others. Governments did not seek institutionalized engagement with teachers, but practices like collective bargaining emerged as a way to defuse potentially destabilizing teachers' politics while simultaneously granting teachers' associations institutionalized access to state decision makers. Against the intentions of nearly all the actors in both cases, these effects interacted with states' disciplinary and repressive techniques, the threat of such techniques, the legitimacy of prevailing jurisdictions over primary education, and teachers' own histories of contentious collective action to produce the process of professionalization, whereby multiple parties compete to provide a service for the same clientele, with at least one party bidding for the support of the state. Selective engagement thereby reconfigures the relationship between state authorities and regime challengers. Chapter 2 explains these dynamics in more detail.

Teachers and State Centralization at the Dawn of the Twentieth Century

During the nineteenth century, across Western Europe and the United States, states were busy expanding their authority over schooling. This consolidation of power had already begun in the more exclusive realm of secondary education, but the expansion of state control over popular primary schooling was unprecedented. Governments expanded state authority over, and popular access to, primary education for a number of reasons. Domestic political emergencies, such as revolutions and civil wars, moved national leaders to deploy public education to reconstruct the social order to "reflect the principles for which the struggle was originally undertaken."[11] Nationalist responses to external threats also stimulated education reform. The Franco-Prussian War, for example, inspired the belief that poor education was responsible for the French military defeat, and the subsequent education reform movements sought to reestablish national unity and reinforce training in basic skills like reading and writing.

World War I transformed public education in America into a security issue, as the movement to "Americanize" immigrants and eliminate "Germanic" sentiments became a federal policy objective. Finally, some states revamped education systems in an effort to stimulate economic development. By the end of the nineteenth century, Western Europe and the United States were in the midst of the Second Industrial Revolution, featuring a vast influx of wage workers and accelerating technological innovation, urbanization, and concomitant social dislocations. Public education came to be seen not only as a "safety valve," inculcating conservative values in a potentially disruptive social class, but also as a positive requirement for building a reproducible labor pool to meet the demands of the new economy.

Beginning approximately in the 1870s, as the stakes and expenses of primary schooling increased, teachers' associations became part of the American and European political landscapes. Their status as autonomous collective actors, however, was highly contested and variable over time. Most of these organizations, often patterned after guild associations and organized not by classroom personnel but by administrative superiors, defined themselves apolitically, conscious as their members were of the sensitivity of their work to their communities and to the polity at large. In the United States, with its established freedom of association and decentralized system of governance, teachers did not face political barriers to forming associations. Although they were state employees, their identity as public servants did not, for the most part, impede their recognition as legitimate collective actors. Teachers in urban centers across the country organized, very often ward by ward, making collective claims on local administrators and, on occasion, the city government. In France, however, autonomous workers' organizations had been illegal since the French Revolution. And they found themselves with an additional impediment: the almost total lack of social networks and associational ties that underpin all sustained collective action. Workers in cottage and craft industries could at least draw on a tradition of guild membership. But the *instituteurs* were isolated in the rural countryside, lacked a cohesive common identity, and were under the thumb of the ecclesiastical authorities in whose hands primary schooling had traditionally rested. In 1880, teachers had a recognized political presence in the United States, but they lacked even a rudimentary political autonomy in France.

These historical legacies dictated different roles for teachers in the politics of centralization.

France

Because French teachers had no capacity for collective action before 1880, their direct role in centralization politics was limited. However, most secular schoolteachers in France supported the legislative overhaul of primary education that took place during the 1880s. These reforms, engineered by Jules Ferry, rendered primary instruction free and obligatory and increased the authority of the school inspection corps and the central administration over local surveillance, teacher employment, and teacher training. Perhaps more important, the legislation of the 1880s transformed the primary education curriculum by extracting moral from religious education, relegating the latter to the Catholic Church, while the secular state secured authority over the former. As I show in greater detail in Chapter 3, the majority of French teachers perceived the Catholic Church to be an oppressor, and the church's influence in rural France had effectively negated the *instituteurs'* potential for collective political action prior to the Third Republic. To the teachers, Ferry and his allies were representatives of a secular order that could protect and empower them. In response to the political struggles over secular education and centralized schooling, the republican regime sought to reshape the teaching force and mobilize it to do the secular pedagogical work that it now valued more highly than ever before. The central administration signaled to the teachers that they had become valuable actors in the French state's arsenal of cultural standardization through a series of institutional reforms—reinvigorating teacher training schools, empowering secular school inspectors, and holding annual congresses for schooling personnel—that spurred teachers to seize some control over their professional destinies.[12]

The United States

In the United States, however, teachers and their organizations generally opposed centralization. In New York City, as elsewhere in the urban United States, teachers' influence in city politics was the product of the decentralized ward system of governance. Teachers and their organizations fought against school reformers' drive to centralize the school system, since centralization meant muting the wards' voices in school politics. Until the late 1880s and 1890s, most city teachers were members of the ethnic groups that hired them, and the wards usually operated as political extensions of the various ethnicities that constituted the city population. Unlike French teachers, New York City teachers were active participants in the politics of centralization, and after their unsuccessful campaign against centralization, they responded with a stepped-up campaign to make their voices heard in city politics. In the years that followed, however, centralized school administrations and city councils began to identify teachers' politics as an inefficiency that needed to be eliminated. This was the era of the professionalization movement in public administration, and the "efficiency experts" of the era saw city schools as an inviting laboratory to implement their theories.[13] In New York City, the efficiency drive was made manifest in the Gary school program to transform the schools into vocational training grounds.[14] In addition, the loyalty of public servants, and teachers in particular, became critically important during World War I, especially given federal and state governments' mission to "Americanize" immigrants. At the heart of the "Garyization" and Americanization programs was the desire to "take the schools out of politics" by putting their administration in the hands of ostensibly impersonal bureaucrats whose only political interest was absolute, unwavering loyalty. According to this vision, classroom teachers were not legitimate political actors, and their salary demands appeared unseemly and inappropriate.

Centralization triggered teachers' resistance to state authority, but the tactics, magnitude, and outcomes of this resistance were shaped by two critical factors: teachers' support or lack of support for centralization, and the degree of official tolerance of teachers' politics when the centralization conflict transpired. French teachers' support for centralization and their lack of associational presence resulted in their quick suppression in the 1880s, followed by quiet, localized mobilization. American teachers opposed centralization in municipalities throughout the country and fought against it, publicly but unsuccessfully. They proceeded to resist city-level efforts to exclude them from public politics. French teachers, meanwhile, had to fight for the very right to act collectively. But in both countries centralization exacerbated preexisting heterogeneities within the teachers' corps. The struggles of teachers' associations to influence state policy happened while they were fighting with each other over the legitimate right to represent teachers politically. The legacy of conflict over centralization, I argue, profoundly shaped the patterns by which teachers overcame these tensions.

Why Teachers?

In spite of the size and political influence of teachers' corps across the advanced industrialized world, political science does not have much to offer to explain their power. Their unions sometimes appeared as interest groups when interest group theory was still in vogue,[15] and several anthologies offer cross-national comparisons of teacher union politics.[16] However, while these studies make passing references to a past in which teachers were apolitical actors, none explore the genesis of teachers' political movements. State-centered studies of the creation of public education systems pay scant attention to the role of teachers.[17] They also pay insufficient attention to the relationship between the state and competing education authorities. They neglect the fact that public school systems are products of not only the social demand for schooling but also political battles between central and local state authorities, ecclesiastical powers, and other organized stakeholders. The literature thus implies that teachers and their relationship to elites are sheltered from these conflicts.[18] But these battles affected teachers by changing the demands that their superiors made of them, and during the late nineteenth and early twentieth centuries, these demands were usually not passively accepted.

Efforts to centralize the school systems in New York City and Chicago around the turn of the twentieth century provide a small demonstration of how teachers are embedded in these larger struggles over public education. In both cities, education reformers—particularly Nicholas Murray Butler in New York and William Rainey Harper in Chicago—campaigned in favor of reorganizing the chains of command in their respective cities to eliminate local governance of schools. In New York, Butler saw centralization of control as a stepping-stone to implementing a vision of education that included a professional, apolitical bureaucracy, but New York City teachers were hostile to the elimination of local representative institutions. So Butler's campaign for the new law during the 1890s included an active effort to win over the largely female teaching force by enlisting the Public Education Association (PEA), an organization of middle-class women, to convince the teachers that centralization would improve the functioning of city schools. Ultimately, teachers' opposition did not stop the reformers. Butler's reform bill became state law in 1896, but the Chicago city teachers, led by Margaret Haley, blocked Harper's bill and subsequent school reform bills for decades by launching organized campaigns against them. The Chicago Teachers' Federation (CTF) lobbied the state legislature during the 1900s and again in the 1910s to stop implementation of centralization. Education reform was not enacted until 1917, after the city outlawed the teachers' union. In both cases, efforts at changing the administrative structure of the school system provoked teachers to protest, but the teachers of Chicago had stronger support from the community, and organized labor in particular, than did their New York counterparts.[19] Administrators could hardly avoid dealing with teachers and their organizations in the administrators' efforts to change the education bureaucracy. Yet teachers' roles in such struggles are not examined in state-centered accounts of education reform.

Teachers are one of a series of actors whom Michael Lipsky refers to as "street-level bureaucrats."[20] Along with police officers, sanitation workers, and welfare and social workers, teachers are distinguished by direct interaction with citizens, "wide discretion over the dispensation of benefits or the allocation of public sanctions,"[21] and relative autonomy from organizational authority. Contrary to the Weberian "faceless" bureaucrat, street-level bureaucrats are profoundly visible in their communities and have unusual resonance because of the value of the services they carry out and because they represent governments. My own analysis treats these qualities as variables, not constants—most rural schoolteachers in mid-nineteenth-century France, for example, could hardly be described as independent of organizational authority—and suggests that by historicizing the occupational category, we can better understand how centralization transformed such street-level bureaucracies into legitimate public claim makers.

The political significance of teachers as street-level bureaucrats is twofold. First, to a great extent, their action is equivalent to policy. No matter what decision makers dictate from above, teachers' autonomy from organizational superiors allows them substantial discretion in the implementation of laws and administrative decrees. In order to confine teachers' discretionary authority, states sometimes go to great lengths to fashion and impose a corporate

identity on them. More broadly, whenever state elites seek to overhaul education systems, teachers become the objects of mobilization processes. Later, I
pursue the theoretical implications of teachers' being both resource-mobilizing
regime challengers and the subjects of elite actors' mobilization. Teachers, however, are not Marxian wage workers (another set of actors distinguished by
being resource mobilizers and mobilized resources), which leads to the other
political significance of teachers: They are embedded in the state apparatus.
When combined with the cultural sensitivity of the work that teachers do, such
embedding creates unusual pressure for teachers to adhere to political orthodoxy. They are, after all, the face of the state in their communities.

The reality of public school teachers as state actors indicates that conflicts
over their right to collectively participate in public politics constitute conflicts
over the contours of the state itself. Like the process of state building, political
scientists' study of state building is an unfinished enterprise, and one of the
loose ends pertains to a particular change in the state structure of advanced
industrialized democracies during the twentieth century—the growth of "bureaucratic insurgency" in law enforcement, postal services, and all across the
civil services, insurgencies that eventually yielded some form of bargaining between state authorities and those civil servants.[22] While scholars like Thomas
Poggi and Thomas Ertman were concerned with the role of bureaucracy in
the development of modern nation-states, they never considered the possibility that those very civil servants might shape the trajectory of state growth in
strange, unexpected ways, as rulers were driven to make deals with disgruntled
state employees in a way that institutionalizes the employees' role as collective
actors in the state apparatus.[23]

Teachers also stand apart from other state workers in some important respects. If education is "the organized labor whose object is the capacity for
social practice," or "capacities for interaction,"[24] then teachers play an unusual
role in a given society. Since different societies value different kinds of social
practices, the workers who labor to inculcate the capacities for those practices are engaged in a particularly value-laden project. As Maria Lorena Cook
writes with reference to Mexico, "Teachers play a unique role in transmitting
a society's dominant cultural values and norms to its school-age children."[25]
They are the workers whose labor creates (and, to some extent, enforces) the
standards of social interaction in particular societies. While other workers can
create such standards through their labor, teachers are the only workers specific to the task. So, to the extent that there are stakeholders who value public
education, how those stakeholders identify teachers, and how teachers define
themselves, becomes politically salient when public education is the object of
political conflict. Such questions are particularly consequential in the case of
nationalism, as Ernest Gellner has theorized and Stephen Harp has demonstrated through his discussion of Alsace and Lorraine from 1850 to 1940.[26] In
later chapters, I explore the significance of teachers' identities in the politics of
centralization.

Another important point about the study of teachers' changing political significance during this time period is the particular relevance of gender. The social construction of teaching as women's work happened at different times, at different paces, and with different consequences in the two countries. Centralization preceded the feminization of the primary teachers' corps in France, while women already constituted a majority of American teachers by 1900 (and an overwhelming majority of New York City teachers). The different rationales for centralizing education, and the different status of working women in the two countries, generated different sets of tensions between governments and organized teachers and, just as important, between men and women teachers. Changes in popular perceptions of schooling interacted with other forms of concomitant social change, including demographic shifts in the case of France, to produce new ways of regulating teachers' corps.[27] As I demonstrate in later chapters, the gendered categories of political orthodoxy with regard to educators that states developed around the turn of the century elicited differentiated responses from men and women teachers and different ways of responding to women teachers' involvement in politics.

If my argument about centralization and selective engagement is correct for understanding the emergence and acceptance of teachers' public claim-making activities, there are two important implications for the study of social movements and states. First, it makes a counterintuitive point about the importance of solidarity for the creation of sustained worker mobilization and the official recognition of their organizations. When state service providers mobilize for collective action, occupational and political heterogeneities within the workers' corps become the basis for contestation over professional boundaries. Selective engagement reinforced preexisting tensions between teachers and teachers' associations of different political orientation. Different groups of teachers sought state recognition not only in their conflicts with governments but also in their conflicts with one another. Governments' responses to these conflicts unintentionally yielded legitimacy to teachers' claim-making activities. Through selective engagement, teachers' associations became acceptable collective actors in public politics. Social movement scholars generally assume that solidarity is a positive boon for labor movements, helping sustain them over time and increasing the likelihood that they will extract concessions from their targets.[28] In the cases explored in this book, however, the lack of solidarity within the teachers' corps, in conjunction with differentiated government responses to teachers' demands, generated the dynamic "power in movement" that led to the anchoring of teachers' unions in the state.

Second, it provides a different way of understanding the state–civil society boundary, a boundary called into question when state workers act collectively in politically unorthodox ways. Political scientists usually apprehend this boundary in one of two ways. Some imagine states and societies to be discrete, unitary entities of relative autonomy that regularly interact through such institutions as political parties and law enforcement and whose socially constructed boundaries are clearest only in times of revolutionary confrontation.[29] Others deconstruct the state itself, rejecting the idea of state autonomy and conceiving of states as inescapably embedded in social relations whose power constitutes the state in different times and places.[30] My own project suggests that the state-society difference is mediated by the creation of, and resistance to, social boundaries. Following Charles Tilly and, to a lesser extent, James Scott, I suggest that when states centralize power over some set of activities, they always deploy some energy toward fashioning categorical identities to mediate relations between state and nonstate actors.[31] This way of understanding the state preserves the concept, along with the idea of, state autonomy without denying the reality of social embeddedness.

Case Selection: Marianne and Uncle Sam in Comparative Perspective

The comparison between France and the United States is useful for a number of reasons. The two regimes represent very different degrees of centralization regarding public education. The difference of degree is clear when looking at their school systems today, although it is somewhat less evident when looking at the systems in the nineteenth century.[32] Specifying the prehistory of centralization is a prerequisite to examining centralization's effects, and for the purposes of this comparison, the very different constitutional traditions tell much of the story. The stability of the American federal structure, as dictated by the U.S. Constitution, is qualitatively different from the shifting constitutional regimes of nineteenth-century France, particularly when coupled with that country's rigid, Napoleonic administrative structure. The American Constitution bounds the centralization of historically localized social services in the United States in a way that the French Revolution prevented from ever developing in France. To conceptualize the difference between Marianne and Uncle Sam along this dimension, I draw on Stein Rokkan and Derek Urwin's distinction between monocephalous and polycephalous territorial structures. In monocephalous territories, only one area has authoritative primacy; in polycephalous ones, central features are diffuse across territory, and different types of resource holders are spatially segmented.[33] France was chosen for its comparative monocephality; the United States, for its polycephality. The implicit wager of this book is that the politics of teacher organization responds in meaningful ways to changes in center-periphery dynamics, and the two types of territorial structure should dictate qualitatively different empirical trajectories. For France, I examine national trends in teacher organizing, which I supplement by looking at local variations. For the United States, I use the opposite spatial strategy, looking at a particular locale, New York City, and examining its place in state and national politics. Taking care not to confuse "the geographic map for the map of effective political influence,"[34] I also try to show how developments at different spatial levels affect each other.

Within the United States, the choice of New York City is advantageous in certain respects, problematic in others. One of the great advantages to studying New York City is the wealth of extant scholarly resources on city education policy and politics, dating back to the nineteenth century. Numerous secondary studies and primary sources on teachers' associations are available in various libraries and archives. In addition, the long history of New York City yields an appropriately long time period to study the effects of causal processes that, I assume, take place over long time periods. Furthermore, New York City administrators also pioneered the urban centralization of public education, which suggests that the experiences of other cities did not impact the planning, politicking, and implementation of the process, thereby controlling for any interaction effects with other cities' centralization efforts.[35]

While all American cities have their own quirks and idiosyncrasies, there can be no doubt that New York is uniquely unique. The enormity of the city, the magnitude of its diversity (cultural and otherwise), and its particular history as both intermediate point and destination for immigrants all suggest that it is not just any "center." Given the role of common schooling in American history as an integrative mechanism, however imperfect, the ethnic diversity of New York City suggests a correspondingly crucial role for the primary school system. Although this problem cannot be completely sidestepped, I would remind readers that what I am after in this book is an explanation of teachers' politics that reasonably demonstrates their politicization as an outgrowth of struggles over centralization and the politics of selective engagement that followed. The peculiarities of New York City surely affect the timing of centralization and selective engagement but not, I argue, the sequence (which, as I suggest in Chapter 2, is crucial). Explaining political outcomes as sequences of causal mechanisms means getting the connections right, and the empirical differences between cities means that some of the specific political circumstances will vary.[36] I pursue the nature of these connections and specificities in subsequent chapters.

Beyond the narrow methodological rationale, the France–United States comparison was also the comparison of chief importance to Alexis de Tocqueville, some of whose major themes I revisit. Tocqueville wrote with concern about the effects of administrative centralization on civic spirit, as increasing government intervention severs people's relationships with each other, rendering them tools of administrative authority. Like Tocqueville, I am interested in the conditions that yield an associational life, especially among a group of people who, in France, lacked the durable social networks that fuel sustained collective action for at least the first half of the nineteenth century. Tocqueville, of course, was not so concerned with the possibility of organized groups gaining the right to make claims on the state—except, as his reflections on the 1848 Revolution suggest, for the sake of neutralizing them. And the thought of state workers rebelling against their employer would surely have repulsed and terrified him. His normative concerns, in that respect, are distinct from my own. But his analytical concerns resonate. Finally, beyond the concern with civic spirit and associational life, Tocqueville was deeply concerned with public education itself in a way that has not been properly addressed in the Tocqueville scholarship.[37] Before reflecting on any of these themes, however, I first develop a theory to examine the relationship between state centralization and teachers' public claim making more closely.

2

✳

Centralization, Mobilization,

and Selective Engagement

Perhaps the most important presumption of this book is that public school teachers are inescapably political actors. Since they represent local or central governments in their classrooms and, often, in their local communities, their interactions with pupils, parents, administrators, and communities constitute state-society relations. They provide services to the polities whose taxes pay their salaries, their labor constitutes an investment of public money, and their identities are a matter of public legitimacy. And they are embedded in a process of social reproduction, with implications for both national cohesion and economic development. A generation of research on Progressive Era school reform in the United States has resurrected teachers from the historical darkness and shown their importance for understanding the education politics of that era. In France, along with the rest of Europe, the importance of teachers has been less in question, since their role in cultural reproduction has been longer acknowledged. I hope that this book can at least reaffirm the idea that depoliticized education—"taking the schools out of politics"—is a fiction with a discursive use-value confined solely to politics. For as long as states have controlled schools, their employees have been political actors.

But the claim that public school teachers are inescapably political actors has multiple dimensions, just like their roles. It means that their actions, identities, and employment status are embedded in power struggles. To the extent that public education is a matter of salient political discourse, teachers' quotidian lives become objects of public scrutiny, as their work becomes revalued according to the prevalent norms of the moment. Loyalty to the state, administrative efficiency, moral righteousness, and adherence to gender norms are just some of the measures of orthodox behavior to which public school teachers have been expected to adhere. Finally, teachers are workers, and like workers in most parts of the world, they have sought, both individually and collectively, to improve their salaries and quality of life. And from time to time, they have even contested the conditions of their employment and the content of their work. Their unions, this book suggests, are the results of long-standing conflicts sprung from the tensions wrought by their involvement in these various roles and missions.

Teachers' unions did not exist anywhere in Europe or the United States until the final quarter of the nineteenth century, and the impetus for teachers to form organizations of any kind, particularly those devoted to collective claim making, was relatively weak. Teachers' involvement in public politics was at best frowned on—at worst, outlawed. Their occupational lives rarely became subjects of direct intervention by central authorities. Collective bargaining was unheard of, as it was in labor relations more generally during this period of history. Furthermore, given the proximity of teachers to the youth of their countries, their private lives were also the subjects of scrutiny. Their leisure activities, summertime travels, religious practices, and marital status were all subjects of concern to the local governments they worked for and the families they served. On the eve of centralization struggles, they were individuals embedded in local communities, interacting daily with the families they served, but they were also government employees and state agents. If "street-level bureaucrats," by definition, provide their services with unusual visibility, flexibility, and relative autonomy from organizational authority, then the teachers of late nineteenth-century Europe and America did not quite fit the label. While they were certainly profoundly visible in their communities, they were not truly autonomous from their employers.

It is these observations that direct me toward the following formulation of the problem: How did teachers mobilize, and how did their collective contestation of state activities become regularized (and, thereby, effectively embedded in the state)? Understanding teachers' collective action requires attention to teachers as social movement actors, challengers of the regimes they work for, and as state actors, members of the regimes they work for. These regimes are simultaneously the sources of their influence and of the limitations of that influence.[1] Penetrating this complexity means that standard formulations of the relationship between human agency and sociopolitical structure must be reconsidered. From the perspective of state theory, the state needs to be "brought back in" again, but it must not be the idealized Weberian state that Theda Skocpol and her colleagues assumed.[2] Rather, we need a more permeable, dynamic state to understand teachers' politics, a state that is "staffed" by workers whose commitment to political orthodoxy is variable, not constant.[3] From the perspective of social movement theory, we need a more sophisticated notion of resource mobilization, one that recognizes that all collective actors within regimes mobilize resources and that, at times, particular regime members can deploy other regime subjects as resources. Before outlining the causal model that can address these matters, I first consider the literature on states and social movements to better explain the strengths and limitations of current approaches to social movement mobilization vis-à-vis the state.

States and Social Movements

Theories dealing with the life cycle of social movements have had a tumultuous history with regard to the state.[4] At one time, political process theorists discussed the state as a critically important element of political opportunity structure.[5] However, in response to critics who have either emphasized the socially constructed nature and/or structural bias of political opportunity,[6] or pointed out the lack of psychological and/or rationalist microfoundations in political process theory,[7] these same scholars have reformed their toolkits and epistemological assumptions to offer a more nuanced, temporally sensitive, and context-dependent framework for understanding the relationship between political regimes and social movements.[8] State structures, whether theorized as dynamic or as static, are only one of many conditions that shape the environment for potential social movement actors.

Studies of the political certification of previously unrecognized collective actors have also gone through a series of permutations. The more recent social movements literature relates newly recognized social differences and values to previously existing social cleavages, while also accounting for the ways in which political institutions represent the new cleavages. Some subsequent literature has provided reasonable syntheses of this approach with political process models.[9] More useful for this project, however, is the *Dynamics of Contention* approach, which offers a theory of actor constitution that views new collective actors as the result of contentious interactions between regime members, challengers, and subjects.[10] The principal merit of this latter approach lies in its focus on interactiveness and dynamism—its attention to the continuous negotiation between differentially empowered actors over identities and social boundaries.

Focusing on the dynamism of not only contentious politics but also the state apparatus itself points a way forward for building a framework to analyze social movements that comprise actors at the fringes of the polity, like state functionaries. As discussed in Chapter 1, teachers are street-level bureaucrats who periodically fight with state authorities, both local and central, over the circumstances of their employment. Like all street-level bureaucrats, teachers are regime members, but they also become regime challengers when they collectively contest the status of their employment. Unlike that of other state functionaries, however, the substance of their work and its very meaning are matters of intense concern to other state agencies, along with families and taxpayers and, more contingently, the business community and organized labor. At crucial periods in the history of public education in the advanced industrialized democracies, all of these actors became stakeholders in education politics. The most distinctive of these crucial periods is the centralization era that, broadly speaking, spans the years from 1880 to 1930. When centralization happens, I argue here, the role of teachers as state resources becomes salient because this process, as well as the politics by which it comes about, revalues teachers and calls into question the political orthodoxy of their actions and identities.

Social movement scholarship usually treats resource mobilization as something that contenders do. But teachers are themselves a resource that the state mobilizes to achieve its own ends. At the same time, teachers are state actors, which is part of what empowers them both as professional workers and as collective political agents. The *Dynamics of Contention* program provides the two important refinements of mobilization theory that deepen the concept in a way that addresses this quirk: first, in its insistence on moving from previously recognized mobilizing structures to challengers' active appropriation of structures, and, second, in its claim that "members and challengers, no less than subjects, confront the problem of mobilizing organizational resources."[11] In this case, state elites are regime members who require previously unavailable or useless resources during critical periods of education reform. These two ideas together call attention to the possibility that challengers might reap benefits from the same institutions that authorities use to discipline them. We should therefore expect elites' efforts to mobilize their own resources to be fraught with unintended consequences, since the reliability of one such resource, teachers, requires more control over their behavior than elites can usually muster.

Centralization, Mobilization, and Selective Engagement

My theory is essentially a sequential one. When state elites initiate political struggles to centralize public education, they unintentionally trigger the causal sequence that yields "bureaucratic insurgency" among the teachers. Stated most simply, I suggest that *centralization causes mobilization and that mobilization, in turn, gives way to a process of selective engagement*. It is through selective engagement that teachers' associations acquire political legitimacy.

Centralization and Mobilization

Centers, following Stein Rokkan and Derek Urwin, are "privileged locations within a territory where key military/administrative, economic, and cultural resource-holders most frequently meet; with established arenas for deliberations, negotiations, and decision-making; where people convene for ritual ceremonies of affirmation of identity; with monuments that symbolize this identity; with the largest proportion of the economically active population engaged in the processing and communication of information and instructions over long distances."[12] Following this formulation, the centralization of education is the process by which these locations acquire their privileged position with regard to schooling. In both France and the United States, between 1880 and 1920, central states consolidated authority over public education, extracting material resources and authoritative decision-making power from local and regional bodies. The spatial distinctions between central, regional, and local are, of course, relative to each other and to external territories. Paris, for example, is central with regard to Lyon, Saint Étienne, and Saint Chamond. New York City is *a* center, with organizational autonomy from other centers (particularly during the time period in question), while the various pre-1896 wards within the city constituted peripheries in relation to the central Board of Education. Centralization meant, in the former case, the extraction of authoritative decision making and resource hoarding with regard to Lyon, Saint-Étienne, and Saint-Chamond and the investiture of such power in Paris and, in the latter case, the elimination of wards from education politics and school administration.

Centralization of education affects teachers in two, related ways.

First, teachers are drawn into the politics of centralization. The politics of centralization always creates a dichotomy between pro- and anti-centralizers within a regime's political elite. Whatever their perspective, teachers will mobilize their resources for political action; they will not fail to take a stand on a matter so important to their work. If they are in favor of centralization, the central administration will bid for teachers' support in centralization politics. If they are against centralization, the central administration will try to recruit dissenters and either convert or suppress the rest. In either case, centralization politics invites teachers' involvement and leads elite coalitions to signal to teachers that their value to the regime has increased.

How teachers mobilize resources in this struggle and what kinds of actions they take—whether they support centralization or not—depend on many factors, but their associational status is most important. Teachers with extant associations have a deployable resource at hand; teachers without associations do not. In the latter case, they will appropriate resources from their environment and generate new ones to take advantage of the new political opportunities that centralization politics affords them. In particular, centralization generates new incentives for teachers to form collective bodies, both as a vehicle for participation in the current struggle and as a tool for attaining the professional goals that centralization creates for them. France is the key case here. Before the centralizing reforms of the late 1870s and 1880s, teachers' participation in any collective action was strictly verboten. But while the republican regime was extracting control over schooling the masses from town councils, the central government began engineering professional solidarity among the teachers as a means of occupational empowerment. Teachers appropriated the regional and national pedagogical conferences that emerged during this period for their own autonomous political goals, even as those same conferences increased the value of teachers to the state. In the urban United States, however, teachers fought against centralization precisely because they recognized that vesting power in a centralized board of education would eliminate the political significance of their close relationship with neighborhood power brokers.

Second, since centralization changes the structure of administrative authority in public education, it affects teachers' ability to influence public politics. It
reconfigures the contours of political authority within which teachers advance
their interests and thereby incentivizes them to change their strategies for influ-
encing politics; indeed, it changes their relationship with the state. As with centralization politics, whether and how teachers adapt to these changes depend on
the specific circumstances of centralization. Teachers' relationship with other
stakeholders in education politics, their role in the politics of centralization,
their associational status when centralization is implemented, and the history
of their relationships with local and central authorities all bear on how teachers
interpret and respond to the changes in administrative structure. So, while centralization might create an objective incentive for teachers to pay less attention
to local authorities and more to central ones, subjective circumstances dictate
how they respond to that incentive. For example, while French teachers were
accustomed to using their community influence to impact their occupational
lives, the relative decline in the magnitude of that influence in the years after the
centralization laws were passed was matched by the central government's signal
to the teachers that they were important in an unprecedented way. It was this
signal that encouraged many teachers to cross the lines of political orthodoxy by
demanding a trade union and also embedded them more firmly in national political affairs. During the course of centralization politics and administration in
the United States, however, public authorities sent a very different signal to the
teachers. For decades, teachers in urban America relied on local networks and
informal relations, buttressed by ethnic and religious ties, to obtain and maintain their jobs and to influence the schools where they worked. They perceived
centralization as a threat to their ability to influence education through these
connections. And, indeed, centralizers did not hide their intentions to eliminate
teachers' political influence and "liberate" them from the influence of local political machinations. This signal was at odds, however, with the administrative
consequences of centralization on the city school system, which generated the
incentive and capacity for organized teachers to make collective claims on the
municipal government rather than on the wards, as I explain in Chapter 4.

All too often, the notion of political opportunity structure is used to refer
to conditions that correlate to contentious politics or social movements, such
that "opportunities come to reside in structures, rather than in specific reciprocal interactions between actors and political and economic conditions."[13] But
the reform of political opportunity structure does not dictate anything necessary about the agency of the actors who work within it. Indeed, teachers are a
part of the state structure, and centralization calls attention to the reality of
teachers as independent agents within that structure. The centralization process constitutes a rupture in the patterns, procedures, and identities of teachers'
occupational lives, and teachers experience these changes in their quotidian
work experiences. But their response to such a rupture cannot be understood
out of context. Teachers' prior political activity, ability to appropriate resources,

identities in their local communities, and perception of the role of centralization in relation to their occupational and private lives all shape the way they respond to changes of such magnitude.

When governments engage in centralization politics, and when centralization happens, teachers become a state resource just as surely as teachers themselves seek out resources from the state. Indeed, appropriation of the newly centralized institutions of public education for political purposes simultaneously constitutes teachers' bid for autonomy within the state structure and signals to elite decision makers and their allies the relative reliability of teachers to assist with their project—that is, their reliability as a resource to be mobilized. Mobilization is thus a dual-pronged causal mechanism.

Mobilization and Category Work

The politics of centralization precipitates teacher mobilization because the work that teachers do places them in the midst of the process of centralization. While state elites can establish educational and pedagogical standards, elites do not implement them. Carrying out centralizing reforms is an administrative task, and teachers are the proximate operators of the schooling apparatus. This process revalues teachers according to the nature of the educational reforms that centralization itself precipitates.

How do state authorities mobilize teachers? One of the constitutive mechanisms of centralization is the reform of categorical boundaries between teachers and other actors, as well as between different kinds of teachers. According to Charles Tilly, "Social categories consist of a boundary and a set of relations across that boundary."[14] Through the process of category reform, state elites alter the boundaries that impute distinctions to one set of actors, teachers, thereby separating them from other stakeholders in public education, including children, parents, priests, school inspectors, and other local and national administrators. Category work distinguishes public school teachers from private school teachers, primary educators from secondary educators, classroom personnel from other school workers, and so forth. Teachers, of course, are involved in "category work" themselves, as they enact a set of curricular and pedagogical standards in an effort to inculcate officially sanctioned knowledge.[15] The category to which teachers belong distinguishes them from others by the specificity of their work and the status of their employment. These categories, particularly during the time period in consideration, are profoundly gendered, as state authorities deployed particular understandings of the role of women in the raising of children to produce teachers' corps that were up to the task of inculcating the right values and in the right manner. Category work thereby creates gendered opportunity structures that interact with political ones.[16] Centrally located political elites establish categorical boundaries, but the specific circumstances of centralization determine how these boundaries are institutionally enforced and reproduced over time.

Why is category work important? It is important because centralization entails the reconfiguration of administrative structures, and such a reconfiguration requires some degree of obedience and political orthodoxy of the actors who work the apparatus. Matthew Lange points out that

> state building must be viewed as a long-term process requiring the construction of a certain esprit de corps that separates state actors from the rest of society through shared norms and identities and increases the possibility of collective state action. . . . [The state] must not be completely separate from society, since the engagement of state and society in active and formal relations is a . . . requirement of state capacity.[17]

Without such an esprit de corps, centralization requires more external resources to regulate public education than if state elites can rely on a cohesive, obedient corps of workers. Teachers are the proximate administrators of the state's pedagogical project, and without coherence within the teachers' corps, state capacity to implement this project is correspondingly weakened.

Teacher training and certification processes are an important way that the inclusiveness/exclusiveness of these categories is regulated. In later chapters, I use them as my chief empirical referent for examining category work. For example, prospective schoolteachers in Restoration-era France (1815–1830), to obtain their basic teaching certificate (*brevet simple*), had to display only the most minimal level of intellectual competence before a school inspector but also had to obtain a certificate of good conduct from the local priest and/or mayor. The question of intellectual proficiency was thematized politically only after the July Revolution in 1830, and the answer came with the regular establishment of normal schools for teacher training. These schools originated during the 1820s, but they proliferated during the July Monarchy years (1830–1848). Annual examinations for the awarding of certificates began in 1833 (the year of François Guizot's benchmark primary education law) for men and 1836 for women, and by 1855, no *département* lacked such a process.[18] The Ferry school laws of the 1880s inaugurated the end of the era of official clerical approval for lay teacher certification, placing it in the hands of secular authorities, and the maintenance of secular normal schools in each *département* was rendered mandatory in 1879. Teacher training in the United States, however, was unsophisticated and generally scarce until the post–World War I years saw a great push, spearheaded by the NEA, to professionalize teaching corps throughout the country.[19] However, the need for competent teachers was first politicized much earlier during the drive to popularize common schools, beginning roughly in the 1830s. By the end of the nineteenth century, normal schools, teachers' colleges, and universities were battling for control over teacher training procedures.[20] Examining training procedures provides excellent evidence for how state elites conceived of the social boundary between state-employed teachers and other stakeholders in primary schooling. In France, these institutions were doubly important because they also brought together teachers and teachers-to-be who would otherwise have had little opportunity to meet one another, much less form associations.

When teachers mobilize for political influence at the same time that state authorities seek to deploy them for political purposes, teachers and their associations can find themselves with unusual leverage in pressing their demands on state elites. Carrying out education policy depends on a relatively obedient corps of teachers, and this dependence generates friction when teachers are trying to affect the politics of education reform. Centralization and its politics do constitute a shift in teachers' capacity to make collective claims on political elites because teachers are both resource mobilizers and mobilized resources during this process. Yet centralization renders teachers dependent on their status as state actors for their salaries and status. The tension between reshaping the category of public school teacher from above and teachers' contestation of this category from below generates conflict over professional jurisdiction.

Professions are occupations whose workers provide a specialized service to a particular clientele in a market that is heavily protected by the state. The process of professionalization happens "when two or more distinct groups of practitioners compete for the same clientele"[21] and at least one group bids for government support in securing jurisdiction over some version of the practice in question (teaching, in this case). Public school teachers are also directly employed by governments; when on the job, teachers are activating their state identity. Therein lies the tension: Public school teachers cannot be professionals without also being state workers, and being a state worker requires adherence to political orthodoxy. The same state elites who regulate the labor market in education also guarantee teachers' professional status in return for obedience and loyalty to the state. To be sure, state elites' concern with controlling their teaching corps varies according to their interest in public education over time and across settings. However, for public school teachers, the struggle for professional status is inseparable from the context of state employment. In the case of teachers, professional status is a way for states to guarantee the loyalty of the corps, exchanging a labor market monopoly for obedience and adherence to political orthodoxy. State elites, in other words, rely on professionalism to ensure that teachers' behavior does not circumvent categorical boundaries. Indeed, professionalism comes to constitute such boundaries. The dilemma for state elites is that although they can impose categories, they cannot fully control the identities of the subjects of this imposition. Different groups of teachers appropriate the idea of professionalism, offer their own understanding of it, and, both individually and through their associations, make claims on that basis.

Category Work and Selective Engagement

When different associations of teachers compete for the recognition of state authorities, those authorities respond through selective engagement. Selective engagement refers to a strategic maneuver by which states "devise differenti-ated responses to [social] movement demands"[22] according to which demands, and which factions within the movement, are most politically acceptable to au-thorities. Governments prefer to engage with movement organizations that "do not threaten their own ability to govern and maintain law and order"[23] and are perceived as legitimate within the broader movement, so as to increase the likelihood that engagement will demobilize activists. Governments' tolerance for threatening action varies over time, as do the relative legitimacy of move-ment organizations within a given social movement, movement organizations' strategies for advancing their interests, and governments' perceptions of the capacity of movements to threaten the regime. Hence, selective engagement is an ongoing, dynamic process.

Not only a government's tolerance for teachers' threatening behavior but also its understandings of what kinds of performances constitute threatening behavior vary over time. Teachers are less of a threat to a government, all else being equal, than secessionist rebels, nationalist insurgents, Communist revo-lutionaries, or the like. However, the process of centralizing a public education system makes the threat of collective disobedience or politically unortho-dox behavior by public school teachers carry more weight than it otherwise would. The importance of teachers' public performances becomes greater, as centralization increases their value (that is, mobilizes them). When public school teachers become more valuable to state elites, regulators can be reliably expected to inscribe categorical boundaries, differentiating social relations within the teachers' corps and between teachers and others to make teachers' deviations from political orthodoxy more costly.[24] Such action changes the way teachers' administrative superiors understand teachers' public performances (and, at times, their private ones). The broader point is that institutional sub-version is relative; the withdrawal of obedience, loyalty, cooperation with the state, or other expressions of political orthodoxy are more or less disruptive at different times and in different places.

Considering the scenarios discussed in the first few pages of this book makes this point clearer. When more than two thousand French teachers gathered in Paris to discuss pedagogical matters at a state-organized teachers' congress, their subsequent demand for a trade union constituted subversion. Twelve days after the congress ended, Spuller responded to the teachers' transgression by issuing a circular to the prefects that formally forbade all autonomous teachers' associations. "The autonomy of the *fonctionnaires* [low-level state workers] has another name," the minister wrote; "it is called anarchy; and the autonomy of the *fonctionnaire* societies would be organized anarchy."[25] In October, Spuller addressed the teachers, telling them that if their job was "the most noble of all, it must remain the most reserved and modest" and that "submission is the first condition of moral perfection."[26] The administration's model primary school teacher was derived from an understanding of the *instituteur*'s role in French society that dated back to the French Revolution, and the role did not allow for autonomous political action.[27] New York City teachers, however, could flood City Hall in droves, men and women alike, during the public debate over the Davis Bill of 1900. It would be two decades before the professional ideology that the centralizers imposed on the teachers' corps would result in a crackdown on teachers' participation in politics. Prior to World War I, thousands of women teachers participated in equal-pay-for-equal-work campaigns, as well as women's suffrage and campaigns for legalized birth control and trade union rights. In these two countries, state authorities interpreted different kinds of actions as politically unorthodox and potentially threatening.

When governments selectively engage professional workers, they are sending different signals to the political factions within the workers' movement. To the moderates, they are signaling a willingness to accept their claim making as legitimate. To the radicals, they are signaling that their claim making will not be recognized and that further contentiousness could be grounds for repression. These signals shift the ways that these two factions relate to each other. Selective engagement incentivizes moderates' labeling of radicals as unprofessional agitators while simultaneously encouraging the radicals to label the moderates as sell-outs. It also encourages other groups within the movement to pick sides as relations polarize and the government starts to engage with part of a social movement that previously went unrecognized.

Selective engagement, in the context of post-centralization teacher politics, constitutes an intervention in a conflict over the limits of professional boundaries. As discussed previously, professionalization is a struggle between groups of workers to corner the market for the service in question in which one or more groups bid for state support. When factions of a workers' movement are competing for state support in matters of occupational jurisdiction, a state's acceptance of a new collective actor's claim making as legitimate constitutes acceptance of a professional boundary. A professional identity invokes a boundary between those who have jurisdiction over a particular work practice and pretenders to such jurisdiction. And it always involves a claim to the exclusiveness of the work that its bearers do for a living. Although all collective identities invoke differences with the potential for politicization, a professional identity is inherently political, since it relies on state support to actualize the exclusiveness of the difference in question: expertise in a particular kind of abstract problem solving.[28] Such a power-laden identity claim is sure to generate tension when a state's category work is predicated on such a claim. Category work, as discussed earlier, is how state elites incorporate teachers into the state apparatus. State elites have the power to create categories, but their ability to enforce compliance with the relations created through these categories is severely circumscribed.

Selective engagement, therefore, is a form of actor certification, constituting a government's "signal of its readiness to recognize and support the existence and claims of a political actor."[29] When a social movement seeks political representation and legitimacy, such a signal constitutes partial, if not necessarily complete, satisfaction of this demand. The reason is that "recognizing the right to make a claim also helps to stabilize and secure that identity."[30] Such a signal can manifest itself quite differently, depending on the relationship between regime challengers and members. For example, the decision of power holders not to suppress a particular claim-making performance could be such a signal if the regime presented a particularly closed political opportunity structure to the regime challengers or if the same performance had regularly triggered repression in recent memory. This is what happened in France. Beginning in 1905, the teachers' movement was split between moderates and radicals, and over the next two decades, French authorities began informally, and unsteadily, tolerating the moderates and marginalizing the radicals. In 1924, after decades of official intolerance of autonomous teachers' organizations, the French government instructed the local school inspectors to maintain good relations with the teachers' *syndicats* (unions). This was the first unambiguous signal from government to teachers that teacher organizing would not be suppressed. In the United States, however, selective engagement did not immediately follow centralization. Teachers were not, at the time, forbidden from political activity, and the city government did not respond through selective engagement to the equal-pay-for-equal-work campaign that constituted the teachers' most important claim-making activity in the period between centralization and World War I. Centralization triggered a decades-long effort on the part of city administrators to maintain a quiescent teaching force, and the notion of professionalism became part of state elites' discursive toolbox for disciplining teachers. At the same time, however, the drive for professional recognition, along with the newly centralized administration, triggered a wave of teacher organizing in New York City. In the years that followed, the moderate-radical cleavage was cross-cut by a series of other identities, defined by gender, religion, and so forth. Only after a coterie of high school and university teachers founded the New York City Teachers' Union (which became Local 5 of the AFT) to fight strident battles for higher salaries and academic freedom and intellectual liberty did a moderate-radical cleavage become consequential in city education politics.

Summing Up

There are two causal propositions to be analyzed in this book:

1. Centralization causes mobilization.
2. Mobilization causes selective engagement.

Locating the process of centralization in time is the first order of business for each case. That means specifying the historical circumstances in which center-periphery tensions with regard to education first became politicized, discussing the dominant and opposing interests and identities that were mobilized for conflict, and examining how the outcomes of the political battles affected the education system and the regulation of the teachers' corps relative to the "center" in question. Rather than conceive of centralization as a teleological process, with a well-defined beginning and end, I look at the precise historical circumstances within which centralization was imagined and enacted in each case, as well as the way the process yielded conflict over the roles that centralizing authorities expected teachers to fulfill. I rely almost entirely on secondary sources for examining centralization.

To detect teacher mobilization, I look for evidence of teachers' public performances. Such performances include not simply strikes and demonstrations, which were relatively rare among teachers during the centralization era, but also public gatherings, meetings of pedagogical conferences and societies, and publications of teachers' associations. I expect that these performances will also reveal information about teachers' identities that are important to their understandings of themselves and their administrators. Since understanding the nature of teachers' radicalism is dependent, I argue, on the specific conditions of their identities in their communities at the time of centralization, I pay particular attention to the ways that teachers saw themselves before and after centralization struggles in their respective environments. Regarding category work, when "a simple verification of mutual membership imposes obligations on actors who have not properly met," a category is strong.[31] For evidence of such verification, I look at the teacher training institutions. By examining normal school curricula, students' lifestyle, and pedagogical conference proceedings, I show that state authorities built a distinctive personality type that resonated across provincial France. Since the normal schools and conferences gave teachers an opportunity to meet one another and secular authorities in a regularized setting, they provide good evidence to accompany what social historians tell us about teachers' interactions with other stakeholders: parents, priests, clerical teachers, and children. In New York, meanwhile, Normal College (later renamed Hunter College) trained women teachers, and City College trained the men. The question of forming networks of women teachers in New York City, I suggest in Chapter 4, was less important than the ways in which Normal's curriculum changed in response to the city's own demographic and the school's uncertainty about what the goals of grammar schooling ought to be. The evidence of these performances and identities is taken from a combination of secondary and primary sources that include rare newspaper articles, annals and minutes from meetings of teachers' organizations, periodicals of teachers' associations, and police reports of early activities of teachers' unions, along with personal essays and correspondence between teacher unionists.

Selective engagement requires attention to government decisions in response to not simply fragmentation within the teachers' corps but also political expressions of that fragmentation. That is, I examine how governments respond to competition between factions of teachers over the state's legitimate recognition of their associations and the acceptability, if not the complete satisfaction, of their demands. This requires some attention to how, why, and whether governments perceive collective claim making by competing groups of teachers to be politically threatening. I expect that governments' evaluation of teachers' contentiousness will be shaped by the relative political salience of public education, the electoral situation of the government in power, and the history of teachers' collective claim-making to date. I also return to teachers' public performances to examine dynamics between teachers' associations in response to the engagement of one group of teachers and the isolation or suppression of others.

What kinds of evidence would serve to falsify this theory? One possibility is that the events under consideration do not follow the sequence that I have laid out. If, for example, there is strong evidence that governments selectively engaged with teachers prior to their efforts to mobilize them, that would suggest that my understanding of teachers' relationship to the state is incorrect. Similarly, if teachers responded in wildly varying ways to centralization politics, and governments respond through selective engagement, that would suggest that centralization itself does not drive teachers to radical or otherwise unorthodox political performances. Finally, if selective engagement either did not happen at all or happened according to some logic other than a response to a potential threat from competition over occupational jurisdiction, then that would suggest that governments professionalize teachers according to some process other than the one advanced in this book.

Looking Ahead

Chapters 3 and 4 examine the politics and process of centralization in these cases. In Chapter 3, I show how a partial, incomplete effort to centralize the French public school system during the 1830s yielded polarization between secular and ecclesiastical educators, a polarization that produced anticlericalism among secular schoolteachers.[32] Animosity toward religious authority was at odds with successive governments' fragmented efforts to build a corps of quiescent allies for parish priests to fulfill their spiritual missions in the countryside. When French republicans triggered a more intensive, wide-ranging centralization of primary education during the 1880s, which included privatizing Catholic schooling, the state mobilized the *instituteurs*. French teachers seized this opportunity to begin placing demands on the state, including the demand for a national trade union. Prior to intensive state intervention in primary education in the 1880s, French teachers had no opportunities for collective action and very little room for individual political action. The earlier, partial effort to centralize public education in the 1830s yielded an atomized, apolitical teachers' corps throughout provincial France, with no chance to act collectively. However, this early effort antagonized the Catholic Church, which tightened its grip on primary education. Tension between secular and ecclesiastical authorities in provincial France created unpleasant environments for local schoolteachers, who found themselves at the mercy of the parish priests, who retained the authority over primary schooling that they typically held. Over the ensuing decades, teachers were not at a loss for grievances—salaries that barely kept them out of poverty, job security that was dependent on local political connections and, as I show later in great detail, their subjection to parish priests, or curés—but until the republicans overhauled the primary education system in the 1880s, teachers lacked the means to make those grievances politically resonant. Teachers internalized anticlericalism until the centralizing reforms of the 1880s extracted religious from moral authority. What enabled them to mount collective challenges to state authorities were the very institutions those authorities created to train them: normal schools for prospective teachers and pedagogical conferences for working teachers.

Chapter 4 examines how centralization triggered animosity from teachers' associations throughout urban America. New York City teachers fought publicly and unsuccessfully against centralization during the 1890s. This struggle drove city centralizers to reform the category of schoolteachers in an effort to remove them from positions of political influence in the city. At the same time, centralization triggered a wave of teacher organizing, producing and reifying heterogeneities throughout the teachers' corps. While many of the new teachers' associations remained politically quiescent, others turned to collectively making demands on city and state governments. The largest one, the Interborough Association of Women Teachers (IAWT), waged a decade-long battle for equal pay for equal work. But it was the activism of a small group of politically radical secondary educators that created the New York City Teachers' Union and spurred the city administration and, later, the New York state government to repress the teachers.

Chapters 5 and 6 examine the politics of selective engagement. In France, not long after the *instituteurs* established a loosely knit national federation of locally organized teachers' associations, a group of revolutionary syndicalists broke away from the moderates. This action prompted the government to engage cautiously with the moderates in an effort to divide the movement. In the years that followed, successive governments reprimanded, suspended, and fired syndicalist teachers, and the moderates did little to complain. These dynamics cemented the divisions between radicals and moderates, which persisted through World War I and beyond. After the war, however, the French government made a tactical error, refusing to involve representatives of the moderate teachers in salary negotiations, thereby driving them to unionize and moving them closer to the political position of the radicals. For the remainder of the 1920s, French governments uneasily negotiated relations between these two groups, as education reform once again became an intense political issue and the Catholic Church's political power showed signs of revitalization. Meanwhile, New York City teachers found themselves politically silenced during the 1920s in the aftermath of the Red-hunting campaigns earlier in the decade. By 1930, however, selective engagement politics had begun, as TU radicals competed with the moderate JCTO for the attention of the municipal government. The city government routinely dealt with the committee instead of the TU until the splintering of the union in 1935 yielded two left-wing groups, one controlled by Communists and the other by anticommunists. After World War II, when the suppression of the TU definitively marginalized the Communist organization, the remaining teachers' organizations struggled to overcome the professionally generated cleavages between primary and secondary teachers and, in particular, conflicts within the secondary teachers' corps. Only after these differences were negotiated could the teachers' associations merge under the banner of the United Federation of Teachers (UFT), the chief organization of New York City teachers to this day.

Chapter 7 concludes the book and suggests areas for further research. First, I move the historical account of teacher unionism forward through a discussion of the events of 1968 in France and in New York City. Both settings became battlegrounds for other social conflicts to play out, with centralized public education serving as the political architecture and, at times, an actor in the drama. After looking at these conflicts, I reexamine the causal theory presented in this chapter in light of the case materials. I also reflect on the distinctiveness of the New York experience and the degree to which claims about this city might hold elsewhere in the United States, as well as offer a gloss on one other European case—Russia. Finally, I suggest two areas for further, cross-national research: the effects of the feminization of teaching on teachers' collective claim making during and after the centralization era, and the effects of changes in twentieth-century political economy and state structure on teacher unionization.

II

✷ ✷ ✷

Centralizing Education and Mobilizing Teachers

3

✳

*Centralizing Public Education
and Teachers' Politics in
Nineteenth-Century France*

D uring the last two weeks of July 1833, lay public school teachers in the cities and villages all across France were greeted with a surprise in the daily post. Each teacher found an official correspondence from Paris, from no less a luminary than the education minister, François Guizot. The minister was sending the teachers a copy of the new education law that had gone into effect on June 28. Even more surprising than that was the personal letter to the teachers, signed by the minister himself. The letter, dated July 18, described the importance of the teachers' mission—"universal primary instruction is from now on one of the guarantees of order and social stability"[1]—and the kinds of benefits and assistance the government would offer the teachers to offset the sacrifices they had to make in terms of prestige and economic well-being. But Guizot went further; he also told the teachers that, beyond enacting the new education law, their duties included maintaining the correct ties with the other parties in their orbit. He instructed them on the proper relations between the teacher and the children, the parents, the town mayor, the parish priest, and "the special authorities that tend to the schools . . . the University itself."[2] In short, Guizot defined the role that teachers were expected to play collectively in France as he prescribed the relationships that they were expected to maintain in their respective, rural locales.

Half a century later, the education ministry again sent a letter to the teachers. But the conservative Protestant Guizot was long gone, as was the bourgeois monarchy of Louis Philippe. Now, the progressive positivist Jules Ferry headed the ministry, and Ferry, along with his friend Ferdinand Buisson, was in the process of transforming the institutional regime that had administered primary education in France since the years of Guizot. And the *instituteurs'* mission, Ferry wrote, was correspondingly different. The challenge for teachers now was to adjust to the fact that the new primary school regime extracted religion from the teaching of morality. From now on, families would deal with religious training, while teachers would be responsible for moral instruction in the classroom. Instead of being the priest's aide, Ferry wrote, "you are the auxiliary and, in certain respects, the replacement of the family father."[3] More than ever before, the teacher would be a kind of representative of the central government in the state's dealings with its citizens in their role as parents.

The republicans of the 1880s reimagined the elementary school teacher and sought to make this image real. They did so, I suggest in this chapter, because they were also remaking public education. Public primary education was mostly religious in its content and in its place in the administrative hierarchy prior to the Third Republic (1870–1940). Ostensibly secular schoolteachers gave lessons in reading and writing that were infused with religiosity, directed as they were toward preparing children for their first communion. In the years after the July Revolution of 1830, the new regime's concern for restoring social stability coexisted with a renewal of Catholic Church influence in provincial France, dating back to the Napoleonic era. The new model schoolmaster (*maître d'école*) would be correspondingly pious, professionally committed, and unquestioningly loyal to local authority figures, particularly the parish priest. Ferry's 1883 letter to the teachers accompanied a more radical shift in the content and administration of primary education than had transpired during the Guizot years. Teachers needed to be specially instructed to carry out the work of the newly centralized education regime, one that was directed by the central state's agents, did not kowtow to religious orthodoxy, and was installed at the risk of enormous political capital.

What is the importance of these letters and education projects for understanding teachers' politics? When Guizot sent his letter to the teachers in 1833, he was writing to a group of mostly untrained educators with little if any esprit de corps. Teachers remained isolated in the rural communities where they were employed. Dependent on town councils and the goodwill of parents for their remuneration, they remained politically quiescent. Furthermore, in the years following the July Revolution of 1830, the central government reinforced its rigid regulations on the formation of associations, as the state moved to suppress working-class unrest. For the teachers, who lacked the social networks that make sustained collective action (including social movement activism) possible, the government's suppression of associations only reinforced teachers' conservatism. It also ensured that the Société des Instituteurs et Institutrices Primaires de France, organized by a young schoolteacher named Philippe Pompée, would be short-lived. For the remainder of the decade, locally organized mutual-aid societies and associations for pedagogical assistance cropped up in provincial France, but they were of a temporary and loose-knit character, often folding after a year of activity. Teachers' quotidian existence consisted of their hours in the schoolhouse, and increasingly over the next couple of decades, they performed a variety of municipal tasks, often tied to religious observance (helping the parish priest prepare for Mass, cleaning the vestry, and ringing the church bells) or the work of the town mayor (transcribing contracts; writing birth, death, and marriage certificates; and surveying land). The primary school teachers of the 1830s were immersed in their local communities, not alone but certainly isolated from other teachers.

By the time that Jules Ferry wrote his letter, however, French *instituteurs* had come to associational life. The state's teacher training institutions— normal schools and pedagogical conferences—had brought teachers together. Associations of former normal school students that had begun meeting regularly during the 1870s proliferated in the decades that followed. Regional pedagogical conferences, which had been disbanded during the Second Republic, began meeting again. Government officials also began to organize national teacher congresses in Paris in a conscious effort to try to build a collective identity among the *instituteurs*. The first of these national meetings was held in 1881 while Jules Ferry was fighting for passage of the compulsory schooling law that would bear his name. The national congresses continued to be held annually up through 1887 and were usually organized by local academic authorities or by members of the central ministry. However, in 1885 and 1887, teachers took the initiative. Teachers worked in conjunction with Jules Siegfried, the Protestant mayor of Le Havre (Seine-Maritime), to organize an international teachers' congress there in 1885. Siegfried had a long-standing interest in school reform and had dreamt for many years about holding an international conference of educators. About two thousand French teachers, men and women, were joined by seventy delegates from other countries and several hundred school inspectors and normal school directors. Two years later, twenty-two hundred teachers attended a four-day teachers' conference in Paris, at which the attendees discussed the possibly of forming a trade union and called for a more robust central teachers' organization with regional affiliates.

My argument in this chapter is that the epistles to the teachers, separated by a half century, evince a shift in the way that the French state perceived its primary school teachers and that this shift was embedded in critical political struggles over the content and administration of primary schooling that were transpiring in France during these two eras. During the July Monarchy (1830– 1848), successive French governments intervened in local education practices with unprecedented vigor, ordering towns to maintain schools with salaried public school teachers, making *départements* fund normal schools for teacher training, creating a school inspection corps, and so forth. These regulations created tension between municipal governments and the Catholic Church, the two authorities with which power over primary education had traditionally rested, and the central government. Public school teachers found themselves caught up in this tension. In response to the secular state's intervention, local and ecclesiastical authorities tightened their surveillance of teachers. By the end of the July Monarchy, the friction between the French state's engineering of the *instituteurs'* public image and the quotidian existence of most rural *instituteurs* had created a subaltern identity among the secular schoolteachers that was quite at odds with the intentions of school reformers. Anticlericalism was at the heart of this identity. The next time that the French state sought to overhaul primary education, during the 1880s, they once again reshaped the teachers' corps. This time, however, central authorities believed that in order to create a corps of truly secular *instituteurs* (and, this time, *institutrices*), teacher training institutions needed to be completely transformed and attendance needed to be mandatory. The resulting training regime enabled teachers from across the regions to create durable networks and even some loose-knit associations. The state tolerated these associations at first, since it needed the teachers' support to carry out the secularization of the primary schools and stave off the challenges from the Catholic Church. But when the teachers, fearing that centralization would replace the tyranny of the church with the tyranny of the state, tried to unionize, the government moved quickly to suppress them.

Centralization in the 1830s

Prior to the July Monarchy, primary education was a matter of local initiative. Towns employed schoolmasters, usually the children of farmers or lower-class laborers with little knowledge of the basic reading, writing, and arithmetic they were charged with teaching to French children. Families and parish priests insisted on limiting primary schooling to the rudimentary knowledge of letters and numbers that children would need for their first communion. Given that teachers' salaries were paid by municipal governments, losing the confidence of parents or the curés meant job loss. Successive central administrations, dating back to the First Empire, inadvertently reinforced these local norms by empowering the Catholic Church. Napoleon Bonaparte partially restored the church's powerful position in France with the 1801 Concordat, believing that young boys and girls ought to learn to be loyal subjects of the empire.[4] Inculcating loyalty, he thought, was a task best undertaken by the ecclesiastics.[5] In 1808, the first emperor invited the teaching congregations—outlawed in France since 1790—to resume their duties in the countryside, and the subsidy of twenty-five thousand francs they were granted was the only money that the first emperor ever spent on primary education.[6] Over the course of the Bourbon Restoration (1815–1830), primary schooling became a regime priority. While the Restoration's constitution, the Charte, did not specify its importance, the chief educational policy maker, Pierre Royer-Collard, proclaimed that with the Charte, "universal instruction was promised because it was necessary."[7] The ordinance of 1816, a compromise between royalists and liberals, empowered the University to license teachers, authorize school openings, and withdraw licenses and authorization when the need arose. However, the ordinance also ensured that the certificates of good conduct required for teachers to start working could not be obtained without the approval of the mayor and curé, thus effectively giving them power over the process of nominating teachers. While "each element of the system could frustrate the other, and no one was strictly accountable to anyone else,"[8] in practice, primary schooling was clearly the domain of local governments and the Catholic Church.

The final years of the Restoration, however, created a lasting rift between ultramontane royalists and the liberals. Until 1828, the trend of the 1820s had been in the direction of greater clerical control in public education: the expansion of the teaching congregations, the requirement for prospective teachers to obtain authorization from a bishop or a committee of priests to teach, the investment of surveillance power in bishops, and a reaction against the "mutual method" of pedagogy.[9] But after the liberals' electoral victory in 1828, and Jean-Baptiste de Martignac's appointment of Antoine Lefebvre Vatimesnil to the new Ministry of Public Instruction, the situation began to change. The ordinance of April 24, 1828, restored University control over teacher certification. Subsequent ordinances drew Jesuit high schools into the University, restored ecclesiastical secondary schools to their role as seminaries, and, although these seminaries were not subject to University authority, capped enrollment in the secondary schools at twenty thousand. In an effort not to alienate the Catholic Church, the April ordinance had granted the clergy a more prominent place on the cantonal committees. But it was not enough. By the end of June, the Martignac government had forfeited good relations with the church. Vatimesnil's policies provoked a group of young, ultramontane Catholics, including such *universitaire* luminaries as Henri Lacordaire, Charles de Montalembert, and Félicité Lamennais, to embrace a new political doctrine with regard to education: *liberté de l'enseignement* (freedom of education). Parents, they argued, should have the freedom to choose where and how (that is, from religious or secular, private or public teachers) their children would be taught. It was this defection of previously royalist Catholics that provided sufficient support for the liberals to work the principle of *liberté de l'enseignement* into the revised Charte of 1830.[10]

Under the guidance of François Guizot, the French government realized this liberty, in primary education at least, with the law of June 28, 1833. The new law was the most far-reaching primary education law in French history to date. Guizot referred to it as the "charter of primary education."[11] It stipulated that every town had to maintain a primary school and established a curriculum, including moral and religious instruction, reading, writing, French language, arithmetic, and the official system of weights and measures. The law made *communes* (towns) officially responsible for providing schoolhouses that could accommodate all of the town's students and their teacher. It also made tuition mandatory to attend the schools, although it was waived for poor families. Teachers were guaranteed a salary of two hundred francs per year, a sum low enough for teachers to continue their practice of taking on second jobs in order to subsist but also a starting point in public *instituteurs'* rise to respectability. In an effort to lure more people to the teaching profession, the law exempted from military service anyone willing to enter into a contract to teach for ten years. The law drew a sharp distinction between public and private schools, the latter being strictly those schools managed by individuals rather than by the central state, *département*, or town.[12] Any eighteen-year-old could found a private school if he had evidence of his intellectual capacity and a certificate of moral fitness (signed by municipal councilors) to present to the town mayor. Guizot also established surveillance committees to oversee the school(s) in each *commune*; two years later, Guizot established a full primary inspection corps. All *communes* with more than six thousand inhabitants had to maintain a public secondary school, as well as a new *école primaire supérieure* (upper-level primary school) for teaching advanced topics in math and science.[13]

The law of June 28, 1833, did not originate with Guizot. In February 1830, education policy had been about to take a crucial step forward. A law was passed that would have fixed teacher salaries, divided communal schools into three types according to size, instructed the *communes* to ensure sufficient funds to establish and maintain public schools, and forced the *départements* to establish primary normal schools. The July Revolution prevented the law's implementation. Furthermore, a series of ordinances were passed in 1830–1831 whose provisions Guizot recycled in 1833: the reduction of clerical representation in the local committees to a single member, the elimination of the certificate of religious instruction as a teaching prerequisite, and the introduction of an exam for *congréganistes* (members of the Catholic teaching congregations) and other private school teachers to obtain a teaching certificate. Guizot's predecessor in the education ministry, Camille de Montalivet, twice tried to create a new legal regime in education in 1831 and 1832 with elements drawn from these ordinances (Guizot became the education minister on October 11, 1832). Guizot's law, in fact, extracted several articles verbatim from Montalivet's education bills.[14] While the government did spend more money on primary education after 1833, the trend of increased spending actually began a couple of years before the 1833 law, as presented in Table 3.1. The only real innovation of his law was his division between the primary school and the more advanced *école primaire supérieure*, an institution that would grow and then temporarily recede before being reborn during the Third Republic.[15] Except for the creation of these schools, few of the changes in primary schooling during the July Monarchy departed substantially from trends that began at the beginning of the Restoration. Quantitative data on the development of primary schooling over time suggest that the 1830s concluded a period of expansion of schools that coincided with local demand dating as far back as 1815.[16] The "Guizot Law" and the expansion of primary education in France during the 1830s should be understood not as the success of one man but as the culmination of a series of efforts that began prior to the 1830 revolution.

As Guizot and his colleagues understood quite well, popular distrust of the central state and the animosity of local ecclesiastical authorities were the two sources of opposition to education reform during the July Monarchy.[17] But, as

TABLE 3.1   PRIMARY EDUCATION BUDGETS IN FRANCE, 1822–1880

Year	Primary education spending as percentage of total education spending	Education spending as percentage of total spending	Primary education spending as percentage of total spending
1822	1.25	0.39	<0.01
1823	0.94	0.32	<0.01
1824	1.30	0.36	<0.01
1825	1.37	0.37	0.01
1826	1.89	0.37	0.01
1827	1.24	0.36	<0.01
1828	1.38	0.35	<0.01
1829	2.75	0.36	0.01
1830	6.94	0.34	0.02
1831	16.21	0.34	0.06
1832	24.54	0.34	0.08
1833	29.32	0.45	0.13
1834	29.42	0.47	0.14
1835	38.65	1.18	0.46
1836	39.35	1.21	0.48
1837	41.60	1.27	0.53
1838	41.36	1.23	0.51
1839	40.26	1.26	0.51
1840	39.38	1.12	0.44
1841	43.47	1.19	0.52
1842	42.83	1.12	0.48
1843	42.54	1.14	0.48
1844	44.88	1.21	0.54
1845	45.98	1.15	0.53
1846	42.41	1.18	0.50
1847	43.85	1.12	0.49
1848	46.17	1.09	0.50
1849	52.55	1.32	0.69
1850	51.12	1.45	0.74
1851	50.96	1.50	0.76
1852	52.71	1.52	0.80
1853	52.71	1.48	0.78
1854	54.10	1.12	0.60
1855	58.45	0.82	0.48
1856	59.44	0.90	0.54

(continued)

TABLE 3.1 *Continued*

Year	Primary education spending as percentage of total education spending	Education spending as percentage of total spending	Primary education spending as percentage of total spending
1857	59.06	1.07	0.63
1858	59.60	1.10	0.66
1859	59.97	0.95	0.57
1860	59.90	1.09	0.65
1861	58.33	1.06	0.62
1862	51.76	1.20	0.62
1863	50.65	1.15	0.58
1864	51.62	1.22	0.63
1865	52.16	1.34	0.70
1866	52.64	1.35	0.71
1867	53.92	1.35	0.73
1868	59.61	1.64	0.98
1869	60.23	1.74	1.05
1870	62.20	1.23	0.77
1871	61.15	1.25	0.77
1872	62.51	1.53	0.96
1873	62.98	1.54	0.97
1874	61.80	1.71	1.05
1875	61.91	1.68	1.04
1876	62.89	1.69	1.06
1877	61.61	2.03	1.25
1878	60.54	2.12	1.28
1879	62.12	1.98	1.23
1880	63.40	1.95	1.24

Source: Calculated from the raw data provided in Charles Nicolas, *Les budgets de la France depuis le commencement du xix* siècle (Paris: Imprimerie Générale A. Lahure, 1882).

Guizot himself wrote, the politicking of the 1833 law was relatively smooth: "The law on primary instruction was welcomed, discussed, and voted upon favorably, and without major impairment."[18] The law was bred from the political and administrative momentum for education reform of the previous three years: "The movement was instilled, the obstacles removed, the public impatient to see primary instruction established; when the cabinet of October 11, 1832, was formed, action was demanded and solemnly promised on all sides but hardly begun."[19] Furthermore, the constitutional document of the new regime, the Charter of 1830, guaranteed *liberté de l'enseignement*. Its inclusion enabled the regime to claim that education reform was a fulfillment of a constitutional obligation. There were some difficult parliamentary debates, as conservative Catholics objected to excessive state control and some extreme leftists detested the power it left to the Catholics. But the outcome was not in doubt.

Although the Guizot legislation and the increase of central state spending on schooling represent an increase in state authority over primary education, a close look at the implementation of the law shows the limitations of state centralization during this period. One important limitation to the state's reach was the power of the Catholic Church in much of provincial France. During the 1830s, ecclesiastical authorities were still very much in active, day-to-day control over the operations of the primary schools, and the lines of authority over schooling remained slanted toward clerical power. In matters of curricula, for example, secular teachers continued to teach what local priests allowed them to teach. The new legislation changed the legal hierarchy among the local committee members from curé-mayor-local notable to mayor-curé-local notable, but given the magnitude of priests' influence on mayors throughout the French countryside, this was not a monumental shift.[20] Priests, in consultation with the mayor, were in charge of nominating teachers to their posts. Even after the creation of the primary school inspectors' corps in 1835, priests maintained a disproportional amount of power because of their influence with parents and traditional role as overseers of educating children in provincial France.

The local implementation of the Guizot law reveals still more limitations on the power of central government over primary education. While there were many men devoted to the cause of primary education (and collaboration with the central government to improve it) in the largest cities and *arrondissement* administrative centers, rural locales lacked secular sponsors for their schools. The mayors of the Somme refused to cooperate with the central or departmental administration with regard to the new legislation.[21] In the West, in Maine-et-Loire, the local committees existed in name only. In the few *arrondissements* where they did exist, they rarely if ever convened. In the Southeast, in the Vaucluse, the July Revolution flushed supporters of clerical education out of the town councils. But across these three *départements*, congregational schooling became more popular during the 1830s, as more families chose them and demanded them, and local ecclesiastics began to retaliate against what they perceived as a return of Jacobinism.[22] When matters of school personnel became contentious during the July Monarchy, local authorities usually deferred to the priest.[23]

Guizot's legislation provoked the French Catholic establishment. Battle lines between state and ecclesiastical authorities hardened during the 1840s. Guizot's belief that an education without a strong religious component was incomplete[24] did nothing to conciliate the church. The question of private education in the secondary schools inflamed Catholic opinion, and Catholic political journals ran hostile stories about the godless *professeurs* and *instituteurs* in the secular schools, as anger over secondary education spilled over into debates over primary schooling.[25] The moderately liberal clerical newspaper *Ami de la religion* declined in popularity during the 1840s relative to the ultramontane *Univers*, which attracted increasing numbers of subscribers after the polemically reactionary Catholic journalist Louis Veuillot took over as editor.[26] Furthermore, while the July Revolution also created large turnovers in the makeup of town councils throughout provincial France, even the most secular local politicians had to contend with the fact that the parish priests met the spiritual needs of rural families. Congregational teachers not only offered their services tuition-free; they were also better equipped to assist families in this regard.

Teachers during the July Monarchy: Category Work and Identity Formation

The identity of the pre-Guizot *maître d'école* bore little resemblance to the professional, socially prestigious *instituteur* that came of age in the Third Republic. Prior to the 1830s, many teachers "saw themselves, not as *instituteurs* but as *clercs-laïcs*: men personally dominated by the priests and occupationally committed to furthering the broad spiritual goals of the Church."[27] Others were *ambulants*, wanderers who signed seasonal short-term contracts with mayors and town councils before moving on to the next village.[28] They taught whatever parents wanted them to teach and generally depended on peaceful relations with priests and parents for whatever job security they enjoyed. Even after the 1833 creation of an official curriculum, there was no uniformity to pedagogical practice. During the 1830s, pedagogical journals proliferated throughout the country, as the demands of the Guizot legislation for more and better teachers spurred national, regional, and local publishers to disseminate teaching aids to working *instituteurs* and, increasingly, *institutrices* as well.[29]

The slow transformation of teachers' identities began with the normal schools. Guizot's legislation required each *département* to maintain one. There were fourteen schools in 1829, thirty-six in 1832, and seventy-four by 1837. The central government regulated them from a distance, and there was little in the way of uniformity among them. According to official regulations, the normal schools were supposed to offer courses for prospective teachers in reading, writing, French grammar, science, history, geography, singing, agricultural education, and land surveying, and even electives like bookkeeping and the grafting and pruning of trees. But most normal schools taught only a fraction of these topics, and normal school graduates would rarely teach most of them in the classroom. Normal schools trained their students to fill a very particular role in rural French communities. Teachers' traditional responsibilities ranged "from the church linen to the parish cemetery,"[30] and normal schools taught prospective teachers to expect such duties. So, while most parish priests and parents viewed the secular schoolmaster with suspicion, they also saw him as being potentially useful. Teachers learned land surveying skills to help local authorities, tree grafting and pruning to assist landowners and tenants, and music to help the parish priests with church services. Teachers often played a central role in preparing children for their first communion, so parents gave teachers tokens of their appreciation that reinforced both the value of the service the teacher was providing and the image of the teacher as *cleric-laïc*. Normal school training was an effort to reinforce these traditional understandings of the local schoolmaster while increasing society's confidence in the teacher to fill these roles. In fact, "Guizot's idea that 'the teacher should know more than he teaches' soon provoked the opposition of conservatives," who foresaw overly intellectual normal school graduates eschewing rural France to "remain instead in the cities as unemployable malcontents and agitators."[31] The government responded by scaling back normal school curricula, keeping the schools in provincial towns, and forcing students to board. Normal schooling was originally a conservative rather than a radical enterprise, but parents, priests, and town councils did not always interpret it that way.[32]

Normal schools reinforced the boundary between *instituteurs* and others in a number of ways. First and foremost, they tended to recruit from the primary schools themselves. Working teachers encouraged their most promising pupils to enter the profession and to do so by first enrolling in the departmental normal school. Furthermore, most normal schools required students to board. Students were under constant supervision, even during their daily walk outside school grounds. Some schools, like the one in Angers, designed uniforms for their students.[33] Military exercises were often conducted in the school courtyard. The Rennes academy rector ordered normal school students to join the Society of Agriculture and Industry in order for the teachers to help meet the needs of the regional economy.[34] Insubordination and intemperance were grounds for expulsion. These disciplinary rituals and isolation from the rest of society concentrated the social boundaries between teachers and the communities that they would come to serve. By the 1840s, most veteran teachers had accepted the superiority of normal school graduates, and they asked to have such graduates as classroom assistants and apprentices.

The pedagogical conferences, a way for working teachers to hone their skills, were also local institutions. Teachers would meet once per month during the winter, twice in the summer, in the administrative center of a canton, often at the normal school if there was one available, to discuss pedagogical issues, exchange tips for improving classroom performance, and listen to instructional lectures given by advanced *instituteurs* or perhaps a *professeur* from a local secondary school. In 1837, the central government issued a circular to regulate the conferences, but its effects were minimal on actual conference proceedings. Although the circular stipulated that religion was to be a major part of conference proceedings, they were in fact fairly secular events, particularly when compared to normal school training.[35] Like the normal schools, the conferences did not create anything new so much as reinforce existing traditions. The particular importance of teaching teachers the metric system was an exception.[36] Although data to assess the question systematically is difficult to obtain, it is likely that the conferences raised the level of knowledge and pedagogical proficiency of hundreds of rural schoolteachers. But the conferences also suggest that primary education was still not socially valued for anything other than its religious significance. Among conference attendees, "no one suspected that there was a science of education."[37] Although the state's 1833 legislation shifted the lines of jurisdiction, primary education's legitimacy remained rooted in the Catholic Church.

The pedagogical conferences also provide strong evidence for the effectiveness of category work. Conference attendance rose unevenly but surely through the early 1840s, before financial problems and a lack of enthusiasm from town councils saw a decline.[38] The primary school inspectors, a part of the new education bureaucracy as of 1835, began to actively watch the conferences and report on them,[39] suggesting enough internal coherence to be commonly recognizable to external authorities. In addition, some teachers, inspired by the experience of independent "normal courses," took it upon themselves to organize conferences. And like any association in 1830s France, the assembled teachers had to draw up statutes for their associations, and they wrote to town councils, prefects, and even the minister to get the statutes approved.[40] In Omer (Pas-de-Calais), for example, a teacher who claimed to be imitating his colleagues elsewhere requested the authorization of a conference so that he and his colleagues could "ameliorate and render elementary instruction uniform."[41] In St. Florentin (Yonne) and farther south in Castelsarrasin (Tarn-et-Garonne), groups of teachers that had previously held unauthorized conferences asked for official clearance for their respective groups to "establish a tie of friendship which binds them together."[42] Teachers in Bar-sur-Aube (Aube) listed "extracting the *instituteurs* of this arrondissement from the state of isolation in which they have lived to this day" as their goal, before listing the pedagogical elements of their task.[43] Teachers were becoming increasingly aware of their common priorities and practices, as well as their isolation from other teachers.

The secular *instituteurs* were not the only option for towns having to hire a teacher. From the time when Napoleon Bonaparte had invited the Catholic Church back to France, parish priests had either taught in the classrooms themselves or invited teaching congregations, such as the Christian Brothers, to found schools. Unlike secular teachers, congregations worked for free. In response to Guizot's legislation, priests began giving parents incentives to avoid sending their children to lay schoolteachers. The pattern became familiar. Congregations would open a school in a *commune*; parents would be attracted by the promise of a free education for their child and the assurance of a teacher with good moral values and/or would be faced with the curé's threat of having the first communion for their children withheld; some children would subsequently be transferred from the lay teacher's school to the Christian Brothers' school; the lay *instituteur* would then lose a number of students and, thus, money out of his pocket, so, in the face of this economic pressure, he would need to either take another job or quit teaching altogether to look for less-taxing work.[44] Brothers would move into schools that lay teachers, under pressure from the clergy, evacuated. If a congregation was not available, a priest would teach the town's children himself. In the Vaucluse, the departmental council pushed hard for secular education after the July Revolution, and municipal councils with secular majorities emerged, but by the end of the 1830s, the ecclesiastics had won the day. When the town councils cut off public subsidies for the religious schools, private donations took up the slack, while supporters of clerical education engineered the closing of many of the Vaucluse's mutual schools.[45]

When competition from the congregations intensified in the 1830s and 1840s, secular teachers found themselves isolated in their communities. Their appeals to local school committees were usually fruitless, since taking a stand against the prestigious teaching congregations tended to be unpopular. The congregations provided good education, they were well-trusted, and the lay *instituteur* cost the community money while the congregations provided their services for free. Religious education was still the norm and the only kind of primary education that was legitimate among most French parents (who were, after all, the principal clients of this service). With little incentive for local authorities to support the lay *instituteurs* and the uneven power relations in which teachers were embedded, their isolation intensified after 1833, when the Guizot legislation (as well as Guizot's own letter to the teachers) signaled to the *instituteurs* more, not less, support from the government. The parish priests were often a de facto surveillance force to accompany, as of 1835, the de jure school inspectors. Any complaints that priests had with *instituteurs* would be taken to the families, the mayors, and the departmental authorities, and given the priests' local influence in most of rural France, many a teacher lost his job for ignoring his auxiliary religious duties. Hence, individual expressions of independence from the clergy during the July Monarchy were nearly impossible and quickly quashed, while collective dissent or resistance against the government was unheard of. The very hint of anything scandalous was enough to disperse associated teachers. When some teachers from the Bas Rhin, for example, formed a conference, they elected a man known for his loudly proclaimed "republican doctrines," prompting the underprefect to suspend the conference.[46] In the canton of Villeneuve-de-Berg (Ardèche), a group of teachers complained to the rector about their conference president's "cold, ironic" treatment of the attendees and his general hostility toward them, moving the rector to suspend the conference "in order to avoid . . . new scandalous scenes."[47] The hierarchical relationship between the curé and the *instituteur*, the traditional religiosity of teachers in the French countryside, and a legal regime designed to maintain both of these constraints all helped maintain docility among teachers. The social boundaries between secular teachers, teaching congregations, parish priests, and the surrounding communities were effectively policed.

The gap between teachers' expectations of secular authorities and the reality of their mistreatment by ecclesiastical ones created a space for anticlericalism to grow. The *instituteurs'* hostility toward the church began to smolder during the 1840s.[48] Most significantly, Arsène Meunier, a former normal school director and ardent socialist who was hostile to the church, founded a teachers' journal, the *Echo des instituteurs*.[49] Broadly speaking, the *Echo* was to be a "permanent petition" to record all the *instituteurs'* complaints, defend their rights and interests, formulate their views and demands, and solicit their deserved moral and material ameliorations—all in order to secure for them "more well-being and independence."[50] The *Echo* was outspokenly critical of the Guizot law of 1833, but the teachers whose letters appeared in its pages had far more to say about the priests and teaching congregations than about the secular government. Teachers accused the Christian Brothers and parish priests of being reactionary enemies of the French people and depicted them as incompetent brutes.[51] They routinely criticized the poor quality of the Christian Brothers' teaching, their ignorance in the subjects they were supposed to teach (math and geometry in particular), their fondness for corporal punishment of children, and their reactionary values. "This is the exploiting class," one *instituteur* wrote of the congregations; "the brother is the *ancien regime* or absolutism, the *instituteur* is the Revolution or liberty."[52] The *Echo* and its teachers also complained about the unfairness of allowing the congregations to compete with the lay teachers while charging fees for parents who did not want to send their children to the Brothers, and they protested the church's practice of refusing to grant communion to children of secular teachers. Teachers wrote to thank the *Echo* for trying to defend the teachers against clerical hostility. One teacher from the Maine-et-Loire wrote that disagreeing with a curé was enough to get a lay *instituteur* in trouble. Another wrote that most curés thought that the *instituteurs* were worthless and would insult and degrade them behind their backs and often in front of the children to undermine the *instituteurs'* authority. The *Echo* agreed with this assessment and was hardly surprised by conflict between these two authorities, since "one has a mission of hastening progress, the other a mission to fight it; how could they come to any agreement? There is necessarily a battle between them."[53] Meunier sent a photograph of Boulay de la Meurthe, the teachers' champion in the Chamber of Deputies, to *Echo* subscribers. De la Meurthe was one of the teachers' few political supporters—he scrutinized and voted against salary bills that he deemed insufficient to alleviate teachers' dire financial situation[54]—and many *Echo* subscribers responded with enthusiasm over their new political spokesperson.[55] By the end of the July Monarchy, relations between secular and ecclesiastical educators had never been more polarized.

Although Meunier founded the *Echo* and inspired it, the journal did not represent a leader without followers. Beyond the letters that the *Echo* published each month, there is further evidence of the teachers' interest in the journal's slant in the demands published there for a political association. As early as the fourth issue, April 1845, a reader from the Maine-et-Loire wrote to the *Echo*, claiming to sense "the necessity for the lay *instituteurs* to form a vast association to act as an interpreter of your excellent journal." The issue came up again a year later. Then, in the August 1847 issue, the *Echo* published a letter from an *instituteur* from Toulon (Var), Vaccon, that set events in motion.[56] Vaccon wrote, in an opinion that ran against the grain as far as the *Echo* was concerned, that the Guizot law was not so bad in principle. However, its application was faulty, and if the *instituteurs* really wanted it, the law could still produce excellent results. So, the *instituteurs* should centralize their efforts in making their feelings known in the Chamber of Deputies by forming a vast association. Meunier asked *Echo* subscribers to write in and promised that if 1,000 teachers wrote that they would be in favor of such an association, he would take steps to organize it. The response was vibrant. In November, the *Echo* reported that 350 teachers had pledged their support, and there were more than 500 by December, 640 in January 1848, and 705 reported in the February issue. After the 1848 revolution began, the *Echo* dropped Vaccon's plan for a "society" and, seeing in the new republic a new set of opportunities, moved on to other matters. But the *Echo*'s supporters, though a small proportion of the teaching force, are clear evidence of increasing hostility toward the clergy.

As a public document with thousands of readers, the *Echo* provides particularly strong evidence of the creation of the teachers' categorical identity. It also demonstrates the limits to the French state's power to regulate teachers' identities. The state could help provide a template for orthodox behaviors and attitudes, but it did not have the repressive resources required to force teachers to conform to it. The teachers' anticlericalism was undesirable and unintended, and secular authorities had little idea of how deep teachers' resentment ran.

Mobilization Failure, 1848–1851

Within two weeks of the February Revolution of 1848, the new republic was already engaged in reforming the teachers' corps once again. The new education minister, Hippolyte Carnot, ordered his rectors to prepare instruction manuals for teachers for them to use to show voters how to evaluate prospective electoral candidates. He even invited teachers to stand for election themselves; in April 1848, thirty-two of them did so. "I am calling on them to contribute their share to found the Republic," Carnot wrote. "It's not a question, as it was in our fathers' time, to defend it against the danger of the frontier; it must be defended against ignorance and lies, and this task falls to the teachers."[57] Although most of the pedagogical conferences had folded by 1848, the remaining ones were now used to organize electoral workshops. The police superintendent of the Moselle, for example, "called together the presidents of the cantonal conferences of teachers, reminded them of their duty to support the government, and granted them one day's leave to coordinate their political action."[58] A similar call was made in Aveyron. In this case, the police commissioner, Alfred Raginel, ordered the teachers to draw up a list of preferred candidates, a list that included the commissioner himself.[59] The new government now saw the *instituteurs*, once understood as a passive tool for reinforcing conservative, religious values, as a force for republican indoctrination.

This attempt at reshaping the teachers' corps, however, met with failure. The political establishment found in Carnot and his *instituteurs* a useful whipping boy following the violence of June 1848. In the first week of July, the legislature censured Carnot, and he resigned. When an extraparliamentary commission met the following year to draw up a new education law, Adolphe Thiers declared the *instituteurs* responsible for the evil forces that had turned the people away from duty and obedience. "Thirty-seven thousand socialists and communists," Thiers called them, those "detestable lay *instituteurs*."[60] He criticized the normal schools for the "demagogic spirit" that had infiltrated them, and he advocated their "absolute suppression."[61] The Catholic press also noted the "evil passions" that motivated many primary teachers.[62] And so it went. The church and the secular state demonized the teachers and punished them for their supposed political subversion. While the evidence is scant, local studies of teachers' political activity during the Second Republic suggest that there was much less subversion than the authorities believed.[63]

The ongoing legitimacy of the Catholic Church, still a bulwark of stability throughout the French countryside, foiled Carnot's attempt to mobilize the teachers to do republican work. Without a substantial change in the legitimacy behind teachers' work, their jurisdiction over primary education remained similarly limited. Ecclesiastical authorities coded teachers' efforts to act outside their jurisdiction as politically unorthodox. By 1851, teachers had clearly cultivated a resonant anticlerical identity, but they lacked the means for expressing it. In addition to the fact that organizational structures were missing, the conservatism of rural French society in the face of political instability curtailed the possibility for teachers to make collective demands of any of those to whom they could attribute responsibility for their misery: the municipal government, the central government, or, most of all, the clergy.

The Second Empire and the Rouland Inquiry

Nothing in the opening seven years of the Second Empire suggested anything other than a trend toward greater spirituality in primary education. Teaching in a primary school became an increasingly unattractive work prospect for young men, and normal school enrollment leveled off and then declined. Even before the coup of Louis Napoleon, the regulations of March 24, 1851, and July 31, 1851, scaled back the scope of normal school curricula to match the requirements for earning basic teaching certification: moral righteousness, religious knowledge, and political docility. Reading, writing, and arithmetic remained in the curriculum, but the courses in history, geography, agriculture, bookkeeping, and the sciences were dropped as requirements, although in some schools they remained as electives.[64] The new curriculum was designed to discourage individual reflection on the subject matter, in favor of recitation of facts learned verbatim from textbooks. Finally, the requirements for entering the normal schools were changed. The 1851 regulation abolished the qualifying examination and was replaced by a private investigation of each candidate by the rector and his inspectors. Entrance to the school generally required the outcome of this investigation to speak well of the candidates' moral righteousness and religious (Catholic) beliefs. While the pre-1851 regulations required students to be between the ages of sixteen and eighteen to study at the normal schools, the 1851 reforms made eighteen the minimum age for a potential student to enter the school and prevented students older than twenty-two from entering. Given that the age requirement for the state teaching certification remained eighteen, the reforms had the overall effect of discouraging prospective teachers from attending the normal school. Now, young men with good personal histories and an interest in becoming teachers had no incentive to enter a normal school at age eighteen, since the normal school program no longer provided students with skills necessary for the classroom.[65] The Hippolyte Fortoul ministry (1851–1856) rendered discipline at the normal schools even stricter and day-to-day life gloomier, "with meals in silence and all movement in the school regulated by the roll of a drum."[66] The religious teaching orders moved to fill teaching vacancies all over France. The church replaced the now-defunct pedagogical conferences with "pedagogical retreats" run by clerics and permeated by religiosity.[67] During vacation months, teachers would gather at a normal school or the local monastery to listen to academy and local authorities speak on questions of pedagogy, morals, or religion. Teachers did not play an active role at these meetings but were required to sit and listen.[68] By the end of the decade, an ecclesiastical authority could confidently write that "within ten years, France will be ours."[69]

The turning point in the history of church-state relations was Louis Napoleon's intervention in the Italian war for independence in 1860. The Catholic Church condemned Louis Napoleon's decision to send troops to aid Camillo Cavour against Austria, and within a year, the church came to be seen as a threat to social stability, not a guarantor of it. The teachers, once feared as subversives, became more orthodox than the church, as the traditionally cooperative relationship between mayors and priests became antagonistic. Now, instead of the mayor and curé allying against the "demagogic and socialist" *instituteur,* the *instituteur* and the mayor came together to oppose the "reactionary and ultramontane" priest.[70] This is not to suggest highly politicized *instituteurs* but, rather, *instituteurs* whose secularism rendered them increasingly valuable in rural France as allies with local authorities and the central state's local representatives. National elites still perceived the teachers as essentially apolitical.

By this time, however, teachers had already fostered a strong sense of anti-clericalism. The best evidence for such an identity is a series of essays that the *instituteurs* wrote between December 1860 and February 1861. Minister Rouland wanted the teachers to report on the problems with primary education as they perceived it in the schools, the students, and the teachers. The ministry received nearly six thousand essays from teachers all over France. Historians have analyzed samples of these documents, dividing them by region, academy, and/or *département*.[71]

While it would be incorrect to say that all these essays reveal animosity toward the ecclesiastical authorities—not all of the essays mention the priests, and not all expressed hostility toward them[72]—animosity toward them was certainly a recurring theme, which cut across geographic and administrative boundaries. "It always seemed that their kindness was accorded to the man rather than to the teacher," wrote a teacher from the Vienne. "The clergy dreams of a day when teaching will be exclusively religious," claimed another, while still another wrote that the parish priest "tells everyone in town that the instruction given by the lay teacher is a poison."[73] Still another, from the town of Rilly (Ardennes), wrote of the "instinct of domination" that was "innate in the priest."[74]

The *instituteurs'* desire for emancipation from the priests extended to their extrapedagogical existence. For example, many teachers placed great value on their gardens, not only because of the extra fruits and vegetables they provided for their households but also because the garden was a status symbol for the teacher as a (very) small landowner, making him feel as if he were on the same level as the priest.[75] The irony of the teachers' desire to be considered the equal of their traditional oppressors is best understood in relation to the similarities between the novitiates and the normal schools, both highly spiritual institutions, well into the Third Republic. Priests and teachers "were often both escapees from poverty or manual labor by dint of education, the one in a seminary, the other in an *École normale*."[76]

Along with the common awareness of the power of religious authorities, the teachers' memoirs also displayed a degree of generational self-consciousness. The older teachers in particular commonly made reference to 1833, 1848, and 1850 as pivotal years, suggesting an awareness of the central government's role in shaping the structures of primary education. Furthermore, there were clear value judgments involved. Members of the generation born 1814–1834, who accounted for 60 percent of the total number of respondents and over three-quarters of the total number of pages submitted, believed that they had begun teaching during the golden age of primary education, having obtained unusually good training, while the teachers born later generally defined their generation of teachers as inferior to its predecessor.[77]

Categorical boundaries were policed at least as rigorously in the years following Louis Napoleon's coup as they had been in the 1840s. Given that most teachers continued to attribute responsibility for their misery to religious authorities, the reaffirmation and enforcement of the boundary between secular teachers and the religious teaching congregations only intensified the *instituteurs'* frustration. The essays are particularly powerful data in this respect, given that these teachers had very few opportunities to interact with one another; their expressions of frustration were generally not the result of extensive socialization or network building with other teachers. The shift in church-state relations after France's intervention in Italy probably had more substantial effects than the legislation of the Second Republic on the evolution of primary education in France. The question of Italian unity was more salient than domestic French politics for the Catholic Church. The Rouland inquiry and the subsequent relaxation of disciplinary oversight came in the midst of a reconfiguration of church-state relations. Although the early years of the Third Republic provide strong evidence that the Catholic Church still had clout in French politics—approximately twelve thousand Christian Brothers operated in France during these years, as well as priests of other religious orders[78]—the friction between teachers and priests was about to become a source of political capital for a new generation of education reformers.

The Third Republic: Centralization and Teacher Mobilization

The Franco-Prussian War and the fall of Louis Napoleon rejuvenated church-state conflict in France. After an abortive attempt by the provisional government of 1870–1871 to despiritualize public education,[79] church-state conflict reemerged on the political stage. With the fires of the 1871 Paris Commune still burning, the Catholic Church's guarantee of social stability increasingly appealed to the nonrepublican political elite. An alliance of monarchists and Bonapartists won the first elections of the Third Republic in 1871, just months after the collapse of the Commune. Adolphe Thiers was the new regime's first president, but he resigned after two frustrating years of legislative gridlock and hostility. His replacement was General Patrice MacMahon, whose army had surrendered to Germany in 1870 and, more important, who led the troops that had squelched the Commune. The military president catered to the monarchist appreciation for order, even as his republican opponents publicly cautioned the country that the monarchists were in league with the Catholic Church to subvert the republic. General MacMahon, however, was bound by the size of the leftist majority in the Chamber of Deputies to appoint consecutive republican prime ministers, Jules Dufaure and Jules Simon, neither of whom could please political allies on either side of the political spectrum. Simon's task was made particularly difficult in January 1877, when his republican comrades demanded that he more vigorously suppress ultramontanism, whose presence in French society appeared particularly threatening after Pope Pius IX's call for universal condemnation of Italy's leftist government generated sympathetic public demonstrations throughout France.[80] General MacMahon abruptly dismissed the Simon ministry on May 16, 1877, and appointed a new government led by the Orléanist Duke of Broglie, in defiance of the republican majority in the Chamber. A month later, in response to the Chamber's call for a vote of confidence, MacMahon dissolved the assembly and called for new elections, further polarizing relations between the advocates of representative government and those of monarchism. Broglie and the general tried to fix the upcoming elections, to no avail; the republicans emerged triumphant once again in October. One of the first actions of the new government was to strip the chief executive of the power to dismiss the Chamber and to establish a system of parliamentary sovereignty that would last for the rest of the Third Republic.

These events generated a more polarized education politics in several respects. The conflict over regime stability forged unity on the French left over the matter of anticlericalism. Although there were multiple battlegrounds in the conflict between church and state, public education was the most salient because "the issue at stake was the control of the minds and loyalties of future generations of Frenchmen."[81] The republican architects of the school reforms that were to come, Jules Ferry above all, envisioned universal, compulsory, and, most important, secular public schooling for French children up until the age of thirteen. This plan was politically polarizing, since it struck out at the Catholic Church, whose connections to ancien régime politics and society had made it the most reliable ally for the monarchism that characterized the French right during the nineteenth century.[82] Furthermore, as I have already described, conflict over public education dated back to pre-Napoleon times. Whenever the matter of the Catholic Church's role in French society reemerged in national politics, the question of education reform was sure to follow. Finally, it was during these years that the myth of the Prussian schoolmaster gained currency in political circles. According to this story, France's defeat in the recent war was the result of the superiority of the Prussian education system, and the Prussian teachers in particular. With the surrender of Alsace to Germany, the French defeat led successive governments to seek out new advantages in its international competition with its neighbor to the east. And Prussia had been one of the "early risers" with regard to top-down primary education reform.[83] These factors, combined with increasing demand for different kinds of schooling, made public education an increasingly important political issue during the later 1870s.

The combination of a republican majority in the legislature, a newly centralized decision-making apparatus, and the embarrassment of conservative political forces in the wake of the MacMahon debacle yielded a fruitful setting for the advancement of the republicans' agenda. After a first year of addressing other priorities of republican ideology—moving the National Assembly from Versailles to Paris, making "La Marseillaise" the national anthem and July 14 a national holiday, among others—the majority began its overhaul of the public education system in 1879. Conservatives, buttressed by an increasingly unified Catholic press, resisted these actions, to little avail. By this time, the political overlap between secularism and republicanism, on the one hand, and religiosity and conservatism, on the other, had become unusually pronounced. The polarizing language associating the priests and the teaching congregations with the ancien régime and monarchism and the secular schoolteachers with the Revolution and republicanism became increasingly commonplace in the national and provincial presses.[84] The moderate left followed up its 1877 electoral success with another strong victory in 1881, followed by more modest ones in 1885 and 1889. With the revolutionary socialists representing only a small segment of the vote, the matter of secular, centralized primary education united most of the French left.[85] And the establishment of parliamentary rule in 1877 meant that the victorious republicans now had the power to advance their agenda with few institutional opportunities for their opponents to stop them.

Jules Ferry's reforms consolidated authority, and most financial responsibility, over popular schooling in Paris. The law of June 16, 1881, made primary school attendance completely free; the decree of July 29, 1881, made moral and religious instruction separate courses; the law of March 28, 1882, made primary instruction obligatory and legally independent from religious authorities; and the law of October 30, 1886, expelled ecclesiastic personnel from public school classrooms. The central government relieved the *départements* of all financial responsibility for public primary education, as shown in Table 3.2. By 1890, all funding for the public primary schools came from the *communes* and, primarily, the central government. The teaching congregations began a slow, legally enforced withdrawal from the primary schools, although this maneuver was not well enforced with regard to women.[86] These reforms collectively constituted the most intensive central state intervention in public primary schooling since the French Revolution.

Given that provincial French communities still harbored some distrust of the secular teachers, Ferry understood that extracting morality from its traditional place in education would be a particular challenge to rural schoolteachers. For this reason, and in an effort to distance itself from the relaxed relationship between the Catholic Church and the Second Empire, the Third Republic began placing unprecedented confidence in the secular *instituteurs*. The minister made his aims clear in his 1883 letter to the teachers, described at the beginning of this chapter, impressing on them the precise nature of their new, secularized responsibilities: "By exempting you from religious education, we don't intend to relieve you of moral education. On the contrary, it appears entirely natural that the teacher, at the same time that he teaches children to read and write, also teaches them the elementary rules of moral life which are no less universally accepted than those of language or arithmetic."[87] The delegation of responsibility for moral education to the *instituteur* and religious education to the curé did not mean that public school teachers were to be atheists, as his conservative opponents argued. Teachers, he asserted, who presented irreligious or antireligious views in the classroom were committing a sin no greater than beating or otherwise physically abusing a child. Furthermore, *laïcité*, this new idea of secularism, did not constitute political neutrality, Ferry and his colleagues believed.[88]

The republican regime's interest in the teachers is clear in its reform of the teacher training institutions. The 1879 reform of the normal school regime obliged every *département* in France to maintain at least one normal school for men and, for the first time, one for women as well. The establishment of

TABLE 3.2   PRIMARY EDUCATION SPENDING IN FRANCE BY ADMINISTRATIVE
LEVEL, 1870–1899 (IN MILLIONS OF FRANCS)

Year	State spending	Departmental spending	Communal spending	Total
1870	10.5	9.3	41.8	61.6
1875	16.4	13.1	48.2	77.7
1880	31.3	19.6	57.3	108.2
1881	47.5	17.9	51.0	116.4
1882	88.6	18.0	27.2	133.8
1883	87.1	17.8	30.1	135.0
1884	91.3	18.0	32.4	141.7
1885	86.6	18.0	66.0	170.6
1886	85.1	17.3	67.6	170.0
1887	85.1	17.6	70.5	173.2
1888	85.5	17.8	70.8	174.1
1889	80.1	17.9	71.9	169.9
1890	120.5	0	56.6	177.1
1891	122.4	0	59.8	182.2
1892	126.0	0	60.3	186.3
1893	139.6	0	67.7	207.3
1894	141.3	0	68.0	209.3
1895	142.8	0	68.7	211.5
1896	143.5	0	70.2	213.7
1897	146.9	0	71.0	217.9
1898	156.1	0	77.4	233.5
1899	157.8	0	79.9	237.7

Source: Adapted from Patrice Grevet, *Besoins populaires et financement public* (Paris: Éditions Sociales, 1976), 348.

a system of women's normal schools, parallel to the men's network of normal schools, virtually assured the recruitment and training of lay teachers of both sexes. A special fund was established to make sure that the *départements* had the necessary funds to build and maintain new buildings.[89] In 1881, Ferry's administration modernized the programs of the women's normal schools to match the academic rigor of the men's schools. Although Duruy's 1867 law on primary education required courses in geography and history in schooling girls, normal school curricula had not been changed to train teachers in these subjects. The eighteen women's normal schools that existed as of 1877 were mostly confessional in nature, with nuns teaching most of the academic courses. Well over half of all women teachers in France at this time were themselves nuns. They were mostly ignorant of the academic subjects in the curricula.[90] After Ferry's reforms, normal schools began instructing teachers in these subjects.

The beginning of official encouragement of pedagogical conferences came earlier, in August 1878, when Education Minister Agénor Bardoux organized a countrywide meeting of *instituteurs* in Paris for the occasion of the Universal Exposition. The Universal Exposition gathered visitors from all over Europe, Asia, and the United States to see the progress being made in schooling the children of the world. The French delegation of primary teachers included contingents from the eastern and southwestern regions of the country, and they all gathered to see the state of primary education in other countries and listen to a series of speakers discuss a set of issues that would have been familiar to conference attendees of the 1830s: pedagogical methods, religious education, the metric system, geography, and so forth. There was even a talk given by an M. Jost, a Parisian school inspector, on the history of the conferences themselves. Bardoux saw the teachers' enthusiasm for these conferences as evidence that the conferences of the July Monarchy needed to be revived. The central government reauthorized the pedagogical conferences in October 1878 and rendered attendance mandatory two years later.[91]

From the teachers' perspective, Bardoux's suggestion that the conference regime be revived was both welcome and surely somewhat surprising since, for the past few years, the teachers of several of the *départements* had begun reestablishing the conferences. Indeed, the teachers were told that conferences were already being held in Nancy, and Jost make specific mention of the Savoie, the Haute-Savoie, the Vosges, and the Ardèche. One teacher, M. Hien from Château l'Abbaye (Nord), wrote in his report on his visit to the exposition that along with the conferences in Valenciennes that he attended himself, teachers in the neighboring Ardennes were also holding conferences every six months.[92]

While the new conferences resembled those of the July Monarchy in many respects, the differences are most striking. One difference was the inclusion of women teachers, the *institutrices*. However, reports indicate that women did not participate much in the conferences. Women were struck by a "sentiment of excessive reserve," one commentator wrote in 1882, with reference to a conference in the Savoie.[93] "Embarrassed by the presence of male schoolteachers," wrote the rector of the Montpellier academy in 1885, "they restrict themselves to listening, so that pedagogical meetings are without interest and almost without purpose [for these women]."[94] Although the silence of the *institutrices* moved some authorities to suggest holding separate conferences for them, the gender segregation of the conferences never happened.[95]

But the most important differences between the conference regime of the early Third Republic and that of the July Monarchy were the aims of the organizers and the revelations of the teachers' discontent. While the conferences of the 1830s were designed to instruct teachers, those of the 1880s were supposed to "stimulate teachers' interest in new books and classroom techniques while encouraging solidarity among teachers."[96] Pedagogical authorities of the 1830s had expressed some sympathy for teachers' isolation, but building solidarity among the teachers was not their chief goal. The conferences of the 1880s, however, were often deliberate exercises in solidarity building. Ferry now asked local school inspectors to focus more of their attention on the conferences and called on the teachers themselves to offer their own voices on matters of primary schooling, including the pedagogical organization of classrooms under a single teacher and the best methods of recruiting for the normal schools.[97] One event is especially telling. At the 1879 conferences in the Toulouse (Haute-Garonne) normal school, evenings were spent singing and listening to songs performed on the harmonium. After an especially stirring performance, the idea of holding a concert was born, so the gallery and court of the normal school were transformed into a concert hall for an evening. The society of Toulousian singers gave a performance, and the prefect of the Haute-Garonne made an appearance with his son, an appearance that was greeted with an "enthusiastic ovation," according to the academy inspector. The merriment at the conference was unprecedented and a far cry from the stuffy, quiet, ascetic atmosphere of the conferences held during the July Monarchy. The teachers clearly appreciated the attention, as they showed in a letter to the academy inspector, signed by all seventy-seven of the conference participants, in which they thanked the relevant authorities for the care that the government gave to primary education, and the teachers in particular.[98]

Apart from organizing local conferences, government officials began to organize national teacher congresses in Paris in a conscious effort to try to build a collective identity among the *instituteurs*. Jules Ferry invited delegates from the cantonal conferences to the Sorbonne in Paris to discuss matters of pedagogical importance. The first of these national meetings was held in 1881 while Ferry was fighting for the passage of the compulsory schooling law that would bear his name.[99] From the republican perspective, the congress addressed a set of fairly uncontroversial issues, two of which became the substance of congressional resolutions (following unanimous votes): relegating the *institutrices* to the lower grades of the elementary schools and making elementary school attendance mandatory for all children, thus supporting the minister in his campaign.[100] The pedagogical conferences became strong networking tools for teachers, particularly after the 1880 regulation's attendance mandate drew increasing numbers of participants. When, at the Paris congress of 1881, Berthereau, a Parisian teacher, concluded the proceedings by declaring of all the delegates that "we quickly recognized ourselves as children of the same family,"[101] teachers understood that their family was the teaching profession. Representatives from the cantonal conferences helped organize the national congresses,[102] which continued to be held annually up through 1887.

During the 1880s, there were numerous examples of conferences in which teachers moved beyond pedagogical concerns to the level of professional grievances. One section of the 1881 Paris congress, in the midst of a discussion on how to assure school attendance, became engaged in a heated debate over the usefulness of the visits of local authorities to the schools, particularly the commissions made up of delegates from the canton. Several teachers recommended that the cantonal delegations be eliminated altogether because of their "incompetence" or the dominance of "the clerical element" in too many of them. Following a call for a vote on the issue, another teacher, M. Périer, noted that the teachers had drifted off to "a terrain foreign to the goal of the meeting and that the maintenance or suppression of the cantonal delegations [was] completely outside the competence of the Congress." Other issues—such as the inconvenience of classes larger than fifty students; the fact that teachers were rarely consulted when local authorities wanted to build, furnish, or otherwise improve the schools; and even the discharge of "all accessory functions" that teachers were forced to take on—were fair game for the discussion.[103] In August of that same year, at a departmental congress of five hundred teachers in Rodez (Aveyron), an *instituteur* from the town of Banhars, M. Carbonel, gave a report on the school contests (*concours scolaire*, in which the children competed for prizes based on their academic performance), which advocated permanently abandoning this institution. While the contests were being held, Carbonel claimed, teachers were working so hard to train their top students to win prizes that the majority in the classrooms were not receiving much attention.[104] Furthermore, these contests created tensions among teachers, who found themselves competing with one another, since highly graded students reflected well on the teachers. But over the past few years, Carbonel wrote, since the contests stopped being held, "the envy, the jealousy, [and] the division" among the teachers had evaporated.[105] The contests were thus assessed in terms of not only pedagogical success but also their relationship to teachers' solidarity. "Our union is our force," Carbonel wrote, and "we separate everything that could weaken this union, which is more necessary than ever in the face of adversaries irritated by the triumph of lay education."[106] By the time the legislature passed the Ferry legislation of 1881, teachers had begun to appropriate the pedagogical conferences and congresses for their own purposes.

For the remainder of the Third Republic, the defense of secular schooling (*école laïque*) was the top priority of the teachers' movement, along with autonomy from the arbitrary authority of their administrative superiors (*l'arbitraire administratif*). All of the auxiliary issues—an end to nepotism and favoritism in employment practices, internationalism, and, of course, salary hikes—were variations on the theme of professional autonomy. True professionalism, for example, would not be possible without salaries high enough to keep teachers out of poverty (and, therefore, free from the necessity of having to work a second job to subsist). The desire for independence was an outgrowth of the *instituteurs'* history of subjugation by ecclesiastical authorities and local political squabbles. During the final six months of 1877, in the midst of General MacMahon's intransigence, the teachers learned anew about the precariousness of government favor. Dozens of *instituteurs* suffered some form of administrative sanction for their suspected republican sympathies during the election campaign in the summer and fall.[107] The one constant still in the lives of most teachers was the presence of the parish priests. Anticlericalism was embedded in the demand for professional autonomy.

Matters reached a head in September 1887 when the four-day teachers' congress in Paris drew twenty-two hundred teachers from across France. Carriot, the director of primary education for the Seine, was the acting president of the congress, and the education minister, Spuller, was granted the position of honorary president. Many of Spuller's school inspectors were there as well, so the administration had a sizable presence at the congress. Indeed, the administration had designed the teachers' agenda, which comprised three issues: the question of whether teachers' associations should be autonomous or federal; the organization of the regional, national, and international conferences; and preparation for the international teachers' congress to coincide with the 1889 Universal Exposition. The discussion of alternative ways of organizing the teachers "sparked a discussion among the teachers which the government later regretted."[108] The teachers favored establishing autonomous associations of teachers in each *département* to protect their professional interests and uniting all these associations into a single Union Nationale des Instituteurs de France. The language of unionism (*syndicalisme*) was prevalent. Twenty-eight testimonies from *instituteurs* who had been unable to attend in person were read aloud, and unionization was recommended, along with a periodical and a mutual assistance fund with an obligatory fee for all members. The attendees also discussed the need for specific guidelines on teacher transfers to new posts, as well as the overwork of both teachers and students. None of the teachers' resolutions directly referred to the education ministry.[109]

The demand for a national congress went beyond what the ministry could tolerate. Even before the conference, in a letter dated September 1, 1887, Jules Ferry expressed his fear: "If Spuller allows this coalition of functionaries to form—a living outrage to the laws of the state, to the central authority, to republican government—there will no longer be a Ministry of Public Instruction, there will no longer be inspectors, there will no longer be a prefect."[110] Ferdinand Buisson later recalled the mood of the government following the Paris congress: "It was with terror that the Minister learned this news. I was called into his cabinet to examine what measures could be taken. . . . For a long time, for months, we were preoccupied with this terror, this phantom."[111] Yet, at the time of the conference, Spuller and the other administration representatives showed no outward signs of dissatisfaction. To the contrary, Carriot encouraged the teachers: "Correct, gentlemen, redress [and] criticize! We need your experience to complete our own. By putting our efforts together, we shall come to realize progress."[112] Carriot's response was the product of a short-lived uncertainty. Twelve days after the Paris conference ended, Spuller responded to the teachers' transgression by issuing a circular to the prefects that formally forbade all autonomous teachers' associations. "The autonomy of the *fonctionnaires* has another name," the minister wrote. "It is called anarchy; and the autonomy of the *fonctionnaire* societies would be organized anarchy."[113]

Another circular was sent to the rectors, requesting them to alert the inspectors of the need to make sure that all the teachers understood "their obligations and responsibilities."[114] The point was reinforced yet again in October, when Spuller addressed the teachers, telling them that if their job was "the most noble of all, it must remain the most reserved and modest" and that "submission is the first condition of moral perfection."[115] Although Spuller continued to allow the departmental and cantonal pedagogical associations to meet, his circular put a decade-long stop to the *instituteurs'* national organizing efforts.

Conclusion

The centralization of primary education made teachers' collective action possible. Before Guizot orchestrated the central state's intervention into primary schooling, the *instituteurs* had no esprit de corps, no durable social networks, few mechanisms for generating them on their own, and relatively little inclination to do so. Both the standard dynamics of provincial French society and the national legal framework discouraged teachers from engaging in public claim making, either collectively or individually. The legislation of the 1830s challenged local control, but it did not fundamentally subvert the legitimacy of parental decisions and Catholic Church authority over primary schooling. Since whatever influence town councils and family fathers had over primary education happened through the local clergy, challenges to local control usually constituted provocations of the Catholic establishment. Over the next quarter of a century, the church intensified its efforts to professionalize the teaching congregations, reinforcing the social boundaries between them and the secular teachers, and bound secular schoolteachers more closely to their religious duties. The combination of the clerical reaction to the Guizot reforms and the growth of secular training institutions, like the normal schools and pedagogical conferences, created a toxic situation for the teachers of rural France, who found themselves at the heart of cross-cutting church-state and center-periphery tensions. The partial centralization of the Guizot era catalyzed the anticlericalism that would become a hallmark of the teachers' organizations of the Third Republic, which I discuss in more detail in Chapter 5.

Centralization transforms center-periphery relations by definition, but in the specific case of France, it also meant secularization. The education reforms of the Jules Ferry era required more political capital than the Guizot-era reforms because Ferry and his colleagues were completely redrawing the lines of legitimate jurisdiction over primary education. The magnitude of this project inspired a comparably radical shift in the mechanisms of training teachers. Religiosity was slowly squeezed out of the normal schools and pedagogical conferences. The requirement that teachers attend these institutions, particularly the pedagogical conferences, created new and durable networks of educators. Teachers appropriated these institutions for their own purposes, culminating in the congresses of Le Havre in 1885 and Paris in 1887. Thus did the regime's mobilization of teachers, by way of the training institutions, beget the teachers' own use of those same institutions as a resource for their own political mobilization.

While French teachers lacked the right to make collective demands as of 1880, their American counterparts had no such obstruction. I now move on to the question of how and why centralization of public education, which began in the urban United States in the 1890s, precipitated the stigmatization of teachers' involvement in politics.

4

✳

Centralization and Its Discontents among New York City Teachers

New York City teachers were active and vocal opponents of centralization. While their French counterparts had publicly supported centralization during the 1880s, they had done so timidly, uncertain of their collective power. But in New York City, teachers were part of a loose-knit, but vocal coalition of city dwellers that opposed what they saw as an elitist intrusion into a matter of local control. Teachers spoke up in a number of ways. For one week in late April 1895, the New York City Teachers' Association organized a series of rallies to protest the centralization bill that was then making its way through the state legislature, a bill that would eliminate the power of neighborhood wards over matters directly affecting the schools and vest it in a central Board of Education. One rally held at City College attracted four thousand teachers, more than 90 percent of the teachers' corps.[1] *School*, a newspaper dedicated to the city teachers' perspectives on education issues, railed against the reform. In March 1896, thirty-five hundred teachers signed a petition against the bill. When the bill came to the mayor's desk for approval in April, hundreds of teachers flooded City Hall to demand, in vain, that the mayor, William Strong, reject it. The teachers had their allies—political party officials, spokesmen for the religious communities, and community leaders from the Bronx and Harlem—but there was little question about where the thrust of resistance to centralization would come from: within the school system itself. Throughout this episode, the teachers' right to make collective claims on the city administration was never questioned.

Two decades later, however, teachers' participation in city politics was less acceptable. By 1916, the Progressive movement in American education was in full swing. The Progressive movement was a cluster of ideas about education that privileged managerial expertise, rigid hierarchy, and impersonal bureaucracy as tools for social justice and social control. Positive change could come about, the argument went, only by extracting administration from the evils of partisan politics—which, for most reformers, was the only kind of politics there was—and putting it in the hands of politically disinterested, civically enlightened experts.[2] By the time World War I began, the administrative "professionals" who had fought for centralization were now entrenched in New York City's schooling apparatus. Leveraging their positions in the Board of Education and the Board of Superintendents, these newcomers sought to depoliticize education, to "take the schools out of politics" in the name of efficiency and cost-cutting. These administrators had powerful political patrons: the Republican Party and a small minority faction of the Democratic Party, along with a series of city organizations devoted to "municipal reform" and "good government." Since teachers were simultaneously the biggest drain on the city's education budget and the most important workers in the education system, their activities came under closer scrutiny than ever before, both in and out of the classroom.[3]

During the two decades between the battle over centralization and the American entrance into World War I, teachers did not cease their political activity altogether. As described previously, teachers agitated over the Davis Bill in 1900. Over the next decade, women teachers demanded equal pay for equal work; fought for the right of married teachers to continue work in the classroom; and participated in movements for birth control, trade union rights, and economic justice.[4] Both men and women classroom teachers reached out in solidarity to teachers in other cities and around the country through the NEA and, as of 1916, the AFT. More so in the United States than in France, teachers brought a rich set of experiences in different forms of political activity into their associational life. However, administrators now labeled their interest in collective political advocacy "unprofessional" and unseemly. There was clearly a gendered dimension to this reaction—most of the city teachers were women elementary school teachers who the "professionals" clearly believed could be exploited more easily than the men. Indeed, the most politically successful of the pre–World War I teachers' organizations was the IAWT, which fought for equal pay for equal work in the teaching profession. There was also an ethnic dimension to the new regime's hostility to teachers' politics. The new immigrants to the city between 1890 and 1920 were primarily Italians and Eastern European Jews, groups that the centralized administration believed would be particularly difficult to assimilate. The teachers' corps slowly but surely changed in response to this trend. "At Hunter College [the teacher training school] Eastern Jews were 8 percent of the graduates in 1906, and one-quarter of the graduates ten years later."[5]

But the city education administration and political establishment responded with the most hostility to the radical politics of the Teachers' League, the forerunner to the TU, a smaller organization made up mostly of male, Jewish high school teachers. The Teachers' League and, later, the TU promoted pacifism, solidarity with organized labor, and the election of classroom teachers to the

Board of Education, to go along with higher salaries and better working conditions. After the Bolshevik Revolution of 1917, the TU, the only advocate for freedom of thought and expression among the teachers' organizations, became an attractive organization for city Communists in the teaching profession.[6] As a result, the union became a target of state surveillance and repression.

The orthodoxy of teachers' participation in public politics clearly shifted between 1890 and 1920. While teachers were never legally forbidden from political activism, by the end of World War I, there was a stigma attached to teachers' public claim-making activities that had not existed prior to centralization. This chapter explains how and why this happened.

As in France, centralization caused mobilization. Centralization spurred political change on the part of administrators and politicians, on the one hand, and teachers and their organizations, on the other. The coalition that fought for centralization followed up its victory with a series of reforms to reinvigorate the teachers' corps and thus to realize its vision for a more efficient, effective, and ostensibly apolitical education system. Doing so constituted category work, as the city's education elite sought to reconfigure teachers' relationship to their work, the administration, and the political establishment. However, while in France the centralizers were secularizers, interested chiefly in extracting rural schools from Catholic Church hegemony, centralization in urban America was an outgrowth of the Progressive movement, an experiment in urban political and administrative reform.

Teachers, meanwhile, responded to centralization by reorganizing themselves in citywide associations, divided by professional affiliations and gender difference, to better avail themselves of the new administrative structure, whose hierarchy, from bottom to top, was the Board of Education, the superintendent, and the mayor's office. While this organizational ferment was taking place, many teachers were participating in the other political struggles mentioned earlier. Between 1896 and 1917, however, the interaction between administrative category work (to mobilize teachers as a resource for the city) and the teachers' professional identity formation (to make claims on the administration) created a politically fragmented teachers' corps, with less solidarity than had existed among nineteenth-century teachers. The city's introduction of the Gary schooling model and the imposition of Americanization (discussed later) yielded a new, important cleavage within the teachers: the moderate-radical split. A minority of politically radical city teachers fought against these policies and became marginalized in city politics. The majority of more moderate teachers adhered to the city's formula for professionalism, relying on a "teachers' council" to deal with the Board of Education. Teachers' participation in collective public politics did not end but was closely monitored in a way that circumscribed mass action of a kind that had been more popular during the nineteenth century.

I begin by discussing the politics of centralization during the early to mid-1890s. Then, I explain how the teachers fought against centralization, paying particular attention to the kinds of identity claims they made in the course of the conflict and the special efforts made by the pro-reform coalition to win over the teachers. Although the teachers failed to stop centralization, the battle over the reform bill had lasting effects on both the teachers, whose responses to the newly centralized education administration bore the residue of what they perceived as the elitist, intrusive character of the centralizers, and the new administrative regime, whose leaders saw the teachers' participation in centralization politics as a perfect example of both administrative inefficiency and self-interested, illegitimate, political activity. Centralization changed teachers' political opportunities, rendering the ward-based associations less politically effective and making citywide organizing more appealing. Centralization also diluted political solidarity within the teachers' corps by forcing teachers with different interests and identities to compete against one another for the administration's attention. Finally, I discuss the wave of teacher activism in the years leading up to, and immediately following, World War I.

The Politics of Centralization in New York City during the 1890s

Like most urban school systems in nineteenth-century America, public education in New York City was organized by ward.[7] In New York City, an 1842 law created the ward system of school administration and gave the city a publicly financed school system for the first time. Prior to that, most of the city's schools were administered by the Public School Society, an autocratic, centralized, emphatically nonsectarian organization that sought to eliminate poverty by eliminating its supposed cause: ignorance. The society's schools served Protestant communities, a practice that became a heated political issue in the wake of massive Irish Catholic immigration in the 1840s and 1850s. The 1842 law made each ward in the city a separate school district. Under this system, each of the city's seventeen wards elected school commissioners, school inspectors, and trustees who were in charge of hiring and firing teachers. "Each local board determined its course of study, selected its own books, purchased its own supplies at its own price, and sent the bill to the Board of Education."[8] The society was absorbed into the Board of Education in 1853, and the society's teachers became teachers in the ward schools. Later reforms enabled the Board of Education to appoint the ward trustees, but once appointed, the trustees wielded unchallenged power; they were not subservient to the central board. Teachers' accountability was guaranteed through informal personal networks. Bad teachers could be dealt with through relationships between parents and ward officials, which were buttressed by ethnic or religious ties.

Although the ward system remained basically stable between 1853 and 1896, a crucial political development during this time set the stage for the centralization conflict of the 1890s: the rise of Tammany Hall, the Democratic

Party's political machine. During the early 1860s, William "Boss" Tweed became the most powerful politician of Tammany Hall, and over the next decade, he engineered electoral victories for the Democrats in the state legislature and in city government. He was appointed a ward trustee in 1864 and won a seat in the state senate several years later, positions that he used to consolidate power in New York City. The city's massive immigrant population supported Boss Tweed. In exchange for Irish and German support, the Tammany network naturalized hundreds of immigrants per day and distributed jobs and other essentials like food and clothing to the faithful. Tammany Hall outlived Boss Tweed by more than half a century. For decades after Tweed's downfall in the early 1870s, the schools were an important site of patronage politics. But they remained in disrepair: poor facilities, insufficient funding, and, most evident and serious, massive overcrowding.

Centralization politics in New York City was the product of friction between the city's political mainstream, as represented by Tammany Hall, and a loose coalition of business leaders, middle-class anticorruption crusaders, administrative professionals, and the Republican Party. A series of structural and ideational changes that had transpired during the final decades of the nineteenth century drew reformers' attention to the city school system. The most important change was that the city's immigrant population had swelled beyond the apparent ability of Tammany Hall to manage its needs in an orderly, efficient, cost-effective manner. The schools, it was well known, were overcrowded and understaffed. The school system was also too expensive, and the biggest item in the education budget, year after year, was teachers' salaries. That the need for more teachers to alleviate overcrowding seemed to contradict an interest in cost-effective management did not matter. The problem, leading reformers argued, was that the corruption of the ward system of teacher appointment guaranteed that the quality of the teachers would not be equal to the tasks before them and that teachers would be the objects of exploitation by ward officials. Nicholas Murray Butler, a leader of the pro-centralization coalition, interpreted the New York City Teachers' Association's animosity toward the reform bill of 1895 as a conspiracy of the school trustees. "I regret that the public school teachers have been misled in regard to the bill,"[9] he said, claiming that the teachers were the victim of a hoax perpetrated by school trustees who saw no further than their own self-interest. Furthermore, as the influx of immigrants created a demand for more schools, the gears of the decentralized school system turned in a way that ensured that the erection of new school buildings and the maintenance of existing buildings would happen at a snail's pace. But the city's problems could not wait, and only a more efficiently organized school system could address them.

The changes in the school system were also coterminous with the rise of a crusading interest in municipal reform and administrative rationalization in urban America more generally.[10] The business establishment exported principles of scientific management like the need for a rigid division of labor between workers and management, the scientific understanding of job execution and labor output, the centralization of administrative structure under a bureaucratic hierarchy, and the elevation of efficiency as the highest priority of management; the municipal reform movement was happy to import them. At the same time, the 1890s was also the first decade of the age of muckraking, with Jacob Riis's photographic exposés of New York City receiving particular attention from the national press. Newspapers, magazines, pamphlets, and monographs disseminated stories about the degraded city school system, the paucity of decent public services in general, and the bright ideas of the municipal reformers to address these problems. Finally, leaders of the reform movement had a particular interest in education, even beyond the question of immigration. Men like Felix Adler and William George, along with Riis, saw education as being the task of elevating the souls of citizens-to-be to extract them from delinquency and make them contributing members of society.[11] Adler claimed that it was up to teachers "to train the moral judgment" of children;[12] for Riis, "the more kindergartens, the fewer prisons."[13] The combination of the popularization of social problems, the appearance of a quick-fix solution to those problems, and the particular significance of education to reform leaders infused middle-class city residents with zealous enthusiasm for reform. By the end of the 1890s, reform groups had affiliates in most American cities. With reference to school reform, the PEA of New York City also emerged during the 1880s,[14] and it would come to play an important role in the education politics of the 1890s.

While the reform craze was not unique to New York City, it arrived there early. Many of the elements of the general trend just described were in full relief by the early 1890s. Two groups from the city's economic and cultural elite— the business establishment and the academy—became passionately engaged in what they saw as a battle for the soul of the city's public services. Centralization, the argument ran, would eliminate the corruption and nepotism that nurtured such dysfunction in city administration, most clearly in public education. The two leaders of the movement in New York City were the founder of Teachers College and president of Columbia University, Nicholas Murray Butler, and a leading Wall Street lawyer, Stephen Olin, both prominent members of the aforementioned constituencies most committed to reform. They found a preconstituted organization that was sympathetic to their aims: the Committee of Seventy, "an influential coalition of anti-Tammany Democrats, prominent business and professional leaders, and Republicans who had had recently succeeded in getting a reform candidate, William L. Strong, elected mayor."[15] Beyond that committee, organizations like the City Reform Club, the People's Municipal League, and the Good Government Club, all made up of middle- and upper-class men and women, supported Butler and Olin's goals.

The centerpiece of the Butler-Olin reform strategy was the elimination of the wards' authority over school practices and investiture of that authority in a central Board of Education. Such an overhaul of the administrative structure of public education would in theory insulate the schools from political wrangling and allow an apolitical administration of efficiency experts to solve the schools' problems. A subcommittee within the Committee of Seventy drafted a bill, known as the Pavey Bill after the state senator who officially submitted it, that recommended all the administrative changes that Butler and Olin were looking for, including, most controversially, stripping ward trustees of most of their authority over schooling. The centralization of the city's public school system was the critical step toward the streamlining of educational administration.

Reform advocates, however, did not initially have a political strategy that could advance their agenda. Their ideas were enormously unpopular in the city. New York City's immigrant population was steadfastly against the reformers' plans. They saw through the facade of antipolitics: "The movement to centralize represented an effort by the city's intellectual and economic upper crust to wrest control of the schools from what they considered to be socially inferior ward trustees."[16] The pro-reform coalition was a predominantly white, patrician, Protestant minority in the city. The loose-knit anti-reform coalition comprised Catholic immigrants, longtime ward residents, and working-class New Yorkers. The coalition also included almost the entire education establishment: most of the teachers, principals, and parents, along with many administrators. Indeed, Butler's early effort to appeal directly to the city Board of Education in 1889 had been brushed off, yet more evidence, for Butler, that the systemic corruption of the Tammany establishment needed to be overcome.[17]

The reformers solved their political problem by appealing not to the Tammany-dominated political establishment of New York City itself but to the Republican administration in the New York state legislature. The New York City Charter required that the state governor, the state legislature, and the city mayor would all have to approve any change in the laws governing the city's public schools, so, in any event, the state political establishment would have to be won over. In the gubernatorial and mayoral elections of 1894, voters blamed the Democratic Party for the economic crisis of the previous year, kicking Tammany out of office and replacing it with the Republican Party. The new governor, Levi Morton, had been vice president under President Benjamin Harrison, and he was a favorite among the corporate and financial giants of the Northeast, having emerged out of that milieu. The new mayor, William Strong, was himself a Republican, but he was elected on a "fusion" ticket, backed by the Republican Party and anti-Tammany Democrats. Most of the rest of the important city officials were in the Tammany fold, but for the first time since Butler and Olin had turned their attention to school reform, the political landscape was favorable to their advances.

After those elections, success did not come immediately. The first attempt to enact centralization in the spring of 1895 passed the New York state assembly but died in the senate. In the days leading up to the senate vote, delegations of teachers made their case before the senators, eventually leading the Senate Cities Committee to issue a negative assessment of the bill. The bill itself was not the Pavey Bill drawn up by the Committee of Seventy but a combination of that bill along with a separate proposal, put forward by Assemblyman Alfred Bell, to create an independent commission in charge of school management. Behind the scenes, Republican leader Thomas "Boss" Platt sought to strike back at Mayor Strong, who had dared to appoint Platt's Republican rivals, not all of whom supported school centralization, to important city offices. "The Platt organization got even less patronage from Mayor Strong than it had received from Tammany Hall."[18] In such an environment, so controversial and convoluted a bill was doomed to failure.

Part of the reformers' problem was that centralization was simply not as popular as the pro-reform coalition wished it to be. Nicholas Murray Butler had been publishing a series of editorials and journal articles that claimed not only that reform was in "everyone's" interest but also that "everyone" wanted it.[19] Butler's articles masked the fact that the various cross-cutting constituencies that he criticized—the lower classes, the ethnic communities, the Catholics, the Irish, the entire teachers' corps—constituted a large, politically influential portion of the city's population. More than half of the city's Board of Education and the city's representatives in the state legislature rejected the reform proposals.

A new centralization bill met with success in 1896. When it was time to vote in the state legislature, the senate and assembly became targets of the reformers' associations. Butler dispatched the society women of the PEA to lobby the senators and, in particular, their wives. Governor Morton did not try to influence the vote, thereby leaving legislators to vote as they saw fit. While the majority of state representatives from the city voted against the bill, a majority of noncity residents voted for it. Teachers protested once again, this time in vain. The centralization bill passed along party lines in both the senate (31 to 13) and assembly (88 to 43). The bill then went to Mayor Strong's desk; while the mayor kept everyone guessing and made a show of listening carefully to arguments on both sides of the issue, he was not afraid to make an unpopular decision. He did not have any further political ambitions, and he found the reformers' arguments convincing. On April 22, 1896, he signed the centralization bill. As of July 1 of that year, the ward trustee system of school administration ceased to exist.

The signing of the centralization bill was actually only the beginning of a protracted centralization process. Less than two years after the bill's enactment, the regions of Queens, Brooklyn, and Richmond joined Manhattan and the Bronx to become a single unit: the consolidated Greater New York City. The city's new charter enabled Brooklyn to maintain a localized system, akin to the one eliminated in Manhattan in 1896, and established a system of borough boards of education. "In Queens, thirty-five independent school districts were merged into one; in the borough of Richmond, twenty-nine districts became one."[20] The new system generated resentment among the borough boards, as they fought for city funds for their own school systems, and collective animosity toward the Boards of Education and Superintendents, which controlled the entire system. Borough boards obstructed citywide initiatives in response to what they perceived as unfair funding allocations. The entire, unwieldy system was overhauled for the Revised Charter of 1901, establishing an administrative structure that would remain until the 1960s. The new charter constituted the final victory of centralization's proponents. According to the new rules, the Board of Superintendents was vested with almost complete control over the city school system. The forty-six-member Board of Education held veto power but could not amend the superintendents' decisions. The centralizers' victory of 1896 was mediated by the 1901 settlement; while the central administration became a near hostage to the new "professional" experts over the ensuing decades, the new charter also granted local school boards the power of school inspection and provided the board with information on local public opinion.

City Teachers and Their Discontents

Teachers had a vibrant associational presence in urban American during the centralization era, in stark contrast to their French counterparts. There were no legal barriers to association in the United States, and the Constitution positively affirmed citizens' right to peaceably assemble. By the beginning of the 1889–1890 school year, and for most of the 1890s, at least ten teachers' associations in New York City had overlapping memberships.[21] Along with citywide groups like the New York City Teachers' Association, the Teachers' Mutual Benefit Association, and the Teachers' Life Insurance Association were groups devoted to occupationally distinct teachers, divided according to subject area, grade level, religion, and/or gender.

Beginning in 1889, Henry S. Fuller began publishing *School*, a newspaper devoted to explaining "to the teachers and School officials of New York what is going on among themselves."[22] *School* not only distributed news; it also informed readers about who the teachers were, what they thought of themselves, and what they wanted. It saw teachers as dedicated, passionate, overworked professionals who did not get the respect they deserved. It paid particular attention to teachers' salaries and benefits, the teachers' voice in city politics, and the teachers' associations efforts to improve their members' economic and professional well-being through collective action, which *School* uniformly praised. For example, the newspaper recounted the five-year-long struggle of the Primary Teachers' Association to win a pay increase for primary school teachers with at least fourteen years of seniority.[23] It praised the Teachers' Mutual Benefit Association for its excellent work in providing annuities to "teachers whom years or illness prevent from active work."[24] It lobbied for Senator Jacob Cantor's bill to establish a state pension fund for the teachers,[25] a fund eventually established in 1894, with subsequent provisions eventually being worked into the 1901 City Charter. It also paid close attention to appointments to the city's Board of Education, looking to see that the voices of teachers would be heard.[26] Rules for occupational promotion came under scrutiny as well, as the case of Emma Seaman became a cause célèbre for the teachers. Seaman had wanted to become a principal of her school but could not because she was not "exempt," that is, "free from all supervision by the superintendents, and under the new regulations only a teacher who has been exempt for five years can be selected as a principal."[27] Given that Seaman had fifteen years of classroom experience, without having become exempt, her interest in a principalship prompted a discussion of rules for classification. *School* was also attentive to the fact that a lot of its readers were women, expressing concern for the Board of Education's rule requiring women teachers to resign as soon as they marry[28] and usually using the female pronoun instead of the male when referring to a teacher. At this point, however, the newspaper did not take up the inequity of men and women teachers' salaries.

Fuller's paper also reveals a strong interest in matters of individual and collective professional dignity and representation. When the discussion turned to the matter of "pensioning" teachers, Fuller pointed out that the city already provided pensions for soldiers, policemen, and firemen. "The teacher certainly does not risk his life in his services, but the ultimate object of his work is quite as much for the perpetuation of good government as that of the policeman or fireman."[29] The newspaper protested the occasional accusation of insubordination when a school principal disagreed with an administrative superior. "Teachers have quite as much right to individual opinions, and to express them, as their 'superiors.'"[30] When members of the Board of Education suggested that teachers were becoming lazy, *School* leaped to the teachers' defense. "The teacher has as much pride in her work, and as strong a sense of duty as an official in any public or private walk of life."[31] It also took note of the accomplishments of their sisters across the river with regard to paid sick leave: "The teachers of Brooklyn are beginning to recognize what may be effected by continuous organization."[32] All along, the newspaper emphasized the teachers' reasonableness and conservatism, whether advocating for the pension bill[33] or praising the Mutual Life Assurance Association for showing that city teachers "possess the full capability of self-government; the prudence and conservatism united with assurance and readiness in action."[34] Indeed, as already mentioned, *School* routinely praised the successes of teachers' collective actions, led by the various associations, whether it was explicitly political or not.

As early as September 1889, the newspaper complained about the lack of an esprit de corps among the teachers. Teachers, *School* complained, did not have a sense of their own collective power. "The trouble is not a lack of inclination or of spirit on the part of New York teachers," the editor wrote, "but a lack of a definite idea how such work is to be effected."[35] One teacher wrote in, claiming that, without an esprit de corps, the city's teachers' associations amount to "almost nothing at all," since "as a rule they all pull in different directions and a great deal of their effort is wasted." They want, wrote the teacher, "some centralization, some cohesion to make them work together, and to sink little petty individual advantages in a general purpose."[36] The teachers' associations took some steps to try to rectify these problems. They organized the "University and

School Extension course of studies," a series of classes, somewhat similar to the French pedagogical conferences and the teachers' institutes of the rural United States, which yielded training opportunities for working teachers and more opportunities to network.[37] They formed a "Teachers' Bazaar," a vast exhibition and fund-raising project for teachers and their Mutual Benefit Association, in order to show "that the teachers of New York are able to work unitedly, effectively, continuously, and patiently to one desired end, and that end is sure to be reached if not immediately, eventually by the means within their power" and, by that example, "bring about . . . the aid of the State" with regard to pensions.[38]

Unlike in France, U.S. teachers' associations participated in centralization politics and did not meet with repression. As discussed at the beginning of this chapter, the teachers protested in writing and in numbers. Teachers attended mass meetings devoted to anti-centralization politicking, gathered petitions, wrote protest letters to Mayor Strong, and conducted public rallies against the Committee of Seventy's centralization bill.[39] A few days prior to the mayor's signing of the 1896 centralization bill, hundreds of teachers flooded City Hall to protest the measure.[40] All this happened without triggering disciplinary action or any overt administrative measures aimed at demobilizing the teachers. Only after the success of the bill did the city administration begin to ramp up the pressure on teachers' politics.

New York City teachers fought against school centralization for a number of reasons. Centralization would eliminate teachers' ability to directly influence the decisions of the school trustees, particularly with regard to the hiring and firing of teachers. Teachers' influence in ward-based decision making was based on their common ethnic and religious commitments, along with more personal connections. The centralizers' plans included the bureaucratization of administration, specifically in order to neutralize the influence of these kinds of relationships and, therefore, the teachers' political voice in public education. Given teachers' distrust of the reformers, the prospect of their work being scrutinized by their representatives, unknown to them, was unattractive. The teachers routinely expressed their displeasure with the reformers' lack of classroom experience. How, they wondered, could reformers presume to have solutions for the problems of the city schools without having taught in them? Such presumptions nurtured teachers' hostility toward the reform proposals and their suspicions of the reformers. But centralization also bore on more parochial concerns. Teachers were sympathetic to the complaints of the immigrant communities whose children they taught. The centralization movement seemed condescendingly elitist and inattentive to the day-to-day realities of city life, both in the schools and outside them. Education ought to be left to the parties that had the most invested in it: the families whose children attended the city schools. The middle- and upper-class New Yorkers who promoted reform did not send their children to the city public schools, a fact that *School* did not ignore: "The centralization of power and its removal from the people . . . comes from those who do not attend the schools; who have no children in them; who have never had any experience, interests or sympathy with them."[41] Furthermore, the reformers, particularly Butler, were insulting the teachers' professional competence, claiming that the teachers were pawns of corrupt ward politicians and school trustees. But after the failure of the 1895 reform bill, Butler wrote about a conspiratorial "teachers' ring" that obstructed the reform movement. It is difficult to imagine both claims being true at the same time. At any rate, the first claim underappreciated the teachers' ability to fight their own battles in the city, while the second claim overstated teachers' political power (since most of them were women, most of them could not vote) and neglected the heterogeneity of the forces opposed to centralization.

One of the more unusual aspects of the centralization campaign involved the PEA, an organization of about three hundred middle-class women whose husbands were active in the worlds of business and politics. Butler recruited the PEA, many of whose members he knew personally, to convince the teachers that centralization would improve the functioning of city schools. The high-society women began organizing get-togethers with the city teachers. The impoverished common schoolteachers were astonished to find themselves "teaed and luncheoned" by the wives of prominent state and city politicians and businessmen. The teachers were not fooled. They saw clearly how they were being used, and they remained steadfastly opposed to the PEA's puppet masters. So, the society women turned to a more pliable set of targets: the Republicans in the state legislature. PEA women not only testified in the state senate as to the desirability of centralization but they also socialized with the politicians' wives. They even "paid a visit to Governor Levi Morton's wife, in short order capturing her for the movement as well."[42] Since the state legislature voted on the centralization bill and the teachers did not, it was a more useful gesture in any case.

The class differences between the teachers and the PEA women made the insincerity of Butler's overtures to the teachers quite clear. "Women schoolteachers in New York were often barred from city women's clubs because membership was by nomination," and the clubs met during the week while schoolteachers were in class.[43] At the same time, Butler lumped the "scores of incompetent teachers" in with the "horde of bandits and barbarians" who supported local control of the schools.[44] For Butler, the typical schoolteacher was a poorly educated girl who was uninterested in her job and whose potential for occupational greatness was held back by ward politicians who cared even less.

Such an identification of the women schoolteachers flew in the face of the reality that most of them knew. Between 1887 and 1895, the proportion of women teachers who were graduates of Normal College, the city's teacher training institution for women, rose from a little over half to about three-quarters.[45] Unlike graduates of French normal schools, the women who attended Normal College did not board but lived in the city. They were familiar with city life and with the neighborhoods where they worked. Although voices within the education system called for a more pronounced esprit de corps among teachers, the

Normal graduates were proud of their training and had an alumnae association that met regularly. Many of the younger teachers who had attended Normal College in the late 1880s witnessed class conflict while being trained. During this decade, the college administration's desire to present Normal's graduates with opportunities comparable to those of a "male" liberal arts education created tension within the student body. Increasingly, Normal College was attracting students of different socioeconomic backgrounds. As a result, when the school system expanded in the late 1880s and 1890s and the college returned to its roots as a teacher training institution, the scaling back of the liberal arts curriculum triggered animosity between lower-class and middle-class parents and their daughters.[46] By the time that Butler mobilized the PEA society women for his campaign, New York City women teachers had had experience with the daughters of the PEA members' generation. Such a background renders the tongue-in-cheek incredulity of one teacher more understandable:

> Have we teachers done anything remarkable? Why should we be invited to their "teas" and waited on by these estimable ladies? Mrs. Ben Ali Haggin's children do not come to our schools. We do not expect that Mrs. Levi P. Morton will drive up to our schools in the Governor's open barouche to take us on a ride in the Park of an afternoon. We have no ambitions to be admitted to the select social circle of the city. I have no doubt we enjoy much more the reading about their splendid affairs in the papers, picturing their elegant toilettes, as we read the long lists of names of those present. We can make tea for ourselves, and we feel more at ease over our own little "teas," without all their delightful attentions.[47]

The animosity bred from this conflict did not soon fade.

Teacher Mobilization and the Mobilization of Teachers: Category Work and Its Discontents

Centralization had an enormous impact on teachers' associational presence and political opportunities. Although the teachers had defended the trustee system, that system had also circumscribed teachers' ability to influence city politics collectively. As long as most of the teachers' occupational interests could be advanced locally, by pressuring or persuading the ward trustees, there were few opportunities or incentives for teachers to work together in a citywide organization. Indeed, the struggle over centralization was an unusual instance of all city teachers participating in a political struggle in which they saw themselves as having a common interest. Under the centralized education system, begun in 1896 and consolidated in 1901, teachers had an incentive, and were free, to organize to fight not for narrow, parochial interests but for broader "democratic rights within the larger institutional structure."[48] However, that did not

happen at first. While centralization brought teachers into a common structural position vis-à-vis the city administration, it also created more fragmentation within the teachers' corps. Centralization precipitated growth in the
schooling apparatus, as the newly streamlined decision-making body enabled
school building projects to commence, several high schools opened for middle-
class children, and the administration went on a hiring binge that tripled the
size of the teaching force in less than a decade. As the school system expanded,
preexisting differences between teachers became socially recognized. Teachers' associations proliferated, representing divisions among occupational interests, city boroughs, school type, and gender. The centralizers' emphasis on
professionalism, combined with many teachers' interest in the same, created
an ideological atmosphere conducive to fighting for the perceived interests of
high school music teachers, male grammar school teachers, Jewish teachers
from Queens, female primary school principals, and so forth. The new administrative structure complemented this atmosphere by regulating the schools in
a uniform manner, thus creating citywide regulations for professional advancement, the provision of school supplies, and salaries and benefits. Some of the
socially recognized divisions among teachers predated centralization. But centralization exacerbated them. "As the city administration centralized, teachers
divided."[49]

The growth of secondary education was a particular catalyst for the splintering of the teachers' corps. As historian Kate Rousmaniere has shown, "The
conditions that unified men and women in secondary schools disunited the
teaching force as a whole."[50] Occupational divisions gave way to distinct professional trajectories, with different training institutions and different sorts of attitudes toward work, politics, and professional solidarity. Differences in social
class between attendees of the elementary and secondary schools were reflected
in the teaching force, as secondary school teachers received higher salaries, attended four-year colleges instead of two- or three-year training schools, and
came from middle-class backgrounds quite different from those of Normal
College graduates. High school teachers saw a clear justification for different salary schedules, and their associations defended them, while elementary
school teachers and their associations advocated a single salary schedule for
primary and secondary teachers. Gender differences within the teachers' corps
reproduced that cleavage, as the high schools were staffed overwhelmingly by
men, since only men had the requisite schooling to fulfill the stiff academic
qualifications for high school teacher certification. Although the borough associations of the nineteenth century remained popular, the centralization of the
school system, along with the growth and consolidation of the city as a whole,
made professionally distinct associations more attractive to teachers during the
first few decades of the twentieth century. These associations represented the
interests and identities of occupationally distinct groups of teachers with more
vigor and more attention to the heterogeneity of the teachers' corps than had
existed previously.

The developments in the associational lives of New York City teachers paralleled developments in other cities. By the turn of the twentieth century, teachers' organizations proliferated. A 1930 bulletin from the federal Bureau of Education compiled data on the status of "voluntary teachers' associations in cities of 100,000 population or more."[51] Of the 137 teachers' associations that responded to the writer's survey, 127 (92.7 percent) were founded after 1890, and the majority of those originated after 1900. The report makes clear that urban teachers' associations were founded for a variety of reasons. Associations promoted teachers' "professional activities," such as lectures or various "cultural" and educational topics, additional course work for the teachers, and educational research projects. They organized social and recreational activities, such as luncheons, dinners, athletic events, "card parties," music performances, and similar activities. They sponsored group insurance plans, gave to charities, did child welfare work, and engaged in various other philanthropic works. They labored to publicize their activities, either in the local media or in their own publications. Finally, teachers' associations also worked to advance their own economic and professional interests at the state and local levels, such as their retirement system, tenure, salary, and certification requirements. The teachers' associations tended to see politics more narrowly. When the New York State Teachers' Association's bulletin advocated voting for "a certain political organization," the city association was quick to pass an official resolution to "strongly deprecate the action of the State association in officially attempting to introduce a political bias into the actions of the teachers of this state."[52] Indeed, the teachers' associations did not usually take part in public politics; nor did teachers see their associations in a political light. These were strictly vehicles of professional development and mutual assistance, not trade unions, which teachers did not consider forming in late 1890s.[53] Because there were no legal restrictions against teachers forming their own associations, urban teachers took full advantage of the opportunities provided to them.

The five years between passage of the centralization bill in New York City and passage of the Revised Charter constituted a critical period for teachers' politics. During this time, city teachers and reformist administrators clashed a number of times, and each battle verified the teachers' distrust of the reformers and their agenda. For example, when the Board of Education was preparing to appoint principals to the three new high schools in 1897, it refused to consider anyone who lacked experience teaching in a high school, a requirement that ruled out nearly all city teachers. Teachers from the Manhattan-Bronx borough fought to keep their salaries based on seniority rather than merit. "The Brooklyn borough board sued the other boards to prove its right to set higher teachers' salaries," and when the Brooklyn board tried to bury the issue, "the Brooklyn Teachers Association brought 2,500 individual suits against the city for the promised salary increases."[54] When the Manhattan-Bronx teachers sued the city for their salary increases, a court forced the city to issue bonds to generate the funds to pay them. In January 1900, the Teachers' Association of Queens threatened to follow suit. When it was time to negotiate what would be the 1901 Charter, *School* recommended restoring power to the local boards and warned against any further centralization, which would only intensify the already difficult city bureaucracy.

The flip side of this process, however, was the way that the Board of Education and the Board of Superintendents intentionally reconfigured the city teachers' corps. Given that teachers provided the service that the reform coalition had fought over during the 1890s, and that teachers constituted the single greatest expense in the City's education budget, it is little surprise that successive political regimes between 1901 and 1913 fought over them. Two national trends yielded local reforms in teacher training and together constituted a new model of public school teacher that, as instantiated in New York City, sparked conflict: professionalization and Americanization.

Professionalism was not the invention of the era's municipal reformers, but the reform coalition united the movement for centralized bureaucracy in education with the professional creed during the early years of the twentieth century. This combination was the essence of the Progressive movement within public education. The notion of professional competence as a guiding principle of the occupation took root in the NEA, the most prestigious education organization in the country at the time, which promoted professionalization through its network of administrators, college presidents, and teachers' college professors. For the second half of the nineteenth century, the NEA promoted an idea of professionalism that revolved around the superiority of the administrator over the classroom teacher and the principal. Administrators had the expertise, and classroom teachers and principals ought to carry out administrative dictates to the best of their abilities. But without a centralized education system, professional administrators could not implement their ideas. Nicholas Murray Butler became NEA president in 1895, as the conflict over centralization in New York City was hitting its peak of intensity. Butler used his new platform to promote the virtues of centralization for all of America's cities, as a mechanism for improving educational efficiency and eliminating corruption, and professional organization, as a mechanism for improving classroom performance and eliminating disorder. As a proven educational expert, with ties to both the academy and the political world, he was an ideal broker between the movements to centralize and professionalize public education.

Around the turn of the century, however, tensions appeared within the NEA over just what professionalism might entail, just as professionalism itself enjoyed a renaissance in popularity within public education in America. Butler had begun to promote "a more modern notion of professionalism, one which embraced educational training and scientific inquiry,"[55] thereby retaining a male-dominated hierarchy, since few women attended institutions of higher education, while more explicitly targeting classroom teachers for the failures of American education. The fact that "administrators were 50 percent of the active membership during the 1890s and classroom teachers only 11 percent" indicates an overwhelmingly male NEA membership.[56] Classroom teachers, however, were just then becoming a more popular group within the NEA; beginning in 1899, representatives of the CTF began challenging Butler's ideas at annual meetings of the NEA. Margaret Haley, president of the CTF, openly challenged Butler himself at the 1903 event. The women of the CTF sought not to eliminate professionalism but to imbue the idea with a different meaning. To Haley and her colleagues, professionalism was about having classroom experience, creating ties to their students' communities to better meet their classroom needs, and being treated with the dignity due public servants. The NEA was traditionally silent on questions of salary and teachers' economic well-being more generally, a silence that became a wedge dividing the growing cadre of female classroom teachers from the male administrators.

Professionalism constituted the contours of teachers' political orthodoxy in the eyes of their administrative superiors. The reaction of New York City's Board of Education to the equal-pay-for-equal-work campaign exemplifies the new attitude toward teachers' politics. When several women teachers "took days off from school to lobby in Albany" for equal-pay legislation, the board censured them, a reaction that carried no penalty for the teachers but "did serve to put teachers on notice that the board disapproved of their activity and would frown upon a repetition of it."[57] When Grace Strachan and her membership agreed "to support the opponent of the governor who had vetoed the 1907 equal-pay bill" in the 1908 gubernatorial election, the Board of Education responded with an investigation of "electioneering" by the teachers "and a proposed board amendment to the school statutes which prohibited political activity by the teachers."[58] The "gag law," as the teachers called it, was very much a sign of the times, as "the organization and rationales for autonomous school bureaucracies directed by self-regulating educating professionals" were becoming embedded in urban politics.[59] That same year, the City Vigilance League, an organization of middle-class citizens devoted to eliminating delinquency from the city and nurturing civic-mindedness, sent a letter, "To the Female School Teachers of New York City," telling teachers that their position as moral guides for the city's children made it inappropriate for any of them to endorse a candidate in the upcoming gubernatorial election (which the IAWT denied doing).[60] The new professional ideology frowned on teachers' involvement in electoral politics, which was now deemed unbecoming. Just as centralization shifted teachers' identities in France, so, too, did the newly centralized administration in New York begin seeing teachers differently in the early twentieth century.

The other trend of the early twentieth century to have an impact on the categorization of teachers was Americanization. The Americanization movement was an effort to acculturate immigrants to a particular construction of American identity, the chief characteristics of which were the ability to speak English, the condemnation of group identities, and an enhanced valuation of the individual, of public institutions, and of cooperation and participation in civic affairs.[61] While it is difficult to pinpoint the genesis of the movement, it was certainly under way by 1900. Indeed, in New York City, the PEA had been using the language of "Americanizing" immigrants since the 1890s.[62] World War I intensified the interest in Americanization, as the federal government nurtured anti-German sentiment in the United States.[63] Teacher training facilities began offering programs in Americanization whose purpose was to show teachers how to teach immigrants to speak, read, and write English. "Of greatest importance, she must appreciate that her big task is Americanization—the making of Americans—and must understand just what that means and how it can best be brought about."[64] Patriotism became more highly valued in teachers than ever before, especially after the United States officially entered the war in 1917. Teachers were expected to "know America and what America stands for and must be able to interpret America to the immigrant in language that he will understand," as well as "what citizenship really means."[65] Their loyalty to the United States also became more closely scrutinized than ever before.

In New York City, as in many other cities, Americanization was implemented in a number of ways. The New York Americanization office had an official task, as dictated by the secretary of the Interior and the National Americanization Committee, to nurture solidarity among the various ethnic communities and, as of 1917, galvanize those communities' support for the war.[66] The office collaborated with the Board of Education to establish evening schools to teach English to immigrants. Mayor John Purroy Mitchell worked with Frances Kellor of the state's Americanization Day Committee during the summer of 1915 to arrange special activities for city immigrants at the new Adolph Lewisohn stadium at City College.[67] The New York state legislature became, in April 1916, the only state legislature in the country to pass a law mandating military training for boys of high school age. Finally, one year later, after American entrance into the war, the Board of Education required teachers to sign loyalty oaths. The refusal of some teachers to sign these oaths led to the administrative sanctions that drew the New York City TU into city politics for the first time.

Between 1896 and 1914, teachers began to mobilize resources for their own purposes, just as the city's education establishment began to mobilize teachers to do their work differently. Teachers developed new associations in response to centralization and its effects on teachers' work and the city's administrative structure. The proliferation of teachers' associations resulted in a more politically and occupationally fragmented corps of workers than had existed during the era of ward governance. At the same time, administrators led by Nicholas Murray Butler, drawing from nationally disseminated ideas about professionalism and Americanization, engaged in category work, using their newfound power in city government to restructure the teaching force. The result was that teachers' own perspective on their work and their role in education politics became quite different from their administrative superiors' perspective on their political orthodoxy.

Mobilization Success and Failure and the Suppression of the Radicals: 1907–1922

The most consequential teacher campaigns of the years leading up to World War I were those of women teachers for salaries and rights equal to those of men. Even before the centralization conflict, male schoolteachers began their careers earning $900 per year and could move up the salary scale to earn as much $2,400 per year. The comparable figures for women, however, were $600 and $1,320. Prior to school centralization, the issue of pay equalization was the subject of isolated campaigns, usually on the part of the Primary Teachers' Association or the Association of Female Grammar School Teachers. After Mayor Strong made an inquiry during a meeting with the Board of Estimate about the gap between men and women teachers' pay, *School* ran a series of letters and reports of public addresses in response, with individual teachers and representatives of the associations speaking out for and against equal pay for equal teaching work.[68] But there was no concerted campaign to promote equal pay for equal work in New York City during the nineteenth century.

Following centralization, however, the equal-pay-for-equal-work campaign gathered steam. In 1905, the Classroom Teachers' Association, comprising about fifteen hundred women and fifty men, initiated a drive for salary equalization, much to the consternation of the association's president, George Cottrell, who had not approved the campaign.[69] The IAWT spearheaded the equal-pay movement. The IAWT emerged in April 1906 with fewer than one hundred members but, within two years, had grown to fourteen thousand and, by the spring of 1915, numbered about twelve thousand: about 60 percent of the teaching force.[70] Their leader and chief spokeswoman, Grace Strachan, engineered the first legislative effort to enact equal pay for equal work, an effort that failed because the state legislature adjourned before it had the opportunity to override a gubernatorial veto.[71] The IAWT emerged out of a smaller group of women teachers from Brooklyn who were understandably hostile to the salary schedule established by the Davis Bill (described in Chapter 1). The Davis Bill had created a single salary schedule for teachers of the five boroughs but also created large discrepancies between the pay of men and women teachers, an injustice felt particularly by the Brooklyn teachers, who, prior to the city consolidation, did receive equal pay for equal work. Strachan's history as a former vice president of the Brooklyn Teachers' Association made her a prime candidate for leading the new organization, as did her association with feminist organizations in the city. Strachan also emerged as a (rather reluctant) leader in the suffragette campaign in the city. New York City had become one of the national centers for women's suffrage organizations, and women's participation in education politics and the suffrage campaign overlapped. The IAWT's equal-pay-for-equal-work campaign began a period of teacher activism that eventually yielded a more politically strident teaching force by the beginning of World War I.

These campaigns illuminated the divisions within the city teachers' corps. In particular, male teachers, overwhelmingly outnumbered within the city, fought against the equal-pay movement. Even before the founding of IAWT, the suggestion of equal salaries elicited animosity between men and women teachers. In the fall of 1904, some women tried to introduce the matter to their association's president, George Cottrell, who refused to take it up. The following year, the Classroom Teachers' Association disseminated a circular promoting equal pay for equal work, but their efforts were unsuccessful. "Bitter attacks were made by Miss Goessling and her associates against the male teachers in the association," the *New York Times* reported. "The men teachers were openly accused of trying to intimidate their feminine coworkers and of getting their own salaries increased."[72] Later in 1907, in response to the IAWT, six hundred men organized the Association of Men Teachers and fought alongside the Male Elementary Teachers' Association against equal-pay legislation.[73]

The other important cause for women teachers was fighting the Board of Education's policy of dismissing married women from their jobs. Married women lost their teaching jobs, by virtue of Board of Education fiat, in most city school systems as late as 1950.[74] Starting in 1911, the New York City Board of Education also began preventing mothers with children under two years old from teaching in the public schools. As the women teachers became increasingly politicized, a number of causes célèbres emerged around these matters. The most famous case was that of Henrietta Rodman, a Teachers College graduate, who taught in the city schools for twenty-five years and was active in a number of political causes in the city. She actively opposed the city's marriage policy. Her opposition resulted in suspension from work without pay from November 13, 1913, to September 1, 1915.[75]

Throughout this time, criticism of the city teachers was limited to women teachers. When the associations of male teachers published campaign endorsements in their journals, which they did during the same period that the City Vigilance League and Schoolmasters' Association publicly criticized the IAWT for its political voice, administrators remained silent.[76] Beyond these two education-related campaigns, women teachers became increasingly active in other social movements during this period. Along with campaigns for women's suffrage were those for birth control and maternity leave and those against the war. In each of these cases, male school administrators and classroom teachers degraded women teachers' participation as unprofessional and unseemly. As overseen by the NEA, professionalism was the domain of male administrators, something for women classroom teachers to aspire to but never achieve. Patriarchy remained a constitutive element of professionalism until after World War I.

The election of John Purroy Mitchell as mayor of New York City in 1913 initiated a five-year period of education politics that drew the battle lines within the teachers' corps for the next half century. Mitchell himself was a reformist Republican, an admirer of the efficiency movement in public education, and a dedicated Americanizer and patriot (he would receive an air force commission after he lost reelection). As an ally, Mayor Mitchell had Comptroller William Prendergast, who stood by nearly every decision the mayor would make. The school superintendent, William Maxwell, had been a follower and friend of Butler but was suspicious of many of the mayor's school reform ideas. By the time the political battles over the mayor's policies heated up in 1915–1916, Maxwell had become Mitchell's opponent. However, Maxwell became ill in the spring of 1916 and receded from the political scene.

To most of the teachers' associations, Mitchell represented everything loathsome about the reformist spirit that had taken hold of the city in the 1890s. "First, he sought legislative authority to control teachers' salaries; second, he supported legislation to reduce the size of the Board of Education; and third, he tried to reorganize the curriculum to conform to the latest progressive thought."[77]

Teachers' salaries and the size of the Board of Education were not only matters of efficiency, Mitchell and Prendergast believed, but also just deserts. Prendergast had insisted that the city eliminate the "public scandal" of salary increases for teachers, who, after all, had summers off and thus did not deserve high salaries. Paying teachers for teaching summer or evening school was tantamount to "graft" and should not be allowed. He described the Board of Education as "the creature of its employees and swayed by the political intriguing of the employers' organizations which rendered the few members of independence . . . powerless against these accelerators and manipulators."[78] Once again, school reformers deployed the chimera of "taking the politics out of schools." Politics, it seemed, had not been taken out of the schools after all; even after centralization, it had remained, in the guise of schoolteachers and their organizations. The teachers' associations were out for the financial gain of their members and appealed not to city officials but to the state legislature for wage increases. Now, under pressures of cost-cutting and the apolitical ideology of professionalism, some Board of Education members were prepared to repeal the teachers' traditional right to lobby the legislature.[79]

The administrative interest in making the Board of Education smaller conformed to the nationwide efficiency movement. A smaller board would mean quicker, more efficient decision making and would also bring the city up to date, given that most other large American cities had reduced the sizes of their boards of education. Teachers' organizations, along with the existing board, fought the mayor and defeated legislation in 1915 and 1916 to change the board. In 1917, legislation was successful, and the board was reduced to seven members.

The most important of the Mitchell-era reforms, however, was the importation of the Gary model of schooling. The Gary school, a reference to Gary, Indiana, was an attempt to merge the goals of cost efficiency and a "learn-by-doing" model of education. According to the Gary model, students would alternate between traditional school subjects for one part of the day and participate in a "work/play" program. The students participating in the work segment "took instruction in art, music, dancing, or dramatics; they studied in school libraries or science laboratories; some went on field trips into the community; by turns, they attended auditorium periods for group singing, movies, student theatricals, or special lectures by outside speakers; girls received training in home economics, while boys attended classes in workshops or on the school farm."[80]

The teachers' organizations suspected all of the Board of Education's reforms as being a front for Mitchell's and Prendergast's publicly expressed desires to cut teachers' salaries. Their response was dominated by the women. The Federation of Teachers' Associations, representing forty-nine groups of teachers, had appointed a committee to generate a formal response to Mitchell and Prendergast, but the IAWT voted to design its own statement in case its leaders believed the federation's statement was deemed "inadequate." The teachers responded as much to cost-cutting and Prendergast's disrespectfulness as to anything specifically having to do with the Gary system. The teachers deserved a pension plan, the IAWT insisted, like those of other professional workers. "The members of the [IAWT] wanted to know why firemen and policemen had this advantage that was denied to them."[81]

About the Gary system, the teachers soon lost reason to worry. In October 1917, public animosity toward the Gary schools spilled over into the city streets. For nearly two weeks, hundreds of students—nearly all under the age of fifteen and some as young as five—gathered to throw rocks at the windows of the Gary schools and scream anti-Gary epithets. During the mornings, truant children would prevent school-bound children from getting through the front doors of some schools. Some scuffles broke out among the children, and many rioters grabbed schoolbooks away from their classmates and tore them apart. Truant officers were kept busy, rounding up rioting children in the morning and taking them back to their schools in police patrol wagons, only to find the students returning to the streets in the afternoon. Under the pressure of popular discontent with the new schooling model, public exhaustion with student truancy,[82] and an upcoming mayoral election, the Gary experiment ground to a halt.

On other matters, however, controversy would not let up. As the American entrance into the Great War drew closer, the Americanization movement intensified. In April 1917, just days after the congressional declaration of war, the Board of Education required all teachers to sign oaths of loyalty to the U.S. government, and the Mitchell administration became more strident in its insistence on teachers' absolute, unquestioning loyalty to the government. The majority of city teachers, many of whom loudly protested the introduction of the Gary plan into the schools, quietly accepted the loyalty oaths. Grace Strachan wholeheartedly supported the war effort, so the IAWT made no challenge. During the war, pacifism became grounds for dismissal. The Board of Education tried a pacifist Latin teacher, Mary McDowell, who refused to sign the loyalty oath, for conduct unbecoming a teacher. One German schoolteacher was dismissed on charges of disloyalty. "She said that, although she wanted the United States to win the war, she did not want to see her native land crushed."[83]

While some individual teachers refused to sign a loyalty oath, the TU was the only organization to protest the oath.

The TU was the brainchild of Henry Linville, a high school biology teacher. Linville and his colleague Abraham Lefkowitz founded an association called the Teachers' League in February 1913, a group that attracted public figures in the teaching profession, such as John Dewey and Charlotte Perkins Gilman. In 1916, it refounded itself as the Teachers' Union, and when several thousand teachers broke with the NEA to form the AFT, the TU became one of its charter members as Local 5. Like the league's, the original TU platform had less to do with economic advancement and more to do with protecting teachers' legal rights, getting teachers represented on the Board of Education, promoting teachers' voice in determining school policy, freeing teachers from administrative oppression, and advancing democratic education within the schools. The one thousand members of the organization were "not in love with principals or superintendents";[84] at a time when the city government was taking a heavy-handed approach to the teachers, speakers at the first TU meeting argued in favor of excluding principals from membership. Meanwhile, Linville's periodical, the *American Teacher*, had become the AFT's flagship journal. Linville saw the *American Teacher* as a powerful tool for advancing the union's views on progressive education and academic freedom. For Linville, teachers were both professionals and trade unionists, and the newspaper ought to disseminate that view and project it publicly. Charles Stillman, the first president of the AFT, disagreed with Linville and wanted to push the union, and its official organ, in the direction of Samuel Gompers's American Federation of Labor (AFL), advocating bread-and-butter trade unionism. Stillman and Linville quarreled over the direction of the *American Teacher* and the AFT itself, a battle that Linville lost.[85] Publication of the *American Teacher* ground to a halt in 1921, temporarily suspended for lack of funds, as the AFT was in the midst of a membership crisis. By this time, tensions within the AFT, between the AFT and the NEA, and between the AFT and federal and state governments had led to a crisis in teacher unionism before it had barely begun. I return to these tensions in the next chapter.

Beginning in 1917, with the TU's publicly expressed opposition to the loyalty oaths, the city education establishment began repressing all teachers suspected of radical politics. Officials from the Board of Education began collecting copies of the *American Teacher* to look for evidence of disloyalty. The newspapers ran editorials denouncing the teachers of "that nursery of anti-patriotism," Dewitt Clinton High School, Linville's workplace.[86] William Wilcox, president of the Board of Education, spoke before the Teachers' Council, a forty-five-member body established by the board that represented the city's entire teaching force, and told it that "Americans must submit to Government organization with autocratic authority, supported by loyal and unquestioning confidence and allegiance."[87] On November 12, 1917, John Tildsley, the associate superintendent of schools, officially suspended three teachers from Dewitt

Clinton and charged them with "conduct unbecoming a teacher." Ten days later, the three of them were tried before the Board of Education, found guilty, and officially dismissed in December. The TU came out in defense of the suspended teachers, along with six others who were transferred in response to charges of disloyalty. Linville began a campaign to raise money to pay for the accused teachers' legal fees when the teachers filed an appeal before the New York State Education Commission. He also sent a letter to the Board of Education, signed by eighty-six teachers, which contained their refusal to sign a loyalty oath.[88] And the TU accused Associate Superintendent Tildsley of "gross misconduct, general inefficiency, abuse of power, and anti-Semitism."[89] Finally, in the spring of 1919, the city officially forbade the TU from holding its meetings in the city's public schools, thus stripping the union of a crucial mobilization resource.

The teachers' appeal before the Education Commission failed. The ruling of Acting Commissioner Thomas Finnegan reflected the mood of the moment in the United States. During wartime, he wrote, questions concerning teachers' loyalty to the state were entirely appropriate: "He must come out in the open and cheerfully and unhesitatingly stand up and make known to the entire community in which he is employed that he is giving his unquestioned support to the President and to the government in the prosecution of this war, and if he refuses to give such assurance he shall not be permitted to discharge the high office of teacher in an American public school system."[90]

The other teachers' associations distanced themselves from the TU after the war began. After hearing Wilcox speak on the matter of loyalty to the government, the Teachers' Council created a special committee devoted to ferreting out undesirables. The Schoolmasters' Association, a group of politically and pedagogically conservative male teachers, prepared a pamphlet entitled *Unpatriotic Teaching in Public Schools*, which attacked the TU and its leaders. The pamphlet was published by the American Defense League, an ultrapatriotic prowar organization that sought out and exposed antiwar individuals and associations in the city. The league's bent, like that of the Schoolmasters' Association, was nativist, and its rhetoric was laced with anti-German sentiments. Grace Strachan, by this time a district superintendent, responded to the matter of the Dewitt Clinton teachers by arguing in favor of a state law to prevent nonnaturalized citizens from becoming classroom teachers, a perspective that echoed the IAWT's suspicion of immigrants.[91] Several years prior, Strachan had distanced herself from Linville's group, objecting to its proposal to put teachers on school boards. Now Linville and Strachan found themselves and their associations at odds once again, this time over the war.[92] While Linville was defending the three pacifist teachers from Dewitt Clinton, Strachan was calling for war preparedness in the high schools and creating the Interborough League for War Service to assist the military in New York City.

In the years following World War I, changes in American politics and society reverberated in New York City and state. The Bolshevik Revolution introduced a new power on the world stage, along with a new, threatening ideology:

Communism. American radicals established two Communist parties in the United States in 1919, attracting tens of thousands of members, many of whom made public, explicit threats of violence against the American government. New York state prosecutors tracked down and imprisoned hundreds of Communists under the state's criminal anarchy law.[93] At the same time, many Communist teachers flocked to Linville's TU, attracted to its public defense of academic freedom and freedom of thought and expression. As the fear of subversives gripped the entire country in the early 1920s, political and social tolerance for public expressions of animosity toward the U.S. government weakened.

The backlash against teacher radicalism came in the form of the Lusk Committee. The state senate appointed this committee, headed by Senator Clayton Lusk, to investigate "seditious activities" of the "Bolshevist or revolutionary movement" in the state of New York.[94] Between 1919 and 1923, the Lusk Committee sought out political undesirables, and Communists in particular. After several months of investigating the Soviet Bureau, an office devoted to nurturing business ties between American companies and the Bolsheviks, the committee refocused its energies onto the public schools. In 1920, the committee issued a report, "Revolutionary Radicalism," that exhaustively reviewed the status of revolutionary politics in Europe and the United States, explicitly implicated pacifism in America with "International Socialism," and called for new laws to establish loyalty oaths for New York teachers, require all schools to obtain a license from the Board of Regents, create a more rigorous Americanization program for teachers, and open more schools in and around factories to offer literacy courses for immigrant adults.[95] In 1921, the state government followed through on some of these recommendations, passing and enacting laws that created requirements of political orthodoxy for private schools to be licensed, along with loyalty and personal morality requirements for public school teacher certification.[96] The following year, the education commissioner of New York State, Dr. Frank P. Graves, created the Advisory Council on Teacher Qualification to monitor compliance with the loyalty oaths. The council's proceedings were private, and teachers were not permitted to bring legal counsel (since the council's activities were technically not legal trials).

The TU was the only teachers' association to protest the council. Linville called it "a spying system within the schools";[97] he argued for the council's hearings to be made public if they had to exist at all. The Board of Education followed Linville in criticizing the council. The president of the High School Teachers' Association (HSTA), Walter Foster, also later remarked that simply being called before the Advisory Council stigmatized teachers.[98] Half a dozen teachers refused to cooperate with the council during the summer of 1922, but by then public opposition to the teacher loyalty oath had begun to grow. In October, when the state commissioner refused to grant teaching certificates to more than twenty teachers, based on the council's secret investigations, Linville wrote to Graves, asking for an explanation.[99] Alfred Smith—who, as governor, had vetoed the initial Lusk legislation in 1919—defeated Nathan Miller in the gubernatorial election several weeks later. Now headed back to Albany, he pledged to end the Lusk Committee and did so in May 1923. For the remainder of the decade, Linville and Lefkowitz waged a largely unsuccessful campaign to reinstate teachers who had lost their jobs during the Lusk era. Their efforts earned them, and their union, a reputation as dangerous subversives, a reputation that polarized their relationship with the Board of Education, even as it made their organization increasingly attractive to Communist teachers.

Until the late 1930s, the TU never represented as much as 10 percent of all city teachers. But it always represented the political radicals within the teachers' corps. The majority of its members were male high school teachers, usually Jewish. That cleavage helped ensure meager membership figures until the 1930s, as women elementary teachers—who continued to constitute the vast majority of the teachers' corps as late as World War II—continued to agitate for equal rights and equal salaries. But the most important cleavage established by the successes, however limited, of the TU was that between political moderates and radicals. The conflict between the TU and the state and municipal governments over the loyalty oath and the Lusk Committee changed the relationship between the teachers and the state. And in the light of the state's repressive measures and the non-TU teachers' responses, these events also verified the cleavage between moderate and radical teachers. Linville's tactics ensured that the teachers' reputations for disloyalty and independence of thought would hound them for decades. However, while leftist teachers joined Linville's organization, knowing that the TU would protect them, others devoted themselves to proving themselves loyal by remaining active NEA members or members of their local professional organization. Above all, they wanted to show themselves as committed to devotion to their work and their government by remaining quiescent.

Conclusion

As in France, centralization in the urban United States had an important impact on teachers' relationship with the state, but the differences between the teachers' perspectives on centralization and their roles in public politics when centralization was being fought for proved to be crucial factors in understanding why newly centralized administrations competed for the teachers' support. The French teachers favored centralization, but New York City teachers, like teachers throughout the urban United States, fought against it. "Far from enhancing the professional role of teachers and principals," as the pro-reform coalition suggested it would do by eliminating the corrupting influence of the ward trustees, the "proposed changes were designed to subject these municipal employees to the discipline of a streamlined bureaucracy."[100] Teachers' resistance to centralization and their subsequent associational ferment signaled to the new administrative regime that they would neither accept centralization peacefully nor behave as obediently as the newly emphasized professional ethos dictated they should. The result encouraged the professionalization movement within the new city administration, as teacher training institutions, especially Normal (now Hunter) College and Board of Education discourse established a new set of categorical boundaries, boundaries that teachers would immediately challenge. The IAWT's "unseemly" and "unprofessional" advocacy of equal pay for equal work and the TU's trade union pretensions and insistence on democratic governance of the schools epitomized the teachers' resistance to the dictates of the new efficiency experts in the field of education. But the politicking of the TU—both in the context of the war effort and in the aftermath of the Bolshevik Revolution—was even more transgressive than the IAWT had been. Indeed, by the time Linville rose to prominence, former IAWT leader Grace Strachan had become an administrator and an advocate of American entry into World War I.

The generation of the union and its fervent defense of freedom of speech might not have been as controversial and provocative had it not been for the Bolshevik Revolution. The rise of a dangerous ideology to the level of national governance on the other side of the world infused U.S. authorities with a reactionary fervor. Americanization programs renewed their efforts to socialize newcomers to the United States. And the Palmer Raids signified a new wave of repression of political radicalism, in New York City in particular. The Lusk Committee polarized the teachers' organizations by forcing teachers to reject Communism and sign loyalty oaths or risk being branded as a political undesirable and thus unable to press claims on city and state administrators. Most city teachers and their organizations distanced themselves from Local 5. By the time the Lusk Committee ended its work in 1923, the cleavage that would shape the contours of teacher organizing for the next twelve years, between moderate teachers committed to NEA-dictated norms of professionalism and radicals committed to social and political reform well to the left of the AFT, had taken shape. Only after the 1935 fragmentation of the radical teachers' movement (discussed in Chapter 6) did these dynamics shift.

III

✳ ✳ ✳

THE POLITICS OF
SELECTIVE ENGAGEMENT

5

✳

Selective Engagement and Teachers' Politics in France, 1887–1950

On the morning of August 3, 1918, a delegation from the Fédération Nationale des Instituteurs (FNSI) congregated in Paris for the annual meeting and was met with a rude surprise. The meeting was to take place at the headquarters of the Confédération Générale du Travail (CGT), located at the Maison des Syndicats on the rue de la Grange-aux-Belles.[1] When the delegates turned onto the impasse Chausson to get to the main entrance of the building, a blockade of police was there to meet them. The CGT members who were with the teachers, including the secretary general, Léon Jouhaux, would be permitted to enter, but the FNSI members were restricted. The government's maneuver was unexpected. Although the wartime congresses of 1916 and 1917 had been conducted under heavy surveillance, the radical teachers had not received any notice that this year's congress would be outlawed. The attendees scattered and reconvened at the restaurant Combes on the rue de la Bretagne, several blocks south of their arranged meeting place. According to a police report, ten minutes after the teachers' arrival at the restaurant, the famous (or, from the perspective of the political regime, notorious) pacifist *institutrice* Hélène Brion left with one of her comrades to meet with Fernand Loriot, treasurer of the FNSI throughout the war years.[2] About an hour later, the teachers reconvened at the Chamber of Deputies, where Jean-Pierre Raffin-Dugens, a socialist sympathizer in the parliament and former *instituteur*, welcomed them.[3] Raffin-Dugens offered the teachers a room to hold their congress and officially made them his guests. For the remainder of the afternoon, teachers came and left the assembly hall, meeting with one another and other Parisian militants. With help from its political allies, the FNSI salvaged their rendezvous and reasserted their opposition to the war, the necessity of class conflict, and support for the recent Bolshevik Revolution.

Thirty years later, with two world wars behind them, the French teachers met in congress to vote on whether to remain affiliated with the CGT. Although the teachers' unions had long been established by this time, the question of their relationship to the broader labor movement remained an open one. During most of the 1930s, all except the most radical teachers' organizations were affiliated with the CGT, but World War II broke these alignments. In March 1948, representatives of the 160,000 teachers—primary, secondary, and higher education—in the Fédération de l'Éducation Nationale (FEN) voted by a huge majority to remain independent of the CGT. More than ever before, the CGT's internal ruptures were costing it prestige and support from within and without its ranks, while the FEN drew most of the teachers' organizations under the same umbrella.[4] This was also a more strident teachers' corps than the teachers of the post–World War I period. The *instituteurs* of the Seine had struck for three weeks in the autumn of 1947 without suffering any sanctions from the central government.[5] The FEN that emerged in the postwar period was a centrally organized trade union. By 1950, the central government had officially legalized public-sector worker organizations, as well as the right to strike. The FEN would become one of the largest trade unions in France until it fragmented in 1992.

Selective engagement politics account for the ultimate success of teacher mobilization during the first half of the early twentieth century. By the time France went to war in 1914, a number of socially recognized differences had congealed into distinguishable cleavages within the teachers' corps, and no cleavage was more politically significant than that between moderates and radicals. Beginning with the 1903 split within the teachers' movement, the French government began selectively engaging with the teachers' associations, dealing with the moderate *amicales* in an attempt to marginalize the radical *syndicats*. Over the course of the next two decades, the French state sought to keep the teachers divided, not only in terms of radicalism but also with regard to gender and professional differences. Now, however, the teachers were organized, politically assertive, and seeking alliances in the broader labor movement. By the end of the Third Republic, the French state had all but ceased to repress teachers' public claim-making activities, and when the teachers' unions returned to public politics after the war, the state dealt with them without molestation. In what follows, I pick up the story of teacher mobilization begun at the end of Chapter 3 with a description of Eugène Spuller's hostile reaction to the 1887 congress. After showing how teachers sustained their local associations during the 1890s and seized the opportunities that the Dreyfus Affair afforded them, I devote the rest of the chapter to tracing the internal politics of the French teachers' movement and the ways that the moderate and radical wings of the movement interacted with public authorities and one another. Once the government engaged with the *amicales* and marginalized the radicals, I suggest, it unintentionally committed the French state to legitimating the teachers' collective political voice. By the end of the Third Republic, successive French governments had begun to tacitly accept the legitimacy of unionism in the teachers' corps.

The Expansion of the Teachers' Movement in Turn-of-the-Century France

From 1887 to 1903, teachers' associations emerged throughout the countryside. These associations went by many titles, usually involving the name of their home *département*, but they were collectively known as the *amicales*.[6] Some 25 such societies existed in 1891, 60 in 1898, 77 in 1900, and 115 by 1903. In 1901, about twenty-five *départements* were without *amicales*; that figure had dropped to twelve by 1903.[7] The March 1904 issue of the *amicales'* national publication announced that at least one *amicale* of teachers was active in every *département* in France.[8] After the 1901 Law on Associations loosened the legal restrictions on collective action, the *amicale* movement accelerated quickly enough so that, by 1907, about 70 percent of all public primary school teachers (approximately 85,000 out of 120,000), men and women, were members of *amicales*.[9]

In light of Spuller's emphatic rejection of the teachers' bid for a trade union in 1887, how were teachers able to sustain and, eventually, expand their associational lives over the ensuing decades? Just as they had begun to do during the 1870s and 1880s, teachers continued to use the normal schools and pedagogical conferences to launch their own associations. Within the teachers' milieu, the word *amicale* was normally reserved for associations of former normal school students until the 1890s.[10] Associations of such students in the Aisne and the Gironde took the *amicale* name in 1892, and the appellation blossomed in the decade that followed. Local organizing, however, was still risky. When a group of teachers from the Vaucluse that same year tried to hold a congress for their association, the prefect forbade it after the education minister, Léon Bourgeois, informed him that the teachers' "pretensions" concerning their salaries were "exaggerated."[11] In some *départements*, teachers were slow to realize their collective power. In the Manche, for example, the first association of normal school alumni did not appear until 1896, and they did not organize a unitary *amicale* until 1903. By then, the national *amicale* federation had already met three times.[12] On the other side of the spectrum, the Seine-et-Oise association of normal school alumni dated back to 1860, although this is an exceptional case.[13] By the beginning of World War I, most normal school graduates took entrance into their local *amicale* for granted. A former *institutrice* remembers: "The *Amicale*? The question wasn't even asked. Upon leaving the normal school, one joined; those who didn't were very rare, I think. Well it's for sure, at least, that all thirteen of us from my entering class met at the first meeting-conference-banquet hall in 1912!"[14]

Meanwhile, the national teacher congresses drew principally from the local pedagogical conferences that had been organized during the 1870s. Indeed, if there had not been a well-organized regime of local conferences from which to draw representatives, establishing a national congress would have been a much more difficult enterprise. Although the congresses were under the thumb of the administration as surely as the local conferences were dominated by the school inspectors, the official encouragement of teachers' solidarity ensured their continuing interest in maintaining contact with one another. As discussed earlier, the education ministry made conference attendance mandatory in 1880 and devoted some attention to the willful generation of an esprit de corps, drawing matters of pedagogical and scholastic improvement together with professional solidarity. The call for regional organizing that had been made by the Union des Instituteurs et Institutrices de la Seine in 1887—the call that triggered the Spuller circular—was repeated in the teachers' regional periodicals in the provinces. Regional conferences in 1892 (Avignon) and 1893 (Toulouse) brought teachers together to discuss their new, post-Ferry professional status, including the possibility of founding a national association "under the aegis of the administration."[15] The Union Pédagogique Française was established in 1891 for the purpose of "making the practical results of the cantonal conferences known."[16] By the end of the century, there were clear linkages between the national congresses and the network of regional conferences.

Although there were local and regional differences between the *amicales*, there were a number of commonalities in terms of what the organizations stood for. Like the associations of former normal school students and conference associations from which they emerged, they met for professional development, including the discussion of academic and pedagogical issues. They were also mutual-aid societies that contributed small sums of money to ill or otherwise incapacitated teachers and their families.[17] They ran primitive group insurance plans. And in 1900, they created a bureau to organize national meetings and the publication of a new journal. The *Bulletin général des amicales d'instituteurs et d'institutrices publics de France et des colonies* began to gather and disseminate information on *amicale* activities around France and, in 1901, published a series of statements from the local associations expressing what they wanted from their new publication. The *amicales* requested that the *Bulletin général des amicales* disseminate information about the state of the reforms that they championed, strengthen the ties that bound the lay teachers together, and favor "the common action of all our associations."[18] Its appearance in 1901 coincided with an increase in local meetings and the beginning of what would be biyearly national congresses of the Fédération des Amicales (FAI).

The *amicales* mostly shied away from overtly political matters, with some exceptions. For example, the FAI demanded higher wages and changes in the seniority system. Since 1889, teachers had been paid directly by the central administration in Paris, but the system of stringently regulated salary increases dated back to the Second Empire. These rules, known as the *pourcentage*, prevented regular advancement, specifying instead that only a particular percentage of teachers could occupy each of the levels of professional classification at any given time. Such a system relegated many teachers to the same position on the salary scale for ten or fifteen years—sometimes more than twenty. A nontenured teacher (*stagiaire*), earning as little as seventy francs per month, could remain without tenure for twenty or even thirty years with only the most modest of pay increases. When the government reformed the *pourcentage*, the *amicales* took credit for the changes, and they also trumpeted the pay hikes of 1903 and 1905 as evidence of their movement's success.[19] The *amicales* were also concerned with political favoritism. Nepotism was "a veritable state doctrine during the first decade of the 20th century."[20] The tides of local politics were widely known to have powerful effects on hiring, firing, and advancement. The Ferry schooling regime, while it centralized the payment of the teachers, still allowed local and regional authorities considerable discretion in determining who taught where. Since the 1880s, teachers had been trying to cultivate autonomy, and the image thereof, and the *amicales'* rejection of nepotism was one manifestation of that effort.

The political climate of the early 1890s revealed a conservative reaction within the young Third Republic. The anticlericalism that was so important to the republicanism in which Jules Ferry rose to prominence faded after the government implemented the laws that bore his name. Education policy had been one of the only threads that held the republican majority together,[21] and Ferry's successors consecutively showed that other policy differences prevented unity within the parliamentary group. After the Goblet Law of 1886, which secularized the teaching personnel, many republicans fell back from the anticlerical barricade and assumed a defensive posture that lasted until the final years of the nineteenth century.[22] In 1889 and 1890, the newspapers stopped chronicling the debate over "morality without God," although they continued to report on the local conflicts between teachers and priests throughout the provinces.[23] Ferry himself, however radical his education policies, was a profoundly conservative politician, especially in regard to the working class, which he believed ought to form associations specifically to curb Communist radicalism and the tendency to violence.[24] Church-friendly politicians, meanwhile, proceeded to regroup. The church supported the candidacy of the authoritarian Georges Boulanger and other candidates who were believed willing to abrogate the Ferry legislation. And with blue-collar labor organizing at a peak and the state elite's growing nervousness about the socialist threat, the political establishment once again embraced the church as a bulwark of social order.[25]

Then the Dreyfus Affair happened. The case of the Jewish officer, framed as a traitor, electrified French society during the second half of the 1890s. It provided a rallying ground for every social force that was dissatisfied with the political order.[26] For clerical politicians, the case provided an opportunity to "re-Catholicize" France. In Angers (Maine-et-Loire), no stranger to religiously based contention, "priests and seminarians spearheaded three days of uproarious anti-Semitic demonstrations during the anti-Dreyfus mobilization of 1895."[27] For defenders of *laïcité* the affair was a true crisis that threatened a secular political order that had been painstakingly fought for. The academy emerged as one of the most strident fighters on behalf of Dreyfus, and it is little surprise that between 1895 and 1905, high school teachers began organizing at a rapid rate,[28] as the threat of clerical power reasserted itself. By 1900, the Dreyfusard campaign had created a widely held belief that the left must educate the masses "if they were not to be an easy prey for demagogic nationalism."[29]

The teachers' *amicales* proliferated in this climate of polarized social relations. With a Catholic Church hostile to the political regime, the idea of an *amicale*, a name chosen by the associations to reflect "a conciliatory attitude toward the government," was amenable to the political establishment.[30] Political authorities were also satisfied with the hierarchical organization of the associations of formal normal school students, with the school director acting as president, such that in the first few years of the twentieth century, the teachers' organizations did not seem threatening to the government and, to Pierre Waldeck-Rousseau, appeared potentially useful. The Dreyfus Affair had reactivated the *instituteurs'* desire to defend the principle and practice of *laïcité* and inspired the teachers to be proactive about voicing their concerns.[31] From the perspective of Parisian political elites, this was a positive development. However, the affair also inspired the beginning of teachers' class consciousness, as the phrase "intellectual proletariat" was first heard in the teachers' ranks during this era.[32] Several luminaries of the radical wing of the teachers' movement, including the Bolshevik sympathizer Louis Bouët, cited the Dreyfus Affair as being at the heart of their radicalism and the basis of "uneraseable memories."[33] "When you are marked by the Dreyfus Affair," Léon Blum said, only days before his death in 1950, "it's for your entire life."[34] In the aftermath of the affair, the teachers' anticlericalism, so important to the organizing of the 1880s, became a valuable asset to a regime perched on the edge of civil war, grasping for a stabilizing influence in the midst of reactionary ultramontanism.[35]

The 1901 Law of Associations was the most important specifically political result of the Dreyfus Affair for teachers. The law was an effort by Prime Minister Waldeck-Rousseau to restrict religious organizations and eliminate the unauthorized organizations that existed.[36] The Dreyfusards of the political left now governed France, and in the anticlerical political environment that persisted in the aftermath of the affair, the republicans were not about to allow illegal and "socially dangerous" organizations like the Jesuits and the Assumptionists to remain.[37] Although the new law placed tight restrictions on religious organizations, it also wiped away restrictions on other forms of association. It permitted functionaries to organize, "as long as they were not 'based on illicit cause or aim' and did not have 'as an aim the injury to the integrity of the territory and the republican form of government.'"[38] State workers took quick advantage of this new legal opening. Between 1901 and 1907, state functionaries organized 515 local and regional associations, including 106 teachers' associations (77 *instituteur* groups, 22 secondary school teacher groups, and 7 associations of higher education personnel).[39]

The teachers' congresses of 1898–1903, discussed in Chapter 1, reveal both the teachers' increasing assertiveness and the regime's internally conflicted perception of that assertiveness. The Paris congress of 1900 was especially important for legitimating the teachers' associations because of the presence of Education Minister Georges Leygues, who gave his blessing to the corporate group. Leygues understood that, as in years past, the teachers could be a valuable bulwark against clerical and reactionary political forces. In the years following the Dreyfus Affair, which had divided the country, Leygues felt that he could take no chances. "What is good for one category of citizens," he told the 1900 congress, "is good for all the others and you do not lose this attribute when you become a teacher."[40] Leygues was thus the first education minister to break publicly with his post-1887 predecessors who had been hostile to the *instituteurs'* associations. The assembled teachers defined themselves and their goals along three lines: pedagogical perfection and defense of professional and material interests, defense of the *école laïque*, and support for "all of the society members in whose defense it will fearlessly fight in the case of unmerited attacks that are aimed specifically at the functionary."[41] At the Bordeaux congress the following year, the teachers' tone was less reserved. The *amicales* adopted a statement of principles that included demands that would become long-standing staples of the teachers' movement: salary increases, the teaching of pacifism in the classroom, and the unrestricted right to organize.[42] The political stridence of the *amicales* at their 1901 national conference in Bordeaux, along with the rush of organizing that followed the 1901 Law of Associations, moved the prime minister to order Leygues to forbid the teachers to meet in 1902, "alleging the bothersome precedent that annual congresses would cause, as well as the harm done to professional work."[43] "In 1903, however, the government not only gave its consent [to the *amicale* federation's meeting in Bordeaux] but sent the new prime minister, Emile Combes, a frequent spokesman for the government against the *fonctionnaires'* organizations, to give its blessings to the Fédération des Amicales."[44]

The teachers did not at first find the political autonomy they sought in the *amicales*. All topics discussed in *amicale* meetings required prior approval from the education minister. During the 1900s, many *amicales* invited and encouraged the participation of local administrators and, in Paris, the minister and his aides. Criticism of the government, if present at all, had to be couched in terms of pedagogical necessity. For example, at the Bordeaux congress of 1901, Marguerite Bodin, one of the most militant of the early *amicalistes*, advanced a motion that called for more pacific history to be taught in the schools. Bodin called for downplaying the history of battles and substituting "the march of civilization through the centuries." And in place of "bellicose chauvinism," she called for teaching students to "respect the right, on whatever side it is found" and stressed the need for establishing "an arbitration tribunal."[45] "The congress had accepted criticizing government militarism on pedagogical grounds,"[46] the only way for teachers to advance such a critique in front of government spokesmen. The *amicale* federation issued a declaration of purpose at the Bordeaux conference that included demands for higher salaries on the grounds that teachers required freedom from economic necessity in order to give a "social education."[47] With the emergence of the *Bulletin général des amicales*, however, the teachers now had another, more strident vehicle for expressing their concerns. The *Bulletin* did not shy away from publishing articles about economic issues.[48] While government authorities did keep careful track of the teachers' activities, what the teachers wrote was, at least during the early years of the teachers' movement, not as important to the authorities as their pedagogical conduct and the way they behaved outside the classroom.

The Origins of Selective Engagement, 1903–1914

While the teachers' movement had never been truly unified, the year 1903 marked a turning point, as two cross-cutting cleavages split the teachers' movement: gender and unionism. For the remainder of the Third Republic, the divisions between men and women and between moderate republicans and radical syndicalists best defined teachers' collective political consciousness.

Between 1880 and 1910, the number of lay *institutrices* in France increased much faster than the number of *instituteurs*. While only 36 percent of teaching personnel in the secular schools were women in 1880, that percentage had steadily risen to 42 percent in 1890, 46 percent in 1900, and 57 percent in 1910.[49] During these decades, teaching had become less appealing to men and increasingly attractive to women, who were now charged with educating the "future mothers of the Republic,"[50] a mission whose importance did not yet justify wages equal to those of men. By 1905, nuns had been phased out of public education, but they were replaced by "lay nuns" who were trained in the new normal schools for women. Notwithstanding that women's wages were lower than those of their male counterparts, teaching was still as good a job as women with white-collar aspirations could hope for, while men with similar aspirations could find more lucrative (if not necessarily more prestigious) work elsewhere. With the *institutrices'* popularity came more intensive surveillance of their professional and personal lives.

The women teachers responded to these patriarchal inequalities by organizing on their own. A radical feminist, Marie Guillot, founded the first Groupe Féministe Universitaire in 1903 in the Meurthe-et-Moselle to "study the role of women, the question of salaries, and the right to vote" and thereby place themselves at the vanguard of the French feminist movement.[51] Over the following decade, *institutrices* founded several dozen of these *groupes*, and at the *amicales'* 1907 conference, they held their own meeting to discuss the issue of equality of salaries for men and women teachers. During the 1907 elections for departmental councils, the first round of voting featured hundreds of ballots in nine *départements* that carried the phrase "equality of salary." The *groupes* were granted a small space in the *Bulletin général des amicales* and started their own publication, the *Action féministe.*[52] These associations provided the *institutrices* with centers of social and intellectual activity, and their influence was felt within the *amicales* and, later, the *syndicats.* Beginning in World War I, the *institutrices* would start to take a more important role in French teacher unionism, as I describe later.

Meanwhile, another split transpired within the *amicale* movement between those who were content with their new associations and those who wanted a more strident political voice. The latter found their first public expression in 1903 at an *amicale* conference in Marseille. Prime Minister Emile Combes attended, along with Minister of the Navy Camille Pelletan, and later made a speech about the importance of the teachers for the defense of the secular republic. The assembled teachers responded with great applause, and the crowd that had gathered outside the meeting place to hear his speech joined them.[53] By the end of the evening, the teachers and the crowd had gathered outside the *hôtel de ville* of Marseille, singing revolutionary hymns. Shortly after the congress, a small group of teachers calling themselves the Emancipation met in Paris and publicly declared their radicalism. By 1905, the Emancipation included thirteen sections, concentrated in Brittany and the Nord, along with the *départements* of Maine-et-Loire, Rhône, and Bouches-du-Rhône.[54]

What did radicalism mean for these teachers? It meant moving beyond the relatively passive "friendly societies" in the direction of trade unionism. The trade unions of this era were revolutionary syndicates devoted to socialist principles and aggressive tactics for realizing them. The *amicales,* radical teachers believed, had abandoned their criticism of the administration's authoritarianism that had spurred the teachers' movement in the first place. Indeed, the *amicales* courted state authority; the fact that school directors and academy inspectors were invited to attend and participate in *amicale* meetings put a damper on political discourse. Teachers' requests for higher wages failed to address the injustices of academic hierarchy and of the capitalist system in which it was embedded. By addressing "the social question," the radical wing of the teachers' movement was calling the broader structure of society into question and also reaching out to another political force in France that did the same: the labor movement. Unlike the *amicalistes,* the radicals identified themselves with the working class. Teachers were "thought workers," the radicals declared at their 1905 congress, who deserved the same guarantees as factory workers.[55] The *Manifesto of Unionized Teachers,* issued in November 1905, made the working-class identification even more explicit. "By their social origins, by the simplicity of their life," the *Manifesto* declared, "primary school teachers belong to the people."[56] True autonomy from local politics and the still-influential priests was not possible within the context of *amicales,* and the Emancipation teachers reflected that belief.

The radical teachers made a number of distinct but related demands. They demanded the establishment of teachers' councils in each school (so that the school directors would never have unchallenged power in the school), freedom from arbitrary administrative authority, and the end of forcing teachers to do work outside their pedagogical obligations. They demanded the legal right to organize unions and to belong to the CGT. And they demanded wide-ranging education reform, including the teaching of class conflict and the elimination of all textbooks that did not advocate secularism and pacifism.[57] As a tactical matter, their journal advised the foundation of regional associations that would be affiliated with the national federation in Paris. The radicals did not, however, want to do away with the *amicales*, preferring instead to co-opt or convert them. Indeed, the groups of Emancipation teachers "were often only *syndicaliste* factions within the *amicales*, and the double appearance, which subsisted in certain areas until 1918–1920, shows the relative complexity of *amicale/syndicat* relations in the militants' minds."[58]

Evidence of the unionist "mentality" began appearing in the provinces two months after the 1903 Marseille meeting, as extremist teachers who had previously stuck with their *amicales* began to express their dissatisfaction. The local periodical of the pedagogical organization of the Var took the name *Bulletin du syndicat*, and several months later, the organization declared itself a union. In the months that followed, teachers' organizations in the Maine-et-Loire, Pyrénées-Orientales, Morbihan, Deux-Sèvres, and Loire-Inférieure had all become unions and submitted statutes to their local Bourses du Travail. The six local teachers' unions had doubled to twelve by the time their new federation, the FNSI, met in October 1906.[59]

Amicaliste and *syndicaliste* teachers attacked each other in their respective journals. *Amicalistes* claimed that radical teachers betrayed the trust of the French Republic by giving the people the impression that all teachers were rebels. The secular state depended on teachers to instill good moral virtues in French children, and revolutionary syndicalists were demonstrating that they were not dependable for the task. The *amicales* also resented the pro-union teachers' condescension of the *amicales*. "Oh yes, I'm an imbecile," a teacher from the Isère sarcastically wrote in his local *amicale*'s journal, "because I don't have your mentality."[60] What was meant by "mentality" was clear enough: class consciousness, along with a conviction that the problems of the teachers were intimately connected with the larger social structure and the exploitation of the working class. Writing in 1911, a teacher from the Calvados union argued that the *amicales* should be transformed into unions and that, indeed, a lot of teachers whose mentality was that of *syndicalistes* were wasting their time being associated with the *amicales*. "The *amicaliste* does not become a true *syndicaliste* in the blink of an eye," he wrote; "his mentality must change."[61] The *syndicalistes* fought for revolutionary transformation. The *amicales*' quest was to contribute to the social order, not overturn it, and they limited their demands to periodic salary raises, a greater voice in decision making, and the recognition of their legitimacy.[62]

The appearance of the Emancipation and publically pro-union teachers happened conterminously with the organization of other state functionaries, including postal, railroad, telephone, telegraph, and law enforcement workers. The postal workers had staged the first functionary strike in May 1899. The functionaries increasingly saw their social status, education levels, and common boss as constituting a common identity, and over the following decades, they fought together for the legal right to organize. Between the end of 1905 and 1909, the functionaries created two organizations, the moderate, *amicaliste* Comité d'Études and the more radical Comité Central, led by the *instituteur* Marius Nègre, devoted to the fight for freedom of association. The Comité Central was inspired specifically by the government's efforts to stop the teachers from organizing a national federation. It was a much smaller organization committed to demanding the right to unionize for the functionaries. In January 1906, it attracted an audience of six thousand Parisian functionaries to the Manège Saint Paul to demand trade union rights, as simultaneous demonstrations transpired in sixty other towns and cities throughout France.

Given what control over the means of production would mean for public-sector workers, state authorities were understandably hostile to the notion of unionized teachers. The general feeling in Paris was that state workers, who numbered more than one million by 1900, and workers in the private industries did not face the same opponent. "State employees do not face private interests," Minister of Commerce and Industry Jules Roche claimed, "but a general interest, the highest of all, that of the state itself." Unionized state workers would be "organizing a struggle against the nation itself, against the general interest of the country, against the national sovereignty."[63] There were some dissenters, but most public officials took the official state line on the matter. "If state functionaries are allowed to unionize," wrote the conservative Charles Maurras, "the state will crumble into small pieces."[64] This was the standard rationale given by politicians for denying teachers the right to unionize.

When some FNSI-affiliated teachers from the Seine submitted their statutes to the prefecture in October 1906, the police ordered the forty chief administrators of the illegal union to appear before a tribunal. The submission of the statutes sparked a campaign in the conservative press against teacher unionization. The prefect declared the teachers' syndicate illegal and refused to authorize it. The forty teachers did appear for the tribunal as ordered, and several days later, several members of the new government of Georges Clemenceau appeared before the Chamber of Deputies to argue the government's case (that the 1884 law did not allow teachers to unionize). The president of the council, Jean-Baptiste Bienvenu-Marin, assured the deputies that the government did not seek to punish the teachers but merely to specify the limits of the law. The Chamber voted overwhelmingly to support the government's position and also declared an amnesty for the teachers of the Seine.[65] The case of the Seine teachers unleashed a torrent of criticism of the government from the teachers, including a statement from the firebrand hero of the early teachers' movement, Marius Nègre. "We are convinced that our interests are tightly linked to those of the working class," wrote Nègre. "Beyond our immediate demands we want to affirm the sentiments of deep solidarity which tie us to the working class and to show our sympathy for the vast movement of organizations and of proletarian emancipation which inevitably must transform the world."[66] Several months later, the government issued a new statute meant to replace the 1901 law, a statute that workers correctly perceived as a regression. It not only forbade functionaries from joining unions but also specified penalties to be imposed on infractions.

The Comité Central responded to the government by posting an open letter to Clemenceau on the walls of city buildings. "For us," the letter declared, "the state is a boss like any other," and the functionaries sold their labor like other workers. Contrary to Spuller's 1887 view that unionized state workers would be organized anarchy, the Comité Central's letter claimed that the right to unionize substitutes "the current administrative anarchy for a more rational and more perfect organization of public services and, at the same time, it defends the interests of production as its own interests." Finally, the letter threw Clemenceau's own words back at him, citing a speech that Clemenceau gave on the floor of the Senate in which he described all the wars, massacres, butcheries, and tortures for which the state was responsible. "You know it better than anyone," the letter concluded, that "the essence of the state is immutable!"[67] The letter was posted on March 30, 1907, at the same time that the annual FNSI congress was concluding in Nantes, where the Parisian teacher Charles Désirat joined Nègre in rallying the representatives to vote in favor of pledging allegiance to the CGT.

Clemenceau's response to the Comité Central came swiftly. Given the strike wave of 1906 and the more recent agitation in the early months of 1907—a shoemakers' lockout in Fougères had just ended, and the electricians of Paris and the dock workers in Nantes were striking[68]—the government had no patience for any more worker militancy, particularly among state workers. He had a letter addressed to Nègre published in the newspapers warning teachers that they were treading on thin ice by associating with the CGT. Nègre and the other signers of the open letter were summoned before their ministers to answer for their subversion. Nègre was fired, along with several of the most outspoken, radical members of the postal workers' union, the municipal workers' union, and several other state workers' organizations. By the end of April 1907, after a series of legal proceedings, seven radicals, including Nègre, were no longer state employees.[69] The government thereby signaled that, first, the official line on teacher unionization had to be drawn (that is, no more teachers could be allowed to form syndicates) and, second, political radicalism within all the functionary organizations would be singled out for administrative sanction. The response from the federal council of the FNSI was quick and telling. The federation rallied to support Nègre and demanded the collective resignation of all town councils in all of France as a statement of protest against Nègre's persecution.

By this time, the spring of 1907, the government had quietly abandoned any concerted effort to break up the *amicales*. One reason was that the threat of teachers' associations was balanced by their usefulness. Given the fact that *amicalistes* were ardent republicans, anticlerical, and Dreyfusard, they were a powerful ally in the ongoing battle to maintain the secular republic in the face of a resurgent Catholic Church. And since their members were rooted in the normal school and pedagogical conference networks, they were also useful professional organizations. Teachers had, by this time, become one of the most socially prestigious groups of workers in the country. This was the era of the *hussard noir*, the vision of the *instituteur* as a crusading secular soldier, a stern and severe servant of the state, clad in black, glorified in novels by Zola, and depicted as an unfairly put-upon public servant in Antonin Lavergne's best-selling 1901 novel, *Jean Coste*.[70] They were now the ardent republicans that the republic had wanted them to be since the era of Jules Ferry, but not in quite the way Ferry had imagined. They supported French democracy, but the ideal democracy of republican teachers was the radical democracy of the socialist Jean Jaurès. They were anticlerical, but the regime did not want to "dechristianize" the nation, as Jaurès and his followers dreamt of doing. Instead of a uniform (and uniformed!) corps of classroom workers, a generation of teacher educators, school inspectors, and politicians had learned the virtues of a diverse, flexible teacher cadre that was as sensitive to preserving certain elements of communities' regional identity as it was of forging a unitary French nation.[71] The trade union movement attracted the teachers who believed in many ostensibly republican ideas but reached beyond them in their demands not only for complete control over the education system but also for the transformation of French society and, through their commitment to socialist internationalism, the world. The union movement "chez les instituteurs" constituted a radical expression of one vision of the French republic, a vision that extended beyond France. "The *amicales* were successful in part because they organized a group of young, vigorous men and women who adhered to everything the radical Republic stood for."[72] They constituted a politically orthodox expression of teachers' esprit de corps; the unions did not.

The Clemenceau government's reaction to the teachers' open letter exposed the fault lines within the teachers' movement, between the hard-liners who wanted to push the *amicales* in the direction of unionization and the mass of moderates who were happy with the *amicales*. Many syndicated teachers, such as those in the Seine, abandoned their organizations, and some *amicales* distanced themselves from Nègre. The syndicates of the Morbihan and the Loire-Inférieure withdrew from the FNSI altogether. The syndicates of the Pyrénées-Orientales and the Var left the Bourse du Travail. The Var was one of the first *départements* to form a teachers' union but, after the firing of Nègre, renounced syndicalism and became an *amicale*.[73] The Seine union did not renounce syndicalism, but it did refuse to pay its share of the salary now owed to Nègre. The more militant syndicates of the Maine-et-Loire and the Bouche-du-Rhône backed Nègre, but in spite of his having been made a permanent secretary and his 1911 reinstatement in the classroom, Nègre's role in teacher unionism faded after the tumults of 1907.[74] Given that his was the main voice of teacher radicalism at the time, many teachers feared for the future of the FNSI. The FNSI's 1908 congress in Lyon was a dismal affair; attendance was light, several affiliates had withdrawn, and an executive committee could not be chosen. Several months later, the federation's headquarters was moved to Marseille, along with the responsibility of publishing the *École émancipée.*[75]

While these fault lines were exposed, the government's strategy signaled some progress in the teachers' organizations' quest for political legitimacy. More than 70 percent of public school teachers, men and women, were *amicale* members by the spring of 1907, but unlike in 1901, the government no longer understood *amicalisme* as dangerous or politically unorthodox. The Clemenceau government did not, at this point, try to ban the radicals from organizing at all but, instead, tried to play the radical and moderate wings of the movement off each other in an effort to marginalize pro-union teachers. Indeed, when Aristide Briand entered the education ministry in 1906, first under Ferdinand Sarrien and then under Clemenceau, he declared that "though he would not disband the existing *syndicats,* he would not allow the formation of any new groups."[76] The new groups did not include the *amicales,* which proliferated, some even joining the local Bourse du Travail. Selective engagement had already begun the process of signaling a new understanding of political orthodoxy to the teachers' movement.

The congress of 1912 provides striking evidence of the progress the teachers had made in securing the legitimacy of their organizations over the previous decade, as well as the strengths and limitations of the government's power to eliminate them. On August 16, 1912, six thousand teachers, representing forty-four local syndicates, gathered in Chambéry for a two-day conference. The attendees voted on a number of pedagogical matters, but they also renewed their commitment to class struggle, to pacifism, and, following the CGT's lead, to participation in the Sou du Soldat campaign, the workers' effort to show solidarity with their military comrades by contributing money to support union members who were doing military service. The Chambéry conference also showed how far along the feminist teachers' movement had come. The Fédération Féministe Universitaire (FFU) held a separate meeting at Chambéry at which Marie Guillot and other women unionists spoke out against the patriarchy of the school system and drew the connection between the radical teachers' movement, the broader syndicalist movement, and civil and political rights for women. Although the Sou du Soldat campaign attracted the most attention outside the teachers' movement, many *instituteurs* saw the FFU as a dangerous, divisive provocation. Political activism, they believed, should be confined to the union.[77] The male teachers' organizations did not acknowledge the profound radicalism of a woman teachers' organization, representing as it did a forum for professional women to be involved in political activism that, given their lack of the franchise, was rare in their lives.

The government responded to the Chambéry conference with hostility. Former war minister Adolphe Messimy criticized the teachers for their participation in the "antimilitaristic" and "antipatriotic" Sou du Soldat campaign; in the weeks and months that followed, a war of words emerged between radical journals like *L'humanité* and *Le radical* and the conservative press and politicians.[78] A week after the congress, Education Minister Gabriel Guist'hau announced that "the government has decided to order the teachers' syndicates to dissolve immediately," declaring them "illegal."[79] The minister instructed the prefects to initiate legal proceedings against teachers who refused to yield to the government. But the timing of the announcement was off since it was summer and the teachers were on vacation. They were unavailable and did not respond to the summonses. There was, however, a critical outlier. The Morbihan syndicate, which was scheduled to take over the leadership of the FNSI in September, before officially taking charge sent a confidential letter to the other affiliates, requesting that they obey the minister's orders.

The other militants responded quickly. The Bouëts wrote to the leaders of all the local syndicates and other teacher militants that they knew and told them to discount the Morbihan's request: "We are going to work together in order to maintain our syndicats."[80] Another manifesto of *syndicaliste* teachers was drawn up, this one more moderate in tone than the 1905 document that announced the birth of the radical teachers' movement to the world. However, the teachers continued to affirm their pacifism and their identification with the working class and the CGT. They offered their support for the new manifesto, both individually and as members of their unions. Marie Guillot was among the teachers reprimanded for their support, while the locals from the Seine, the Rhône, the Bouches-du-Rhône, and the Maine-et-Loire were summoned before tribunals where the penalty of dissolution was pronounced. But an amnesty was granted for the teachers in December.[81] The amnesty was preceded by the testimonies of leftist politicians in the Chamber of Deputies who presented information to the effect that teachers were not so much pacifist as full of confidence in the spirit of international cooperation. Finally, the amnesty was pronounced, with Prime Minister Raymond Poincaré, a sympathizer, expressing the opinion of the regime. "The government," Poincaré stated, "far from making the totality of teachers responsible for a few individual transgressions, never doubted either patriotism or the spirit of discipline that animates the teachers' corps."[82] For the second time in five years, the teachers' union movement survived a credible government threat of dissolution.

The "Chambéry scandal" marked the end of prewar teacher militancy and also demonstrated the progress and limitations of their resistance against state authority. While the FNSI did hold a congress the following year in Bourges, it was a quiet affair, reported neither in the major press nor in the federation's flagship journal, the *École émancipée*.[83] The government's divisive strategy had succeeded in marginalizing, if not eliminating, the radical teachers' associations. But the strategy had the effect of rendering normal what had once been verboten: the *amicales'* meetings and publications were now an acceptable mode of action for the teachers. The onset of war, however, would jeopardize this development.

World War I and the Teachers' Movement

World War I brought economic and demographic ruin to France. The value of the franc plunged, the cost of living escalated, and the national debt quintupled.[84] Well over two million Frenchmen were killed or wounded between 1914 and 1918, and male life expectancy plunged from 48.9 years to 39.5 years.[85]

The war effort took an enormous toll on the teachers' corps. By 1915, twenty-five thousand male teachers had traded the classroom for the trenches.[86] Most were replaced by women, although about fifteen hundred Parisian *instituteurs* were replaced by *intérmiaires* (temporary workers), who were paid well under the standard teacher's salary.[87] For the teachers' movement, this meant that the women, the *institutrices*, were forced into leadership positions in the FNSI and its local affiliates. In 1914, after the general secretary and undersecretary of the FNSI, Charles Joly and Marcel Cottet, were conscripted into the army, Hélène Brion and Fernand Briot assumed leadership of the federation. The *École émancipée* was officially suspended as of October 24, 1914, but reappeared soon thereafter under the less provocative title *École de la fédération*. New leaders emerged, as Marie Mayoux, Julia Bertrand, and Gabrielle Bouët, along with Brion and Guillot, kept the *École* in publication and periodically met with CGT and Section Française de l'Internationale Ouvrière (SFIO) members. Delegates from the depleted teachers' corps continued to meet in conference under the weight of intensive governmental surveillance. World War I shook but did not destroy the foundations of the movement.

While the overall structure of primary education was not altered during the war years, the prevalence of prowar propaganda in the classrooms increased, and the surveillance over teachers' activities—both private and work related—intensified. Not only the government was especially attentive to teachers' private and professional lives; the children themselves were reporting suspicious activities of their schoolmasters and schoolmistresses. When ten-year-olds reported comments that suggested anything less than unqualified opposition to the Germans, the result was enough to attract the school inspectors and, sometimes, the police force. "One must not confuse hate for the German people with hate for their teachers," a teacher from Dordogne told his class, meriting a six-month prison sentence on the charge of "having given subversive talks."[88] Teachers were also ordered to read a brochure, written by members of the administration, entitled *Their Crimes*, about their German enemy.[89] The federal committee of the FNSI publicly protested against the state's efforts to cultivate war hysteria in the classroom.

Speaking out against the war became increasingly difficult for the teachers outside the classroom as well. Marie and François Mayoux wrote an antiwar pamphlet entitled *Syndicaliste Teachers and the War* whose publication in May 1917 provoked a hostile response from the government. The two teachers were suspended from their functions in July and, in October, imprisoned for six months each, while a stock of their pamphlets was impounded, along with other pacifist literature.[90] One month after their sentencing, the police arrested Hélène Brion for her antiwar propagandizing, an arrest that provoked a series of protests from her syndicate comrades.[91] She received a three-year prison term with a suspended sentence and was forbidden from the classroom until 1925, when she resumed teaching in a Paris suburb.[92] While dozens of individual teachers were disciplined for their wartime and immediate post-wartime *syndicalistes* opinions and activities,[93] Brion and the Mayoux had become especially popular within the radical teachers' movement. Even CGT leaders made overtures to the radical teachers' movement, their disagreement over the war notwithstanding.[94]

During the war, relations between moderate and radical teachers grew more polarized. The *amicales* supported the government's war effort, and despite the internal division within the FNSI's wartime leadership, most of the radical teachers were antiwar. A statement from the FAI in September 1914, reprinted in a number of newspapers and journals, is illustrative: "The soul of the school, melted into the great French soul, is expressed in a sublime, patriotic surge, in an indomitable will to overcome, in the acceptance of all the sacrifices, in a generous outburst of the highest feelings of solidarity and fraternity."[95] The FAI's *Bulletin* regularly carried articles that "praised the act of dying for the Republic,"[96] as well as reports on teachers killed in battle, all of whom were described in heroic terms. The president of the *amicales*, Emile Glay, wrote an open letter from the front to his students in which he depicted the Germans as "enemies of liberty."[97] The federation also released a pamphlet addressed to "the children of France" that tried to inculcate "a feeling of indebtedness" in its depiction, in text and illustrations, of children paying respect to killed and wounded soldiers and their families.[98] And the *amicales* joined the administration in branding the unionized teachers as *défaitiste* (defeatist) for their pacifism. As early as 1913, Glay had recommended that the unions be dissolved and transformed into "study groups" within the *amicales*.[99] As I discuss later, the radical branch of the teachers' movement did not forget Glay's divisive tactics, and the rigidity of the division between the moderate and radical teachers' federations persisted well after the war.

Although there was some dissension within the leadership, the FNSI was generally antiwar. For hard-line unionists, committed as they were to internationalism, the war was a blow against the working classes of Europe, all of whom were bound to suffer. In June 1915, Marie Mayoux organized a conference of unionized teachers in Tours "in order to formulate a position on the war with her colleagues."[100] The conference attracted mostly antiwar teachers, including wounded soldiers returned from the front. The only question, the majority believed, was how publicly demonstrative the teachers should be of their pacifism. Mayoux herself drew up a new *Manifesto of Unionized Teachers* that called on the French government to negotiate peace. The FNSI's affiliates in the Charente and the Bouches-du-Rhône, along with individual teachers from a dozen other *départements*, expressed their support for a new manifesto of unionized teachers, drawn up by Mayoux for publication on July 1, 1915. This document, in which teachers were described as "members of the grand family of French and world workers,"[101] was essentially an antiwar statement. But the FNSI's federal council, with Hélène Brion at the helm, initially refused to support it. Brion claimed that the war could end only with a French victory. Several weeks later, about thirty FNSI representatives from local affiliates throughout France met in Paris to continue the argument, and Brion and Loriot were won over to the pacifist cause. "I was wrong," Brion later recalled of her prowar stance, "and I consider this error the most serious mistake in my life."[102] Meanwhile, the *École* regularly published letters from teachers at the front who remarked on the horrors they witnessed.[103] And Brion herself was the recipient of many letters from war-mobilized teachers that, even after government censorship, expressed the fear and frustration of being under fire.[104]

The disagreement between the *amicale* and the *syndicat* federations extended beyond the simple question of whether France should be at war. Their positions also led to differences in how they used their resources. The FAI and its affiliates encouraged all *instituteurs* and *institutrices* to donate money to support the war effort and charities that helped the families of the war dead. The FAI also retracted its long-standing salary complaints and endorsed the government's pay scale, an issue that would become salient again as soon as the war ended. *Amicale* leaders believed that their charity and support of the war effort would "strengthen their organization by creating a middle-class image of 'respectability'" and "advance their public image. . . . They expressed confidence that once the war was over they would be rewarded for their outstanding support."[105] The FNSI, meanwhile, started a collection to support teachers who had been suspended or fired for their antiwar and pro-union positions.[106] The *École* also ran stories that exposed war profiteering and the government's engineering of inequalities within the teachers' corps through the *intérmiaires*, the teachers who replaced those at the front.[107]

The obstacles to teachers' political mobilization were more formidable during this period than at any other time during the Third Republic, all the more so given the fact that women teachers were, in the popular imagination, still only a step removed from the convent. Merely being the recipient of a magazine or newspaper of questionable political orthodoxy was enough to attract police surveillance. However, only a small portion of teachers actually participated in politically salient activities. Just as the upheavals of the 1848–1851 period attracted suppression of teachers that was out of proportion to the small number of teachers who had actually been politically active, only a small minority of teachers had really engaged in politically unorthodox activity during World War I (even granting a more stringent understanding of orthodoxy at the time). Although the teachers were a well-organized labor group by this time, the vast majority were members of the prowar, progovernment *amicales*, not the *syndicats*. Only about 3 percent of French teachers were affiliated with the FNSI on the eve of the war. The FNSI, whose leaders were inspired anew by the Bolshevik Revolution, was ready to resume its international outreach to teachers and the broader labor movement, while the *amicalistes* were ready to reap the rewards of their patriotism. By the end of 1918, the moderate and radical teachers' organizations were more hostile to each other than ever before.

Remobilization, Selective Engagement, and Certification, 1918–1940

Between the November 1918 armistice and the end of the Third Republic, teacher organization experienced its renaissance. Driven by wartime and postwar social dislocation, a spike in industrial labor militancy, and discontent with the conservative government elected in November 1919, the teachers' postwar unionization drive bore fruit. The radicals at first reaped the benefits of having consistently stood for peace, "attracting a younger generation of militant teachers radicalized by the Great War."[108] Before the war, the radical FNSI had never comprised more than six thousand members but, by 1920, about twelve thousand were in the federation, a peak number for the radicals; membership plummeted soon thereafter and, for the remainder of the 1920s, never rose above forty-eight hundred.[109] But the moderates experienced a surge in popularity that extended into the 1930s. Membership steadily rose from fifty-five thousand in 1920 to seventy-nine thousand by 1929 and exceeded one hundred thousand by 1937.[110] By then, both federations reached out beyond the *instituteurs* to the higher educators as well, the *professeurs* of the *collèges* and *lycées*.[111] Yet for most new primary school teachers, "joining the SN[I] became a veritable right of passage . . . in the years between the wars."[112] By 1923, both federations identified themselves as trade unions, demanded the legal right to organize as such, and launched campaigns to ban national chauvinism and bellicosity from textbooks in the name of pacifism.[113] While the government continued to persecute teachers for their open involvement in politics as late as the 1924 election campaign, and teachers remained wary of taking part in strikes, teachers' collective claim making over the next fifteen years, both autonomously and in joint actions with other *fonctionnaire* associations, became tacitly accepted by French governments.

What happened to radicalize the *amicale* organizations? And how did the regularization of their political activity happen? Although the impact of the war had an understandably enormous impact on teachers' understanding of French politics and society, independently of the structure of teachers' organizations, the answer to both of these questions relates to the dynamics of selective engagement. Basically, the government miscalculated the degree of loyalty that the *amicales* were willing to give the regime. Following the war, the state granted teachers the most meager pay raise they had received in years. The FAI had not been informed when the government would meet to discuss the pay scale, in spite of having made a specific request to have an FAI representative present at that meeting and all other state workers having sent representatives to participate in salary decisions.[114] The teachers were no longer hesitant about making their demands heard; almost six thousand of them had been killed in the war, and much of the conservative press was still accusing them—and not just the more stridently antiwar radicals—of being *défaitiste* and even enemies of the state. Given their expectation of rewards from the state in return for their support of the government during the war, FAI members felt betrayed. It was this sense of betrayal that drew Emile Glay and other *amicaliste* teachers to the radicals' conference in August 1919. The *amicaliste* teachers now complained of "administrative mistrust" and, in a joint statement with their *syndicaliste* brethren, "hostility toward primary teachers."[115] In the quarter century that followed, relations between the teachers' organizations, the labor movement, and the government shifted.

The willingness of the teachers' organizations to affiliate with organized labor must be understood in the context of the broader labor movement. In the spring of 1919, the CGT general secretary, Léon Jouhaux, renounced the union's commitment to revolutionary syndicalism. For now on, Jouhaux told the CGT rank and file, it was the duty of the working class not to bring about a social revolution but, rather, to work for the maximization of industrial production. The split between the majority of workers who followed Jouhaux and those who followed the hard-line revolutionaries metamorphosed into an organizational split between the CGT and the CGTU (Confédération Générale du Travail Unitaire) in 1921. Jouhaux had long been a friend to the teachers, but he was also the target of suspicion by the more pro-union teachers because of his overtures to the government. The teachers had not forgotten Clemenceau's history of suppressing teachers' organizing efforts, and they were dismayed to hear Jouhaux, several months before the armistice of 1918, praise President Clemenceau for his "revolutionary" credentials.[116] When the FNSI met in Tours in August 1919, Emile Glay and Louis Roussel, both luminaries of the *amicale* federation, were in attendance. They approved of Jouhaux's moderation, and Glay expressed both reluctance in joining the revolutionary syndicalist movement—since he believed that there could be no social revolution without the teachers first educating and organizing the masses—and eagerness to bring the *amicales* into the CGT.[117] Neither Glay nor his proposal was warmly welcomed by the *syndicalistes*, represented by Louis Bouët and Fernand Loriot. The *syndicalistes* had forgotten neither Glay's prowar propaganda nor his advice that the syndicates be dissolved, while Loriot rejected the very possibility of pursuing social change through democratic political institutions.[118] In the end, the radicals, believing that the result of uniting with the moderates "could be to introduce into our milieu elements hostile to the essential goal of the CGT: the extinction of wage workers and employers,"[119] rejected a union with their *amicaliste* colleagues. Instead, they reinvented themselves as the FMEL, an organization that drew secondary and higher education workers into its ranks. The only exclusions were school inspectors and directors, along with the teaching congregations.[120]

One month after the Tours congress, representatives of the local *amicales* met in Paris and voted 242 to 2 (with 4 abstentions) to unionize, as the aforementioned SNI, and 170 to 43 (with 34 abstentions) to affiliate with the CGT.[121] The objections to these decisions came most notably from the Parisian *instituteur* Abel Sennelier, who refused to take part in political activity. During the discussions leading up to the vote for syndication and affiliation with the CGT, Sennelier rejected the language of class struggle, claiming that teachers "must be everything to the nation and not to a single class."[122] He then founded a "professional" association that, while avoiding political persecution, never attracted the membership of the other two organizations. By the end of 1921, Sennelier's group had between six thousand and seven thousand members, compared to about fifty-five thousand in Glay's SNI and about twelve thousand in the FMEL.[123]

Tension between the SNI and the more radical FMEL continued unabated. Militants greeted Emile Glay with derision at the Tours congress of 1919, as they remembered the *amicale* leader's prewar criticism of the FNSI. After the FAI's subsequent congress in Lyon, when the *amicales'* representatives voted to transform their organization into syndicates, Emile Glay wrote that "because our neighbors want to bar the road . . . we will crowd into their weak troops to attain our objective."[124] Glay refused to speak out against the government's surveillance and persecution of his fellow teachers. "I am not," he claimed, "like Bouët, against any disciplinary measure for one's beliefs."[125] Meanwhile, the *amicales'* Roussel and the *syndicats'* Bouët argued, in print, over why the two organizations could not resolve their differences and unify.[126] The question of labor affiliation also inspired public bickering. "When Louis Bouët wondered about the sincerity of the rallying of the ex-*amicalistes*—'Are we allowed to doubt the sincerity of the neo-*syndicalistes* who do not even have the courage to perform the act of individual adhesion?'—Emile Glay retorted: 'With or without our adversaries, we will go to the Rue la Grange-aux-Belles to help realize the *cégétiste* ideal, and the more that it is desired that we move away from the battle, the more that we will strive to fight.'"[127] When the CGT national committee decided to allow the Fédération Générale des Fonctionnaires (FGF) to join the blue-collar worker organization, thus indirectly connecting Glay's organization to the CGT, Bouët argued that "you cannot reasonably approve a proposition that has, as its exclusive objective, to admit, concurrently with our federation, the entirety of the teachers' *amicales*, whose leaders have fought too often against syndicalism."[128] Reasonable or not, the FGF decided to adhere to the CGT in May 1920. The CGT accepted its new comrades, thus allowing the local teachers' syndicates to participate in institutionalized labor politics.[129]

These disputes between the labor federations transpired while the Bloc National government, which ruled France from 1919 to 1924, intensified its disciplinary activities over the teachers. The government reprimanded, suspended, or fired teachers "for participating in May Day activities, for writing pacifist articles, for publishing in socialist newspapers, for publishing in *L'humanité*, for expressing ideas publicly, for having 'watched the sale' of a brochure."[130] Just as in the prewar years, teachers who joined unions and *amicales* were subject to persecution. During the Bloc National years, local affiliates of the radical teachers' organizations were brought before tribunals, legally disbanded, and their members fined.[131] Hundreds of individual teachers became the subjects of police surveillance,[132] and local affiliates of the two national teachers' federations began issuing statements of protest and collecting funds to support their persecuted comrades. During the 1919–1920 school year, the pages of the revived *École émancipée* were filled with reports of disciplinary measures taken against the teachers.[133] In the Rhône—the site of long-standing anticlerical activism and, along with the Bouches-du-Rhône farther south and Maine-et-Loire in the West, an early bastion of teacher unionism—the local authorities were wary of worker activism of any sort after 1918. When antiwar teachers in Lyon threatened to organize a strike in protest against persecution by the government, the prefect took the threat seriously. "The leaders will not content themselves with a threat," he wrote, and recommended that several hundred troops be stationed in Lyon specifically to guard against labor unrest.[134] The Catholic conversion of one teacher, Jacquet, from Saint-Igny, was enough to have him transferred, while Marie Farget from Oullins was accused by her school director of being absent too often.[135] The teachers' union in the Var— another *département* with a history of teacher radicalism—quietly resumed its affiliation with the workers' movement, though not without fears about legal retribution.[136] By May 1920, they were no longer quiet, as the Var teachers opted to lend "moral and financial" support to the strike movement in Toulon.[137] The minister of the interior requested information on an *instituteur*, M. Gueran, who was trying to create a syndicate chapter in the Finistère.[138] Within a year and a half, Gueran was successful and then some: The Finistère affiliate was refusing to run any candidates in the elections for the departmental council because it rejected all collaboration with the stagnant political administration.[139] In the spring of 1921, Education Minister Léon Bréard asked his rectors and inspectors to alert him to any deviations from politically orthodox "conduct or language."[140] On the first day of 1922, about 300 of the 360 teachers from more than seventy-five of the departmental councils sent resignation letters to their respective prefects.[141] The vast majority of them were reelected two months later on a campaign against the use of transfers to discipline teachers and other, related persecution.[142] Later that year, at a meeting of the Loire FMEL affiliate in Saint-Étienne, some younger teachers implicitly acknowledged their apolitical past in their complaint that "the politicians of the Bloc National and the prefectoral administration wanted to transform the teachers into docile electoral agents."[143]

By the time the French electorate returned to the polls in 1924, the feminization of the primary teachers' corps had accelerated. After the wartime spike in the number of working *institutrices*, the percentage of women teachers dropped to 61.2 percent for the 1921–1922 school year before rising to hover around 65 percent for the remainder of the Third Republic.[144] While all French women lacked the right to vote in national elections, *institutrices* also faced the legacy of two depoliticizing labels: the nun and the mother. Women public school teachers no longer came from the convent, but the image of the religious schoolmistress was even more firmly embedded in the French national consciousness than the image of their male counterparts. Still more important though, given the secularism that had become so important in public affairs, was the maternal image. The innately maternal qualities of women, the story went, were conducive to the role teachers were expected to play in the secular education of the republic's youth. It was this image, along with the government's pronatalist policy and fear of demographic decline (especially in relation to Germany), that helps explain the government's facilitation of teacher marriages, when most other countries in Europe and North America discouraged them.[145] Women were active suffragists and did have voting rights in elections to departmental education councils, but the institutional and informal social constraints on their ability to contest government decisions or engage in other forms of autonomous collective claim making were formidable.

Yet pacifism, particularly as expressed through the union movement, was a way for *institutrices* to express themselves politically, "through the back door," as it were.[146] No fewer than a third of *institutrices* were affiliated with the CGTU between 1921 and 1934, a figure that suggests a degree of "underrepresentation" given the feminization of the teachers' corps during this era.[147] But through their union affiliates' Groupes Féministes de l'Enseignement Laïque, the more moderate Groupes Féministes Universitaires, and other associations, women teachers made their presence felt in local and national politics through their strident advocacy for pacifism.[148] Their voices could be heard through their local union newspapers and journals, their speeches at national and international congresses that included their organizations, and a variety of locally organized campaigns: to boycott toys that glorified war, outlaw textbooks that glorified militarism, and raise money for German children who were thrust into poverty after France occupied the Ruhr in 1923.

While the teachers' organizations found much to disagree about—their relationship with the working class and the CGT, their political affiliation, tactics for advancing their agenda, and methods of mediating between organization and membership—there remained one subject that united teachers' associations throughout France: anticlericalism. The Bloc National provoked the defenders of *laïcité* several times over, with the reestablishment of ties with the Vatican, the expression of antisecular sentiment in Alsace and Lorraine (now French territory once again), the infusion of church schools in western France, "and the attempt to get state financial aid for private religious schools."[149] These policies, along with the ongoing persecution of *fonctionnaire* unions, alarmed the teachers. The image of the teacher as a secular warrior, refined and popularized by the turn of the century, persisted into the 1920s, and the unions continued to defend *laïcité* as a political cause. The SNI and FMEL made the clerical reaction and the *école laïque* the central themes of their 1923 congresses. Thousands gathered for meetings in Lyon (Rhône) and nearby Saint-Étienne (Loire) to hear speeches protesting against the influence of ecclesiastical authorities in the schools. Political persecution of teachers came to be more closely associated with the *école laïque* than ever before. When Paul Laguesse, a teacher from Semeur (Seine-et-Marne), was fired for the crime of being a Communist, the leftist press referred to it as "an episode in a great battle undertaken against the *école laïque*, a battle which is sometimes manifest by the dismissals of communist teachers, sometimes by the closing of rural schools in order to allow *congréganistes* to open new private schools."[150] A comparable case was made in the Yonne newspapers for the dismissal of a school inspector, Lebossé, who was an ardent defender of the *école laïque*.[151] The persistence of church-state conflict guaranteed the continued salience of the *instituteurs'* categorical identity as secular warriors first activated by the French state during the centralization politics of the early Third Republic.

The return of church-state conflict to the political stage was coterminous with a renewed political interest in overhauling the entire public education system. Just as the Franco-Prussian War had stimulated a latent interest in overhauling the French education system, so, too, did World War I bring public education reform back into the national spotlight.[152] A group of *lycée* and university teachers founded an organization devoted to educational reform, the Compagnons de l'Université Nouvelle, to launch a press campaign for the *école unique*. Although *école unique* would become something of a catchphrase phase for educational reform in the ensuing years, it initially referred to a liberalization of the public education system. The Compagnons fought for the establishment of equal educational opportunity for all students, regardless of class or gender. Secondary schools had long been the training grounds for the bourgeoisie and the elite. These schools were selective, charged tuition, were located chiefly in urban areas, and offered courses, like Latin, that were not taught in the *écoles primaires*. Although the idea of equalizing educational opportunity dated back to prewar years, the teachers' unions began to promote large-scale educational reform during the Bloc National years. There were even some signs that new forces in the Catholic establishment might be willing to support the *école unique*. During the 1920s, French Catholicism moved a step closer to conciliation with the republic, a step that, as the Dreyfus Affair made clear, had not happened during the republic's early years. Now, with the reestablishment of the French embassy at the Vatican and a positive attitude on the part of Pope Pius XI toward Paris, the French right became less solidly Catholic. In particular, "the Church did not look with favor upon the continued collusion of French Catholics with the forces of the extreme Right."[153]

But the *école unique* floundered. The traditional Catholic view on the class-based segregation of primary and secondary education prevailed. Many on the religious right viewed this project as another attempt to realize latently the antireligious legacy of the French Revolution by stealth, "another attempt to extend the state monopoly over the educational system."[154] Catholics also did not miss the fact that the Cartel des Gauches government of Édouard Herriot consisted of anticlerical radicals, which made any large-scale education reform illegitimate in the eyes of most ecclesiastical authorities.[155] "In a December, 1925 encyclical, Pius XI had identified laicism as 'the plague of our era which has corrupted human society.'"[156] In spite of having thirty *universitaires* in the ranks of the Cartel, including Herriot, reform did not happen.[157] Not only was the expense of rebuilding the school system too great for a country in the midst of a financial crisis, but "the entanglement of the religious policy of the Cartel des Gauches with the problem of education reform"[158] was also too controversial and too great a threat to the government.

Although the teachers' unions supported the idea of education reform, some of the specific proposals for the *école unique* antagonized them. The reforms clearly privileged secondary schooling. More seriously, one reform bill, presented to the Senate in August 1926, "involved the abolition or at least the transformation of the teachers' training colleges, which had an especial place in the emotions of most of the primary school reformers."[159] Indeed, the normal schools became increasingly important institutions during the Third Republic, particularly insofar as they trained the *institutrices*, who outnumbered the *instituteurs* by the end of World War I.[160] Many FMEL teachers predicted the failure of reform even before the 1924 election as a result of the French economic system. "It is indeed evident," wrote one teacher, "that the realization of the *école unique* will never happen in a capitalist regime."[161] In response to the Compagnons' program, the SNI advocated a more complete nationalization of the school system. "Conceived partly as a threat against those the school teachers considered the adversaries of *laïcité*, nationalization was a distant goal at best."[162] Essentially, the SNI's plan amounted to a kind of University, "independent of the state, composed of representatives of the state, of parents, and of teachers."[163] What was most important to the teachers' unions, even more than the political independence of the educational system, was that the confessional schools, if they had to exist at all, be dependent on secular authority. For the SNI of interwar years, *laïcité* and this notion of state control (*étatisme*) were wrapped up in each other. But socialist ideology now provided an emancipatory telos that earlier visions of secularism did not supply. "The notion of *laïcité*," wrote the socialist teacher Marceau Pivert, "must lead the working class to intellectually emancipate itself from all dogmatisms, as well as that of the fatherland and that of property."[164]

The 1924 election campaign was a critical moment for the teachers' unions. The Cartel des Gauches, an alliance between the SFIO and the radicals, fought the 1924 election against a coalition of conservative parties and the nascent Parti Communiste Française (PCF), which was competing in its first national election. The Cartel's architect was Édouard Herriot, a former *professeur* who was a strong advocate for the *école unique* and an ardent secularist. Herriot steered the socialist left away from a platform of social change, thereby paralleling the CGT's reformism, leaving the political ground of radical transformation to the PCF.[165] For the first time in French history, the *fonctionnaires'* associations entered national politics en masse, their spokesmen claiming that while they did not want to participate in politics, politics was all around them.[166] They sent questionnaires to candidates for office, soliciting their viewpoints on a range of issues, and then submitted their responses to the newspapers.[167] Spokesmen for the Bloc National government publically cautioned the *fonctionnaires* against participating in politics as early as the spring of 1923, a remonstration that pushed the *fonctionnaire* organizations even more firmly in the direction of the Cartel.

The *fonctionnaires*, and the teachers in particular, had gone to great risk to participate in the electoral campaign of 1924, and the victorious Cartel did not forget them. Shortly after the May 11 election, a series of administrative motions opened the legal doorway for teachers to unionize without fear of legal sanction. In June, Herriot declared that "the government does not forbid [the *fonctionnaires'*] professional organization" and "thus grants them the *droit syndical*."[168] Two months later, he granted a limited amnesty to many *fonctionnaires* who had been suspended for a variety of wrongs, from the railroad workers' strike of 1920 to *instituteurs'* presence at union meetings to *institutrices'* dissemination of material about contraception. Then, early in September, the Cartel's first education minister, François Albert, authorized his academy inspectors to reopen the lines of communication with the local syndicate organizations.[169] Two weeks later, Interior Minister Camille Chautemps sent a circular to his prefects, encouraging them to maintain good relations with the *fonctionnaire* unions.[170] The following year Education Minister Anatole de Monzie empowered the teachers' "corporate groups" to participate in departmental consultation committees.[171] In February, Chautemps told the Chamber of Deputies that a law guaranteeing the right for state workers to unionize was imminent. This law, the Chabrun-Bertholet Bill of June 1925, never made it out of a Chamber committee, but the Cartel's overtures to the *fonctionnaires* constituted a tacit but de facto recognition of state workers' freedom to participate, peacefully, in public politics.

The teachers took full advantage of this new freedom. Between 1924 and 1939, teachers' political lives became increasingly rich and varied. Their commitment to unionism escalated; by 1928, the CGT and CGTU had organized more than 70 percent of the teachers, compared to about 10 percent of blue-collar workers.[172] That same year, the SNI formally aligned itself with the secondary teachers' association, led by Ludovic Zoretti, to become the Fédération Générale de l'Enseignement (FGE), the third-largest association of workers in the CGT. The FMEL continued to compete with the FGE for members; the groups were divided over ideological and tactical matters in spite of broad agreement over a range of issues: higher salaries, pacifism and antichauvinism in the school curriculum, and, most important, defense of *laïcité*. Teachers from both associations routinely participated in public rallies in support of the *école laïque*, pacifism, and other causes dear to the teachers' union movement. During the 1930s, teachers began to actively participate in the SFIO. They campaigned with increasing vigor for the defense of *laïcité*, sometimes generating tension with extant groups aiming at the same goal.[173] By the early 1930s, the SNI had founded low-price insurance programs, while union teachers increased their efforts to organize day camps for schoolchildren that promoted peace, internationalism, and *laïcité*.[174] Union leaders took strident positions against war and fought, publicly but unsuccessfully, against reductions in pensions and state funding of public services in general. In February 1934, in the aftermath of the Stavisky Affair (in which the financier Alexander Stavisky committed suicide, leaving behind a paper trail that implicated a series of high-ranking government officials in his embezzlement schemes) and the reactionary street politics of that winter, the CGT called for a general strike, and the teachers' organizations publicly offered their support. By 1939, the SNI's membership level had reached 110,000—well over 80 percent of the entire teachers' corps[175]—and teachers headed twenty-five hundred of the four thousand local sections of the SFIO.[176] The education and interior ministries monitored the teachers' behavior and sometimes persecuted union leaders through sanctions or transfers. The moderate *confédérés* drew less administrative attention than the militant *unitaires*. "In the late 1920s, unitaire teachers, including the Bouets, continued to be harassed, fired, and in the case of one teacher, jailed for spreading antimilitarist propaganda."[177] But this persecution had less to do with political action in general than with the radical tactics and ideologies of revolutionary Communism. By the time World War II began, the vast majority of French schoolteachers, at every level of secular education, had a political presence in France, be it through a trade union or through individual activity.

Vichy and the Building of the FEN, 1945–1950

During the Vichy years, two contradictory outcomes of the war nearly tore the teachers' syndicates apart. First, just as was done after the Franco-Prussian War, the French public attributed responsibility for the defeat of France to the teachers. The legacy of two decades' worth of pacifist propagandizing had earned the *instituteurs* and *institutrices* the label of *défaitiste* well before the Nazi army stormed the Ardennes Forest en route to Paris. After the defeat of the French army and the fall of the Third Republic, the label acquired new resonance. The Vichy government sanctioned teachers at every level of the education system.[178] The second development was the resurgence of Catholic Church power, resulting both from the teachers' newly unorthodox anticlericalism and the Vichy government's Catholic-friendly policies. Under Vichy, the normal schools were closed, its students were integrated into the high schools, and religious training became mandatory for all teachers.[179]

Just as surely as teachers fought an unsuccessful battle against fascism in the 1930s, they were actively involved in the successful resistance movement during the early 1940s. They clandestinely wrote and published journals that advocated overthrowing their German occupiers, taught units on opposing anti-Semitism in the classroom, and otherwise opposed Nazi ideology.[180] Many of the Communists who were important to the French Resistance were also *instituteurs*, and the teachers emerged from the war in a politically more advantageous position than they had been in 1939.

The postwar years were a time of political opportunity for the teachers. The Catholic Church's political influence was unusually muted due to the collaboration of many prominent clergymen with the occupation forces. Although no large-scale education reforms emerged between 1945 and 1950, these years were consequential for the teachers' movement as teachers emerged as an unusually large, cohesive member of the labor community. The primary school system emerged from the war as a martyred institution; just as in previous wars, military defeat had been blamed on bad schools, and the Vichy Regime had dissolved the normal schools and cracked down on the civil service. By 1946, the normal schools had been fully restored.

The debates among teachers and between teachers and the labor movement suggest that the battle for political legitimacy had already been won. While the new postwar legal order gave teachers the legal right to unionize, teachers' attention was already focused on other matters. The principal question for the teachers was one of internal structure: How should the teachers be organized? The basic contours of teachers as political actors were much as they had been in the 1920s and 1930s.[181] Beginning in 1928, the FGE had begun representing the mass of teachers. But the FGE was no longer deemed sufficient. Under the guidance of Paul Delanoue and Adrien Lavergne, the FGE reinvented itself as the FEN, a federally organized structure that sought both to address the concerns of as many different categories of teachers as possible and simultaneously to appear united. The basis for teachers' cooperation was never in doubt; it was the spirit of *laïcité* that drew the teachers together. The FEN was an institutional expression of the teachers' movement as it had developed in the interwar period.[182] Its strategic concerns were embedded in political consideration. For example, FEN leaders considered the possibility of severing the FEN's formal connection with the FGF in order to make a broader appeal to the teachers. Their organization would be more appealing if members, potential or otherwise, paid fees to only one organization (membership in the FGE had also meant paying a fee to the FGF).[183] Meanwhile, the CGT's internal divisiveness repelled many in the teachers' movement who remembered the long struggle for unity that dated back to World War I. The vote for autonomy described in the introduction to this chapter was the product of these concerns.

Perhaps the best evidence that teachers and their unions had acquired legitimacy as collective political claim makers came in the first five years after the war, as the FEN organized a series of autonomous teachers' strikes for the first time in the history of French teacher unionism. As discussed previously, the majority of French teachers were reluctant to embrace work stoppage as a political tactic. Teachers' structural dependence on the French state made the strike appealing to only the most radical revolutionary unionists. When the national functionary organization engineered a general strike of state workers in February 1933, the first time such a radical tactic had been attempted on such a grand scale, teachers participated. After the war, however, teachers staged their own strikes, autonomously from the other state workers, and suffered no retribution from the government.[184] The teachers' conference of 1948, described briefly at the beginning of this chapter, began what was to become more than forty years of a relatively unified FEN. The law legalizing public-sector unions was passed the following year, but by then, in the immediate postwar years, most of the *fonctionnaires* had seized this right de facto. Fears of class conflict and a generally more amenable political environment after World War II ensured that the teachers' unions could operate unmolested, and by the end of the Fourth Republic (1945–1957), bargaining structures were in place that institutionalized teachers' relationship with state elites.

Conclusion

The ultimate success of the French teachers' movement followed decades of conflict over its legitimate right to exist. Successive governments found themselves in a difficult situation. Along with higher salaries, an end to nepotism, and various kinds of curricular reform, the *instituteurs* and *institutrices* demanded the right to form associations and make political demands autonomously, free from state control. Political elites' understanding of the teachers' corps, and the identity of the teachers that they most wanted to disseminate, was that of the apolitical tool of the state, a manifestation of the republican regime in the towns and villages of the countryside. However far from reality this image may have been, and however impractical it was for the quotidian duties of the teachers, the state's justification for forbidding trade unionism in the teachers' corps was derived from this image.[185] As historian Judith Wishnia has noted, the French state of the early Third Republic was never friendly to the trade union movement among civil servants, but it was downright hostile to such organizing among the teachers.[186] The suppression of the teachers' movement, however, came at a cost: the alienation of a valuable political ally during the secularization struggles, the Dreyfus Affair, World War I, the renewal of church-state conflict during the 1920s, and the battle over the *école unique*. Beyond those conflicts, the French state had committed itself, as of the early 1880s, to providing the French populace with free, secular, high-quality education and had rendered school attendance mandatory. These commitments meant, among other things, creating a high-quality teachers' corps. The tools for creating such a corps, however, were the normal schools and pedagogical conferences, which the teachers appropriated for political purposes, slowly at first but with increasing success during the 1880s and 1890s. And the republicans knew that if they alienated their political allies in the teachers' movement, many teachers could be lost to the radical wing of the broader French labor movement. In the context of the blue-collar labor unrest of the 1880s and 1890s, such a fear was justified. Denying teachers the legal right to associate at all evaporated by 1901; after that, only trade union rights, the *droit syndical*, were in doubt. But, as described previously, the 1901 broadening of the right to associate yielded such a massive wave of teacher organizing that the state outlawed the *amicales*' 1902 national conference. The state's inability and unwillingness to crush the *amicale* movement entirely yielded another, more durable mobilization structure: the *amicales* themselves. While the state needed the training institutions to mobilize the teachers, the polyvalence of these institutions, as well as that of the teachers, enabled the teachers to mobilize themselves.

The emergence of the *amicales*, however, did not constitute the success of the teachers' movement, given the state's discretion in dealing with them. What is more important is how tolerance of the *amicales* yielded internal conflicts within the national teachers' movement over political radicalism. The 1903 breakaway of the revolutionary *syndicalistes*, who identified with the working class and sought alliances with the labor movement, initiated a process of selective engagement by which successive French governments sought to marginalize the radicals. That strategy, however, had the unintended consequence of breathing life into an *amicaliste* movement that, on the eve of the Dreyfus Affair, struggled to conduct its activities openly. During the affair, and with the renewal of church-state conflict on the eve of the 1905 Act of Separation, the state relaxed its stance with regard to teachers' associations for fear of alienating a powerful secular ally. By 1907, the *amicales* constituted a corps of moderate teachers that the state could use to keep the radical pro-union teachers at bay. Selective engagement was thereby a useful tool, given persistent labor unrest during the early years of the twentieth century. The intensity of the polarization within the teachers' corps became clear in the aftermath of Clemenceau's suppressive measures. However, selective engagement was also a dangerous game for the state; allowing, however grudgingly, the moderate teachers' associations to exist legitimated them and encouraged teachers to join them in increasing numbers.[187] By 1914, the vast majority of teachers were associated with an affiliate of the national *amicale* federation. After the French government signed the Treaty of Versailles, the government was faced with two possible threats: the radicalization of the *amicales* and the unification of the teachers' movement. The former happened, but the latter did not until after 1945, and only partially. The teachers won political certification then, not because of an agreeable French state, a new epoch in the history of French (or world) capitalism, or as a leveraging device for the purposes of social control, but through a series of protracted, uneven struggles among themselves and against the state.

6

✳

Selective Engagement and Teachers' Politics in New York City, 1920–1960

During the early 1920s, few teachers were actively involved in New York City politics. One reason for their political passiveness was practical: The volume and stressfulness of their work discouraged most teachers from expending more energy after their working days were over.[1] Beyond that, administrators stigmatized demands for higher wages and other political activities among teachers as being "unprofessional." The preeminent national education organization, the NEA, issued multiple public statements to the effect that trade unionism was anathema to professionalism. City administrators told teachers, and believed among themselves, that the "individual moral mission of teaching" precluded turning to organizational assistance for the sake of political activism, notwithstanding the dozens of teachers' associations in the city.[2] Furthermore, of the twenty-three thousand teachers in New York City in 1920, only two thousand were men, the majority of whom worked in the high schools. These male high school teachers dominated the teachers' union movement during this time. Masculine or not, Superintendent William Ettinger frowned on the teachers' union movement, claiming that "nothing can be more detrimental to our schools than the assumption that the classroom teachers constitute a laboring class, a sort of intellectual proletariat."[3] Finally, in 1920, Local 5 was just becoming the object of the state legislature's attention to radicalism in public education, as discussed in Chapter 4, and teachers throughout the city were intent on avoiding accusations of disloyalty, or even disobedience, by school administrators.

By 1960, however, the patterns of teachers' politics in the city had changed dramatically. In the time between the mid-1930s and 1950, the TU had become a shell of its former self. The AFT had revoked Local 5's charter in 1941, in response to pressure from the AFL and from the Teachers' Guild (TG), a group of teachers who had, in 1935, split from the TU. Over the next two decades, a series of federal and local investigations into Communism in the schools gutted the union, driving hundreds of teachers out of work. By 1960, its membership was fewer than three thousand, even as the number of teachers in the city schools topped forty thousand. During the 1950s, with the Communist-dominated TU's influence dwindling, the other city teachers' associations battled the city and state governments over wage hikes and working conditions. However, the various associations fought as much with one another as with state and municipal governments. In late 1959, some members of the HSTA, frustrated by the failure of the TG and the HSTA to form a unified front to fight for them, engineered an alliance between the HSTA and the TG. This alliance became the UFT, which staged a one-day strike in November 1960, spurring its board to conduct a referendum "to determine whether teachers wanted collective bargaining."[4] The teachers overwhelmingly approved of collective bargaining, and the UFT won the bargaining election of 1961. The UFT continues today as the sole bargaining agent for New York City teachers and is a key player in school reform projects in the city.

Between 1920 and 1960, the acceptability of teachers' involvement in politics had changed enormously. After World War I, teachers' aspirations to "professional" status clashed with administrators' apolitical understanding of professionalism. Both city and state officials (and, during the 1940s and 1950s, federal officials) suppressed radicalism in the teachers' corps, and even the more mundane politics of most teachers' associations was frowned on. But by 1960, teachers' participation in public politics had become routine and was on the verge of becoming institutionalized through the mechanism of collective bargaining. This chapter explains this change.

As was the case in France, the dynamics of selective engagement are crucial for understanding the shift in the acceptability of teachers' involvement in collective claim making. However, there were three important differences between selective engagement in the two cases. First, at the time of centralization, French teachers were not recognized as legitimate political actors. In the United States, however, teachers participated in the politics of centralization. The legacy of their political action in the mid-1890s yielded the Progressives' emphasis on professionalism, an apolitical ideology that sought to delegitimize teachers' collective claim making by making it seem an inauthentic and inappropriate expression of teachers' interests. As discussed in Chapter 4, it also encouraged teachers to form associations according to narrow occupational interests, thereby increasing the fragmentation of a teachers' corps whose heterogeneity was already quite pronounced (according to borough, gender, religion, and so forth). While city teachers did not completely withdraw from public politics, professionalism decreased their associations' ability and willingness to mobilize resources, as well as the potential for teachers to create a unified front of the kind that fought against centralization in the 1890s. The history of teachers' mobilization prior to centralization shapes the way that states respond to it after the centralization process begins.

The second difference between the cases is that the dynamics of selective engagement work differently when social movement organizations do not group activists strictly along moderate-radical lines. In New York City, between 1924 and 1935, the JCTO represented the majority of teachers' associations in city politics, while the TU was the radical voice of the teachers' movement. However, several factors complicated this situation. First, the JCTO was an internally heterogeneous organization, comprising more than sixty overlapping associations of teachers, most of which played little or no role in public claim making. The inability of JCTO leadership to maintain unity within the organization prevented it from harnessing power in numbers. Second, in 1927, the TU became a JCTO affiliate. Over the next decade, the TU's radicalism produced tensions within the already heterogeneous JCTO, even as the TU's leadership became increasingly instrumental to the JCTO's legislative successes. And third, until 1935, the TU itself became increasingly beset by internal dissension, as an increasing number of rank-and-file unionists were either members of the Communist Party or had Communist sympathies. Until these tensions split the leftist tendency in the teachers' movement in 1935, the union had as many problems dealing with internal cleavages as with city and state governments. These three empirical factors made it easier for the city government to selectively engage with teachers' associations by decreasing the capacity for any teachers' group to pose a serious threat to the Board of Education's plans, let alone to public order.

The third difference is that in the United States, neither radicals nor moderates dealt with a single, unified state authority. Between 1920 and 1947, the city and state governments interacted with city teachers' associations in different ways, while the federal government's involvement in city education politics was minimal. There was relatively little collaboration between these governments in their mobilization or repression of teachers. After World War II, as the political atmosphere in the United States became increasingly hostile to Communism, municipal, state, and local authorities became unified in their interest in not only neutralizing it but also trying to combat it in a more unified way. After 1947, the American state apparatus—with an unusual degree of coordination between the various levels of governance, administration, and law enforcement—began to target the TU, home to hundreds of teachers who were suspected of Communist Party membership. The influence of the TU in city politics thereby dwindled during the 1950s, clearing the way for the remaining, more conservative teachers' organizations to compete with one another for attention from city and state governments.

These differences suggest that selective engagement created a set of opportunities for New York City teachers to make collective demands on their government that were quite different from those for French teachers. While radicalism facilitated a greater willingness of the French state to accept moderate teachers' associations as legitimate collective actors, it also polarized relations between moderates and radicals. The ideological and tactical differences between the moderates and radicals haunted the teachers' movement long after successive French governments had recognized teachers' collective claim-making activities as legitimate. The radical cleavage in the New York City teachers' movement, however, actually limited teachers' ability to make collective claims on the state during this time period. The city and state governments isolated the TU by restricting its access to public places, subjecting it to investigations, and stigmatizing it and its members as disloyal, unwholesome, and unprofessional. Meanwhile, most city teachers relied on the less overtly political JCTO for representation in public affairs and stayed clear of direct action. But the shifting relationship between the TU and JCTO, and the entrance of the TG into the fray in 1935, created complexities without a clear parallel in the French case. Selective engagement generated pressure on the moderates that was qualitatively different from the way the French government treated the *amicales* and the moderate unionist tendency in the teachers' corps of the inter-war years. American governments treated Communism as a more substantial threat than French governments did, and for that reason, the neutralization of radicalism in the American case had more far-reaching consequences for the teachers' movement than in the French case.

Teachers' Politics and the Beginnings of Selective Engagement, 1923–1935

By the time the Lusk Committee disbanded, the national teachers' union movement had been set back. While NEA membership swelled from 8,466 members in 1917 to 53,000 by 1920, and continued to expand with unprecedented rapidness during the 1920s, the AFT declined in membership over the decade following its peak year of 1920.[5] From the moment of its inception, the AFT was basically a loose federation of locals, with Chicago being the center of influence. There was little in the way of central coordination. Its organizational thinness, along with internal dissension in the locals, prevented it from responding effectively to the Red Scare of the early 1920s. Leadership was another problem. The AFT had, at its inaugural meeting in 1916, elected Charles Stillman (formerly of the Chicago Federation of Men Teachers) president of the organization. Unlike the majority of AFT members, as well as AFL president Samuel Gompers, Stillman was prowar. By electing a male high school teacher to the president of a federation of mostly women's locals, the AFT caucus ensured that the federation's appeal to women teachers would be minimal. Margaret Haley soon withdrew her large and influential CTF from the AFT, and Stillman was left with fewer than one thousand members. For the next three decades, elementary school teachers kept their distance from the AFT, while the NEA remained the country's most influential education organization.

Henry Linville attracted attention in the national community of teachers for being the editor of the *American Teacher*, the AFT's official publication. "Linville wanted to present in it a forthright defense of academic freedom, which was part of his overall vision of unionism," while Stillman "consistently tried to muzzle Linville's more militant tone."[6] The TU leader's vision of the AFT was of "an organization of professionally prepared teachers taking the reins of progressive educational leadership."[7] Stillman saw trade unionism as a more conservative movement for economic advancement. Linville and Stillman would fight over the direction of the *Teacher* for years to come.

Meanwhile, sixty-three New York City teachers' organizations, representing twenty-eight thousand teachers, formed the Joint (Salary) Committee of Teachers' Organizations (JCTO) in 1924. The JCTO quickly became the teachers' political face in city affairs, albeit a fairly conservative one, while the smaller, specialty associations worked to advance teachers' narrower occupational concerns. Representing the vast majority of city teachers, the JCTO was a loose-knit organization, initially without a constitution or bylaws, but through the voluntary contributions of city teachers, it became a powerful force in state and city politics. The city's most important, influential teachers' associations were JCTO affiliates, including the Brooklyn Teachers' Association, comprising seventy-five hundred education personnel; the HSTA, which organized six thousand (about two-thirds) of the secondary school staff; and the Kindergarten–6B Teachers' Association, which consisted of about eighty-four hundred primary school teachers (as of 1935).[8] The TU was also a member, although it was also more likely than other associations to take stands at odds with those of the JCTO. The JCTO did not require associations to support every bill that it endorsed (and it lacked the power to compel such support), but in practice, most member associations followed the JCTO line. The JCTO's twenty-one-member executive committee worked primarily to reconcile factions within the JCTO in order to take united action whenever possible. Although the executive committee was initially concerned only with teachers' salaries, it broadened its scope during the 1930s to include teachers' tenure, pensions, and state aid to the city.

The TU remained a more radical group, albeit a chastened and cautious one after the Lusk hearings. Linville's group, although part of the JCTO, was different from the other teachers' groups. Unlike every other teachers' association in the city, it was a public friend to organized labor, identified itself as a trade union, was unusually bold in making its salary demands, and most important, was the most strident teachers' association in the city regarding matters of academic freedom and involvement in city and state politics in general. When lobbying in Albany, Local 5 had something that the JCTO did not: affiliation with the New York State Federation of Labor, which was the largest, most powerful state labor organization in the United States. School supervisors were hostile to Local 5's "unprofessional" union affiliation, and they saw Linville and Abraham Lefkowitz themselves as subversives and agitators.

In regard to public politics, the Board of Education and the superintendency (and, at the state level, the Albany legislature) opted to engage with the JCTO and to marginalize Local 5. It is not difficult to see why. The JCTO clearly had the support of the greatest number of teachers. Local 5 was not only a very small organization but also one with a fairly narrow constituency; it comprised mostly high school teachers, the majority of whom were men, most of them Jewish. Gender and religious cleavages remained quite salient in the teachers' corps, and the union spoke chiefly to the constituents that had been in its corner since 1916. From the beginning, Linville and Lefkowitz supported the maintenance of a salary differential between elementary and high school teachers, a matter that would sustain tension within the teachers' corps for decades to come. Matters of academic freedom and intellectual liberty, which were most precious to Linville, were not primary educators' top priorities; salaries were. Furthermore, the representativeness of the JCTO was matched by its conservativeness. It neither called itself a trade union nor sought out labor affiliation. It engaged in lobbying and letter-writing campaigns, and while it pressured the state to spend more money on teachers' salaries and on education in New York City more generally, it backed away from more controversial matters. For example, it opposed the repeal of the 1934 Ives Loyalty Oath Law, which mandated loyalty oaths for all teachers in New York State. The JCTO appeared both less threatening to state and city governments than Local 5 and more representative of the city's teachers.

The JCTO quickly accumulated a record of legislative success. Its first major accomplishment was winning salary increases. Almost from the moment of its founding, the JCTO had been working to secure the support of a wide variety of labor, parent, business, and taxpayer associations for an increase in teachers' salaries. After the governor vetoed a salary bill in April 1925, along with seventeen other bills aiming to increase salaries for public-sector workers,[9] the JCTO and HSTA president, William Lasher, initiated a lobbying effort that persisted through the spring of 1927. By the end of that year, more than one hundred associations had backed the passage of a new salary schedule, and the city's Board of Education yielded to the unexpected display of organized pressure. After the success of the 1927 campaign, Lasher maintained the "Joint Salary Committee," as it was then called, to wage salary campaigns over the coming years and broaden its scope in the defense of teachers' well-being. In 1930 and 1931, the JCTO fought successfully for legislation that protected the salary schedules thus established by way of a statute that, for the first time, legally extended New York State's authority over the teachers' salaries. The JCTO fought against Mayor James Walker's proposal, announced while most teachers were on their summer vacation in 1932, to induce all city workers to "voluntarily" give up a month's salary in 1933. Throughout the later 1920s and 1930s, JCTO officials were regular attendees at legislative sessions in Albany, and their opponents noted their diligence. "When an educational bill is pending," wrote one social scientist of the time, "representatives of the teachers' organizations, especially from New

York City, are so much in evidence in the corridors, galleries, and on the floor of the legislative chambers, that such uncomplimentary epithets as 'racketeers' and 'nuisances' have been hurled at teachers' representatives."[10]

The city administration signaled to teachers and the public at large that Local 5 was not welcome. The union "was denied the right to meet in the schools, and its leaders were hounded by city, state, and national authorities."[11] In the fall of 1926, Superintendent William O'Shea turned down the promotions of some union members because they "berate American institutions and principles" and "are considered by medical men of eminence as psychopathic."[12] Linville publicly challenged the board to provide evidence for these charges. When Associate Superintendent of Schools Edward Mandel suggested that Lefkowitz was a Bolshevist, the union responded with a letter to the Board of Education that struck back, pointing out "the recrudescence of the spirit of Luskism in the dictum of Mr. Mendel, that 'as a school teacher, he [Lefkowitz] has not the same rights as other citizens to print, publish, or declare his thoughts and opinions. He is no longer at liberty to freely write, speak, or publish.'"[13] For the rest of the 1920s, Linville, Lefkowitz, and their colleagues in the TU routinely defended teachers who were dismissed without hearings, and the Board of Education and mayor's office accused them of subversion and "unbecoming" conduct in return.

Notwithstanding Local 5's reputation among both teachers and administration, the JCTO's greatest legislative successes came after the TU became a member of the JCTO in 1927. The TU's place in the AFT, an AFL organization, gave it special significance in the city's labor community, as did its relationship with the New York State Federation of Labor. Its reputation as a left-wing organization, and the leadership of "agitators" like Linville and Lefkowitz, earned it plenty of press in the city and state newspapers. Few members of the more moderate teachers' associations had any experience with city politics, much less state politics. But Abraham Lefkowitz was a skilled legislative representative, which explains why "the Teachers' Union frequently plays the directive role in campaigns for legislation."[14] Its influence was out of proportion to its small size.

While Local 5 did not actively campaign against the JCTO prior to 1935, it did take stands that were at odds with the umbrella group. When Mayor Walker announced his salary-cut plan, Local 5 was both the only teachers' organization to come out against it immediately (others would eventually speak out publicly) and the only city employees' organization to fight the mayor on this policy. The president of the Board of Education, Dr. George Joseph Ryan, made light of this maneuver, dismissing the TU as "only about 2 percent of the 40,000 teachers" and as out for only itself and its own members.[15] Only later did the JCTO, under Lefkowitz's influence, publicly fight the policy. In addition, the JCTO opposed the repeal of the Ives Loyalty Oath Law, while Local 5 publicly spoke out against it. After 1935, relations between the JCTO and the TU became increasingly polarized, as the union began to take up causes and forge alliances in keeping with the Communist Party line.

Despite Local 5's influence, all was not well within the organization. Linville's defense of academic freedom during the Lusk years had made his organization an attractive one for Bolshevik sympathizers. Linville was no Communist, and he and those close to him certainly saw the Communist membership as a threat. But that did not stop Communist teachers from joining the union or many union members from openly declaring their Communist sympathies. The new members proceeded to lash out at their "reactionary" leaders in the union. For the Communists, the leaders of Local 5 were vestiges of an old order destined to be swept away: the old guard, the "right-wingers." By 1923, Communist leadership saw the schools as a provocative tool for undermining authority in the United States. The following year, however, the focus shifted from the children to the teachers themselves. *Teachers International,* a periodical produced by the Educational Workers International (EWI), promoted the idea that the teachers were victims of capitalist exploitation and that "the workers of the world were with them as long as they had no fraudulent delusions about being 'professionals.'"[16] Prior to 1929, the Communists were a small minority in the union. Beginning that year, however, Communists began entering the union in larger and larger numbers. The union's appeal certainly had to do with the stock market collapse and ensuing social catastrophe, but the more proximate cause of the union's popularity had to do with the end of a leadership battle within the American Communist Party (CPUSA). William Foster, Stalin's champion in the United States, defeated the reformist Jay Lovestone, who broke with Comintern's analysis of American capitalism and took stands at odds with those of the Kremlin. Most of the TU's Communists were "Lovestoneites," and in the wake of Lovestone's defeat, they saw the TU as a potential beachhead to advance their interests in New York City. Between 1929 and 1931, their numbers grew rapidly. Between 1931 and 1935, Soviet-backed Communists began entering as well, fighting with the Lovestone sympathizers for control over the entire organization. Linville did not, at first, care about these battles. For him, as for the Board of Education, both groups were undesirables.

The 1935 "Split" and Its Aftermath

During the early years of the Great Depression, the city school system was in dire financial straits. The education budget was cut, enrollments in the public schools increased, class sizes went up, and in an effort to control costs and overcrowding in the schools, "New York City was only hiring substitute teachers and paying them little more than half the salary of regular teachers."[17] The substitutes did not require teaching certificates, did not have to pass standard examinations, and were not subject to reference checks. In 1935, the Works Progress Administration (WPA) sent thousands of teachers to the city.

Given the particular prominence of substitutes in the high schools, whose teachers had a heavy presence in Local 5, Linville was especially sensitive to the matter of substitute and WPA teachers in the union. Linville and Lefko-witz demanded that only properly credentialed teachers be employed in the city schools. Since Linville's power and influence in the TU had come from the sup-port of more senior, licensed teachers, he sought "to defend the professional prerogatives of the established teaching staff and to limit membership" in order to maintain his support base.[18] By 1933, Linville had consolidated tremendous formal power in Local 5 "through constitutional revisions that limited general membership meetings, allowed tighter control of discussion at those meetings, ended recall of the Executive Board, and gave the board power to fill its own vacancies (previously the responsibility of representatives from each school)."[19] While he defended these maneuvers as necessary responses to the obstruc-tionist tactics of the Communists, his opponents accused him of Red baiting, dictatorship, and elitism. Local 5 certainly paid a price in membership terms; by 1932, barely twelve hundred of the city's thirty-five thousand teachers were union members.

The union's Communist bloc took up the contrary position. They argued that all substitute teachers' employment should be rendered permanent and that they deserved the same rights and privileges given to other teachers, in-cluding suffrage in union elections. In 1935, the administration and the op-position took parallel positions with regard to WPA teachers. The Communists framed their demands in terms of the internal structure of the TU itself, which they claimed was insular and undemocratic. Given their interest in mobilizing "the masses," the Communists pushed for a definition of *teacher* that included not only substitutes and WPA teachers but unemployed teachers as well. In the face of Linville's refusal to abandon his "professional" stance, both Communist groups formed independent associations to mobilize the excluded teachers.

The executive committee of Local 5 found itself in a difficult position. The Communist opposition was not a majority, but it was much better organized and politically active than the union administration and its supporters. Rank and filers and Progressives flooded union meetings and dominated the pro-ceedings, refusing to give up the floor when they were granted it, and shouting and chanting when they were not. These tactics dismayed union leadership. At the same time, Henry Linville was committed to Local 5's being a democratic organization. As the problem was put in the union's official publication, "The question which our Union members must settle is how to deal with teachers who in general in our meetings refuse to recognize as valid any of the principles of common decency and cooperation."[20]

Matters came to a head in 1933, when Linville called for the expulsion of six of the Communist opposition leaders. Charges of "disruption" were filed, and in accordance with the union constitution's provisions for expelling mem-bers, the executive board commissioned a grievance committee to consider the charges and offer a recommendation to the assembled membership. Linville appointed his old friend and charter TU member John Dewey to chair the com-mittee. Dewey presented the committee report and made a presentation before eight hundred members of the union on April 29, 1933. His remarks on the committee report were clearly sympathetic to Linville's position and contemptuous of that of the opposition groups.[21] Dewey and his colleagues made two recommendations: first, that basic union powers be vested in a delegate assembly in order to prevent coherent minorities from taking over union decision-making power, and second, a six-month suspension for the six teachers on trial. Regarding the suspension of the teachers, "the vote of 451 to 316 was a few short of the two-thirds majority needed, under the union's constitution, to convict."[22]

The Dewey presentation precipitated a quarrel that brought all the union's dirty laundry out onto the table. The cleavage between Communists and administration loyalists overlapped solidly with the difference between youth and seniority. Earlier in the meeting, one of the accused, Isadore Begun, reminded the membership that "in the early days of the union, 'Dr. Lefkowitz was a dangerous agitator and Dr. Linville a red Bolshevik,' but two decades had passed, and 'life goes right on and leaves some people behind.'"[23] Dewey wrote in his own report that "there is a certain amount of cleavage between older members who have come in recently who incline to the idea that new conditions require new methods and that the older membership is imbued with too much conservatism."[24] After the report was presented, Begun had the opportunity to defend himself, during which "he turned to Dewey and said that 'it is with great regret that I see a former teacher of mine who taught me about democracy in education, and liberalism, signing this report.'" After the vote on the suspensions had been taken, an irritated John Dewey turned to Begun and said, "I do regret that I was not more successful with my pupil."[25] Accusations of obstructionism met with accusations of Red baiting. Right after Dewey's report was adopted, attendees began leaving the hall.[26]

By 1935, Linville and Lefkowitz realized that their standing in Local 5 was irreparably damaged. The Communists were successfully taking advantage of the economic depression by recruiting more unionists to their camp, and Local 5's image in the labor community was tarnished. When AFL president William Green wrote a letter to the local, urging the expulsion of Communists from the union, Linville's administration drafted a mild response that the delegate assembly rejected. In its place, the assembly passed a resolution that not only opposed "any discrimination or disciplinary action against any worker because of his political opinions or activity" but also called President Green's correspondence "a Red-Baiting letter, which is in violation of Union democracy and Union principles."[27] "In my judgment, you are out of place in your affiliation with the American Federation of Labor," Green responded. "You properly belong to the communist organization and the communist movement."[28] "Local 5 thus went on public record as condemning the president of the American Federation of Labor for 'red-baiting' and 'anti-union activities.'"[29] Linville had lost his battle with the minority, and when the AFT convened in Cleveland that year, he turned on his own organization, recommending that the AFT revoke Local 5's charter. During the convention, a telegram from William Green arrived, requesting the revocation of the charter. Linville told the convention that if the request was denied, he and the other union officers would resign their posts and leave the union. The membership voted 100 to 79 against revocation. On September 5, Linville followed through with his promise. He and nearly all the other officers of the union left Local 5, and approximately eight hundred of the twenty-two hundred union members followed. Later that year, they formed the New York City Teachers' Guild.

The administration's break from the TU had a powerful impact on city teachers. It came to be known as "the split" for decades to follow. "A few members [of the Teachers' Guild] continue to look back with mixed feelings," Linville wrote in a letter to Dewey, "including some indications of longing regret, to our inglorious past, but that uncertainty will doubtless fade in time."[30] He later claimed that "if another local of the AF of T neglects to see the lesson of Local 5, it deserves to be destroyed."[31] Many former members of Local 5 nurtured animosity toward their old organization. Selma Borchardt, still faithful to Linville, referred to Local 5 as "a weird combination of Lovestoneites, Rank and File, Militants, and lots of other maladjusted, psychopathic human material."[32] She later expressed her frustration with the idea "that to oppose dishonest Reds is any less liberal than to oppose any other dishonest person."[33] Well into the 1990s, old-timers in the teachers' movement of New York City continued to debate the merits of "the split" and of the Communist minorities' tactics.[34] The proximate effect of the split, however, was clear: a splintering of the progressive tendency within the teachers' movement.

Meanwhile, the JCTO continued its modest, but successful efforts to influence the city on bread-and-butter issues. On the initiative of the TG's Abraham Lefkowitz, the JCTO gave questionnaires to all candidates for state office to learn their views on key issues like state aid, teachers' salaries, taxation, and the maintenance of teachers' tenure rights.[35] It also formalized its organization with a constitution and bylaws.[36] More important, the JCTO fought to restore teachers' salaries that had been cut in the 1932 budget, a battle won in February 1937. Although the TG and the TU both tried to take credit for this victory, it was the JCTO to which Governor Lehman sent the ceremonial pen with which he signed the bill.

There were, to be sure, great tensions within the JCTO. Even before the split within the Progressive teachers' movement, the JCTO executive board was often split on policy matters. For example, when the salary cuts of 1932 were announced, JCTO affiliates were divided; the Women Teachers' Association (WTA) and HSTA wanted to work with the mayor, but Local 5 was hostile to the cuts.[37] Although the JCTO spoke out, mildly, against the cuts, it gave up the fight fairly quickly, while Lefkowitz of Local 5 insisted on continuing the battle.[38] Some of the JCTO's policies were fairly conservative. For example, it did not oppose loyalty oaths for teachers. It appealed to the NEA in its campaign to guarantee tenure rights to teachers, promoting tenure on the grounds of the professionalism that administrators claimed was their goal.[39] However, after the successful pay restoration campaign, when the committee adopted a constitution with bylaws, Lefkowitz declared that the JCTO would become a force for social progress and deal more broadly with community and the social issues of the day.[40] While this was not a widely held perspective, Lefkowitz's position in the influential TG and his proven record as the JCTO's legislative representative lent weight to his position. Finally, under Charles Hedley's post-1935 leadership, the TU was unrelentingly critical of the JCTO's undemocratic structure, demanding that the committee be proportionally representative so that the larger associations would wield more influence, especially in the executive committee.[41] At the JCTO's first meeting under its new constitution, Lefkowitz and the TU's new legislative representative, Bella Dodd, fought over the issue of increasing the pay for substitutes, with Dodd in favor and Lefkowitz, concerned with preserving the merit system of pay increases, against. Exasperated with her colleagues, HSTA president Katherine Reif stormed out of the meeting.

While these conflicts were playing out within the teachers' corps, the federal programs of the New Deal brought new ideas to life in public education. Programs in adult and remedial education, parent education, cultural awareness, health services, nursery schools, and school lunches all came into existence. "Federal money also made possible the construction of twenty-four schools, adding 60,000 new settings" in New York City.[42] Thirty-six thousand teachers continued to work throughout the country courtesy of the WPA. And the "activity" program became increasingly popular in city schools. Begun in 1934, inspired by Dewey's ideas, the activity program was centered in the idea that children would learn more (and more easily) if teachers offered them more interesting assignments in the classroom. The program deemphasized textbooks and discrete subject areas, promoted "pupil experience rather than subject matter,"[43] and encouraged activities that would supposedly enhance students' abilities to determine for themselves what they enjoyed and needed to learn. Over the next year, New York City implemented the activity program in sixty-nine public elementary schools with seventy-five thousand students and twenty-five hundred teachers. Students and teachers would collaborate in selecting subject matter, creative and dramatic work became increasingly emphasized, and children became involved in current events, community activism, and self-government. Each child would be autonomous from other children, as far as learning was concerned. The experiment was not implemented very thoroughly. Reports given at the end of the six-year period noted that classes spent three hours per day at most on the activity program, while some classes did not deviate much from the regular curriculum.[44]

Meanwhile, changes in the labor community, as well as in the broader political climate, created problems for the national teachers' organization, the AFT. The financial pressure of the Depression led the AFL to withdraw its financial support from the AFT, and the AFT's increasing support for radical changes in social policy created animosity between Presidents William Green of the

AFL and Jerome Davis of the AFT.[45] As of 1936, the AFT had begun to compete with the Congress of Industrial Organizations (CIO) for membership. The CIO's model of industrial unionism was attractive to teachers, and its presence stopped the AFL from moderating its agenda too much. More important, however, the AFT, which was the only AFL affiliate whose charter included a no-strike clause, worked with increasing intensity through the 1930s to suppress radicalism within its ranks. Local 5 was a thorn in the AFT's side. Its presence, post-1935, earned the AFT the unwanted (and unwarranted) reputation of the union with the Communist leadership. With the CIO's competition to fear, the AFT was slow to move against the TU. Many teachers across the urban United States wanted to join the CIO, although the CPUSA actually discouraged teachers from joining the CIO, seeing in the AFT a foothold with which to gain influence in the AFL.[46] In any event, the influx of political radicals into the AFT throughout the 1930s was a mixed blessing. While the increase in membership was a blessing for the growing organization, the radicalism of many teachers who joined the union movement during the Great Depression disturbed the AFT's image of itself as the true organization of professionals. "Even at its most militant, the AFT pursued improved benefits and working conditions, as well as higher standards for entry-level teachers, in language which appealed to teachers' desire for occupational respectability."[47]

Mobilization and Repression, 1935–1941

During the six years between the split and American entrance into World War II, the TU took on a variety of causes. Many of them were familiar: higher salaries, more state aid, reduced class size, better and more secure pensions, equal treatment for substitutes, and solidarity with organized labor. Others were newer, in keeping with the times. Antifascism became an important part of the union's discourse, as the threat of "Hitlerism" loomed and the Spanish Civil War intensified. The union took up donations of food, clothing, and medical supplies to send to the republicans in Spain.

Those matters notwithstanding, the union's two greatest passions were for academic freedom, which survived the departure of Linville and Lefkowitz for obvious reasons, and civil rights, which had been a relatively quiet issue for the union before the split, only to surface in 1936. The passage of the Ives Loyalty Oath Law of 1934, which required all state teachers to take loyalty oaths, elicited a renewed interested in matters of academic freedom. The union fought for its repeal and against the McNaboe investigations, which sought to crack down on "subversive activities" in the schools. In April 1939, the anthropologist and union member Franz Boas announced the creation of the American Committee for Democracy and Intellectual Freedom; among other things, it investigated and reported on racial biases in social studies textbooks. The union called for the veto of the Coudert-McLaughlin Bill, which passed both houses of the legislature in April 1940 and would have created regulations for religious instruction during the school day. And the union took up a number of causes célèbres pertaining to freedom of thought, the two most renowned of which were those of Morris Schappes and Jerome Davis.

Schappes was a junior English professor at City College in April 1936 when the college tried to fire him along with a dozen other politically active professors on campus. He was an active member of Local 5's college section, as well as a charter member of the college's Anti-Fascist Association, affiliations that did not endear him to the college president, Frederick B. Robinson. Dr. Robinson was unpopular with both the student body and the college's alumni association, particularly because he dismissed several dozen students because of their antiwar and antifascist activities on campus, while the senior class had voted Schappes the most popular and respected professor on campus. The announcement of Schappes's dismissal triggered widespread protest within the college community, including sit-down strikes and mass meetings. The union announced that "reaction rides high at city college" and reported on the union's outreach in defense of Schappes and his colleagues.[48] At the end of the semester, the Board of Education overrode President Robinson's decision and reinstated all thirteen of the dismissed professors.[49]

Jerome Davis held the Stark Chair of Practical Philanthropy at the Yale Divinity School when Yale dismissed him, citing the university's "pressing financial situation." Professor Davis had been teaching at Yale since 1924 and had an excellent record of teaching and scholarship, but he was also president of the AFT, an early advocate for American recognition of the USSR, and author of *Capitalism and Its Culture*, a deeply critical examination of capitalism that foretold its demise. The AFT put together an exhaustive critique of Yale's actions toward Davis.[50] The TU noted his radicalism and suggested that the Yale administration's decision had more to do with his politics than with his scholarship or teaching.[51] The AFT's Academic Freedom Committee secured a year's leave with pay for Professor Davis, but Yale did not rescind the dismissal.

In the years following the split, the union also became increasingly involved in community activism, particularly in Harlem and the Bedford-Stuyvesant neighborhood of Brooklyn. It formed the Harlem Committee "to focus attention and garner resources for the Harlem schools,"[52] and it formed the Permanent Committee for Better Schools in Harlem from a coalition of church groups and community organizations. Among other activities, "the coalition held a mock hearing in which they put the New York City Board of Education on trial."[53] For nearly three decades, the TU sponsored courses on black history and race relations and developed curricula to promote the study of "Negro history." This was an era of racist and bigoted textbooks, and the union was an early watchdog on this matter, as well as an advocate of "intercultural" education. What is today known as Black History Month in New York City is a legacy of the TU's advocacy campaign and activation of its community alliances.

Any doubt as to the nature of Local 5's post-1935 leadership became clear with the onset of World War II. For four years after the split, Local 5 had been enthusiastically pro-Roosevelt, pro–New Deal, and in favor of standing up to aggressor nations. After the Hitler-Stalin Pact of 1939, the union dropped its support for all three and took up a pacifist banner.[54] The *New York Teacher* reflected on the damage done to teachers, schools, and freedom of thought during the last world war and called on teachers to expose and criticize warmongering. "Teachers must be especially aware of their function in maintaining and strengthening forces that work for peace."[55] In June 1941, after two years of firmly avowed pacifism, the TU turned on the dime of the Nazi invasion of the USSR. When war broke out at the end of December, the *New York Teacher News* announced that the teachers were ready to serve their country.[56] The union's executive board clearly followed the CPUSA's line on the conflict in Europe.

The New York legislature created in the spring of 1940 a special joint committee to investigate school financing and subversive activities statewide, including a subcommittee specifically assigned to examine New York City teachers.[57] The subcommittee was co-chaired by Assemblyman Herbert Rapp and Senator Frederic Coudert, the former focusing on budgetary issues and the latter on subversion. The proximate motivation for the Rapp-Coudert Committee was the case of Bertrand Russell. The previous month, the Board of Higher Education had appointed the professor of philosophy to the faculty of City College, effective as of February 1941. The appointment prompted an outcry from the city's religious communities. Bishop Manning of the Protestant Episcopal Diocese denounced the appointment, claiming that Russell would be a classroom "propagandist" against "religion and morality."[58] The *Tablet*, mouthpiece of the Brooklyn Catholic Diocese, expressed outrage at the appointment and demanded an investigation of the Board of Education. The Knights of Columbus also spoke against the appointment, their state council chairman, George Timone, claiming that all the local Knights affiliates stood behind Bishop Manning.[59] Two weeks later, the Board of Higher Education refused to reconsider the appointment, prompting a petition for a court order to revoke the appointment.[60] Writing for the state Supreme Court, Justice John E. McGeehan revoked the appointment on March 30, calling it an "insult" to the city and accusing City College of creating a "chair of indecency."[61] In the midst of the uproar over the Russell case, the state legislature established its joint committee. The state assembly had already considered the Coudert-McLaughlin Bill to allow absence from school for religious instruction and permit the New York City Board of Education to cut part of the teachers' most recent salary increases provided by general legislation in 1930. In addition, the previous two state education budgets had been slashed, leading to less state aid money earmarked for New York City. The case of Bertrand Russell came at a time when both budgetary pressures and social mores were very much on the minds of New Yorkers.

The Rapp-Coudert Committee did most of its work between September 1940, when private sessions began (public hearings commenced in December), and December 1941, when the bombing of Pearl Harbor and ensuing war mobilization shifted the legislature's priorities. During this time, the Coudert subcommittee focused on the TU. In October, the subcommittee requested that the union surrender its membership list, a request that yielded an official subpoena. Over the course of the next year, the subcommittee interviewed 460 individuals with regard to Communist activities in the city schools, "interrogated 404 witnesses at private hearings and 76 witnesses at public hearings."[62] Drawing from this information, the committee released a report arguing that it was not possible to be a public school teacher while also being a Communist Party member.[63] The committee's logic was not that there was something inherently problematic about Communist politics but, rather, that "the Communist method is the method of conspirative fraud," requiring "discipline and a course of conduct which are incompatible with the public service, in that they are thereby obliged to do improper acts in furtherance of those objectives."[64]

The union, of course, fought the Rapp-Coudert Committee from the outset. The TU withheld its membership lists, obtaining a stay in October that was struck down by the Supreme Court's Appellate Division at the end of November. Former activist Bella Dodd later recalled robust activism, sponsored clandestinely by the CPUSA, against Rapp-Coudert, including the creation of a "Friends of the Free Public Schools" committee, which raised $150,000 to fight Rapp-Coudert; the creation of "Save Our Schools" community clubs consisting of parents, students, teachers, and unionists; and the distribution of pamphlets advocating free public schools, which were sent to teachers' organizations, trade unions, women's clubs, and public officials.[65] The union did not ignore the relationship between Rapp-Coudert's focus on the matter of subversive activities and the Russell affair, or the state's relating subversion in the schools to the justification of cutting state aid to education and denying teachers' demands for salary raises.[66] Boas's American Committee for Democracy and Intellectual Freedom took up the teachers' cause. As early as April 13, 1940, Professor Ned Dearborn of New York University spoke at Carnegie Hall on behalf of Boas's committee, calling listeners' attention to not only cuts to state aid and the Coudert-McLaughlin bill but also the Rapp resolution currently in the state legislature, the Bertrand Russell case, and an American Legion–sponsored investigation of textbooks. The union also put the Coudert proceedings into the perspective of its own organizational history, as a defender of academic freedom in the face of the Lusk Committee, of which Coudert was a "lineal descendent."[67] The union accused Rapp-Coudert of being soft on fascism and anti-Semitism, and after the committee had ceased its work, the union also called for reinstatement of the forty teachers who had been purged as a result of the Rapp-Coudert proceedings.[68]

Among other associations, the AFT, CIO, American Civil Liberties Union (ACLU), Lawyers' Guild, City Industrial Council, New York State Federation of Labor, and Teamsters' Local 807 all came to the teachers' aid in one way or another: sending petitions to the state government and various media outlets in support of the teachers' right to withhold their lists, helping the union in its legal battle with the state, and sending delegations to Albany to protest Rapp-Coudert's activities.

However, as a portent of things to come, the other major teachers' organizations in the city did nothing to show solidarity with their beleaguered comrades. The JCTO had already expelled the union back in 1938, and now it proceeded to criticize its ex-affiliate. The JCTO called the TU's picketing of City Hall in April in protest of Mayor Fiorello La Guardia's cuts to the education budget "unwarranted" and "uncivilized."[69] In June, the JCTO wrote to President Franklin D. Roosevelt to repudiate the union's opposition to U.S. rearmament.[70] Later that year, the president of the Board of Education revealed to the press that JCTO leader Frank Whalen had asked for the board to create a committee devoted to ousting "unfit" teachers from their jobs, a committee that would include both Whalen and Abraham Lefkowitz.[71] At the Bronx Boro-Wide Association of Teachers' third annual luncheon, in the midst of the Rapp-Coudert investigations, JCTO officials and local councilmen spoke out against the union and in favor of weeding "subversives" out of the school system.[72] Meanwhile, the TG was even more directly complicit in the attack on the TU. Rapp-Coudert specifically noted Henry Linville's cooperation in helping bring the story of Communism in the city teachers' corps to light.[73] The guild had no objection to the Coudert subcommittee's work; in fact, when the other, more financial side of Rapp-Coudert's work began, the guild was happy to find that many of its own policies were endorsed by the committee's 1943 report.[74] As mentioned earlier, guild members had been trying to subvert the union almost from the moment Linville and his colleagues abandoned it. The guild leadership saw itself as trying to undo the damage done to teacher unionism, and unionism in general, through its "professional and economic program."[75]

While the two Communist-dominated locals dealt with Rapp-Coudert, they also had to deal with their comrades in the AFT. The AFT executive committee voted, at its meeting of December 1940, to hold a referendum on the expulsion of New York City's Locals 5 and 537, along with Philadelphia's Local 192. The AFT charged Local 5 with an inability to stem factionalism in its internal affairs, disruption of the AFT's decision-making process, bad publicity directly resulting in loss of membership, failure to win reinstatement to the Central Trades and Labor Council following the local's 1938 expulsion from that council, and, finally, engagement in "certain organized tactics and practices inimical to democracy."[76] "By ridding ourselves of this influence," the AFT's executive council declared, "we are wresting from reaction the strongest weapon it has against us."[77] Two months later, the union's president, Charles Hendley, officially appealed to the AFT "on the principles of tolerance and democracy" to cease its course, accusing the federation of ignoring "the advance of fascism right in your own field of education" and underestimating the resolve of the minority groups to acquiesce in the executive board's decisions.[78] "Did you think we would be so overawed by you," he asked, "that we would be speechless and helpless in the face of any move you would make to eliminate us from the scene?"[79] Robert Speer, a professor of elementary education at New York University and chair of the Committee to Save the American Federation of Teachers, similarly argued that the AFT was adopting a "totalitarian attitude" and accused the executive board of subverting the federation's own constitution in order to expel undesirables.[80] But their efforts were in vain. In May 1941, the AFT officially expelled Locals 5 and 537 from its ranks, along with Philadelphia's Local 192.

Teachers' Politics in Postwar New York City

In the decade following war's end, two matters dominated teachers' attention in the world of city politics: the intensification of anticommunism in the schools and the shifting lines of competition within the teachers' movement. These two issues shaped the trajectory of organized teachers' conflicts with the city government all through the 1950s.

After the inauguration of Harry Truman, the cold war turned inward. Domestic surveillance and persecution of political subversives, already simmering since the 1935 establishment of the House Committee on Un-American Activities (HUAC), became institutionalized. For the first time since 1917, federal, state, and local governments were in sync with one another and law enforcement authorities with regard to crushing Communism. Given the considerable representation of the CPUSA in and around New York City, crushing Communism became a particular focus of federal and state attention. Between 1948 and 1955, the entire repressive apparatus of the American state slowly destroyed the radical teachers' movement of New York City.

At the federal level, Truman started early. He had, by executive order, established the Commission on Employee Loyalty in November 1946 to investigate federal government employees. He followed up the commission with another executive order in March 1947, creating the first peacetime federal employment loyalty program in U.S. history. Several years later, Attorney General Thomas Clark invoked the Smith Act of 1940, which made it a crime to "teach and advocate the overthrow and destruction of the Government of the United States by force and violence,"[81] to indict a dozen leaders of CPUSA, whose convictions were upheld in the Supreme Court case *Dennis v. U.S.* (1951). Then, in the fall of 1950, with anticommunist sentiment white hot, Congress passed the Internal Security Act over President Truman's veto. This omnibus legislation, which synthesized a series of HUAC-sponsored bills, was the brainchild of Senator Pat McCarran of Nevada, an ardent pre-McCarthy anticommunist. It contained provisions that required Communist and front groups to register with the Subversive Activities Control Board and open their membership lists, forbade Communists from holding government jobs, made it easier for the government to deport aliens, removed citizenship from naturalized aliens who had any relationship with subversive groups, and created a bureau of passports and visas under the auspices of the State Department. Finally, in December

1951, Senate Resolution 366 created the Senate Internal Security Subcommittee (SISS), which was charged with examining the implementation of the McCarran Act but also had the authority to investigate "subversive activities."[82] New York City teachers began appearing before the SISS in September 1952.

At the state level, Governor Thomas E. Dewey signed the Feinberg Law of 1949. It was one of numerous mini-HUACs signed into law across the country during the late 1940s and 1950s. The law required the New York State Board of Regents to make a list of subversive organizations, subversion being understood as advocacy for overthrowing the U.S. government by force, violence, or other unlawful means. "Membership in a listed organization . . . constituted prima facie evidence for disqualification for appointment or retention in an office or position in the public schools of the state."[83] The law's impact was not direct, since state authorities could not bring teachers up on charges under Feinberg until the regents drew up their list. However, over the next five years, municipal authorities, particularly the superintendent of schools, William Jansen, and his legal advisers, used the Feinberg Law as justification for their interrogations.

The city municipal government entered the fray in 1948, on the heels of the Hartley Labor Committee's investigations. The Hartley Labor Committee had subpoenaed TU members in response to a five-week-long picket at the Radio Electronics School of New York, organized by the TU's private school unit. The committee also interviewed Superintendent Jansen about Communism in the schools. Jansen refused to indict teachers before the committee, instead praising TU members for their professionalism and leadership. However, by the end of the year, he had begun summoning suspected Communist teachers to his office for interrogations. Abraham Lederman and Samuel Wallach, both executive board members, were summoned multiple times between 1948 and 1950. After Jansen threatened first-grade teacher Minnie Gutride with conduct unbecoming a teacher, Gutride went home that evening and committed suicide, eliciting condemnation of Jansen's investigations.[84] On May 3, 1950, he suspended eight teachers, all members of the union's executive board, for refusing to answer questions about their Communist Party affiliation, officially terminating their employment in February of the following year. On June 1, the city Board of Education passed the Timone Resolution, which committed the board and its affiliated personnel to "negotiate, confer, or deal with or recognize" the TU.[85] In the summer of 1952, Jansen delegated his investigative authority to Saul Moskoff, the corporation counsel for the City of New York. Over the next three years, Moskoff interviewed more than three hundred teachers. Moskoff gathered lists of teachers from SISS, HUAC, and similar organizations to find potential subversives.

The pursuit of Communism, both in the country at large and in public education in particular, not only united federal, state, and municipal governments but also drew law enforcement into the fray. The New York City Board of Education regularly exchanged information about city teachers with the New York Police Department, as well as with federal committees and agencies, including

HUAC Immigration and Naturalization Services. In March 1951, Senator Mc-Carran and Federal Bureau of Investigation (FBI) Director J. Edgar Hoover established a formal liaison between their organizations. "The FBI would act as a kind of private detective agency for SISS" from then on, sharing its files with the subcommittee.[86] By the end of 1952, the legal and law enforcement apparatus of New York City and state, along with the federal government, had set its sights on the New York City teachers' corps.

As anticommunist fervor accelerated, divisions within the teachers' movement remained sharp. The JCTO still organized the vast majority of the city's sixty-eight teachers' organizations. While the guild, and Abraham Lefkowitz in particular, remained influential within the JCTO, the TG also strained to go beyond the committee's relative conservatism and become a more politically assertive organization. The TU had become isolated from the other organizations by 1947, having had its AFT charter revoked and its JCTO affiliation terminated, and its membership levels had begun to decline. In 1943, it became Local 555 of the CIO. Although there was a pronounced cleavage between radicals and moderates in 1947, the unusual position of the TG complicated the scene. As a militant, labor-affiliated association, it regularly pushed against the moderation of its colleagues, until it finally withdrew from the JCTO in 1954. However, its radicalism was clearly distinct from that of the TU.

In the summer of 1947, on the eve of this flurry of anticommunist activism, another matter electrified the teachers' organizations of New York City. Governor Dewey prompted the state legislature to pass a single salary scale for city teachers in July, thus marking the first time in the city's history that all teachers—whether in an elementary, junior high, or high school—would receive the same salary. Teachers would henceforth start by making $2,500 per year, with a sixteen-step scale that could go as high as $5,125. Prior to 1947, high school teachers had been paid an average of 25 percent more per year than elementary or junior high school teachers. Although the HSTA argued that the pay differential was justified because of the special licensing exams and advanced degree required of high school teachers, it was an open secret that high school teachers saw teaching younger children as easier work. The system of remuneration was thereby stacked against the elementary schools because the best teachers (and teachers-to-be) were attracted to the higher rewards of the high schools. The state legislature had been trying to eliminate the elementary school teacher shortage, which had become increasingly pressing as a new generation began entering the school system. Furthermore, the men returning from war had been more attracted to the better-paying high school jobs than elementary school jobs. Equal salaries were a mechanism to address the shortage of elementary school teachers, and Governor Dewey publicly justified the law on those grounds.[87]

The new salary schedule sparked a battle between the teachers' organizations. The TG, still a popular representative of high school teachers, backed the single salary schedule, as did the TU. For Rebecca Simonson, a former elementary school teacher, the equity of salaries was a matter of simple justice for all teachers as well as long-overdue acknowledgment of the work and accomplishments of primary school educators.[88] But high school teachers thought otherwise, and hundreds of them fled from the guild to join the HSTA. Prior to 1947, the HSTA had been a small organization and not especially influential in city politics. But with this infusion of new members, the HSTA became a major player in the cluster of teachers' organizations. In November 1949, the HSTA, by then two thousand strong, withdrew from the JCTO, citing "insurmountable difficulties between the two organizations" and the lack of "effective, vigorous, professional leadership" from the JCTO (meaning that it supported the single salary schedule).[89] When the HSTA polled high school teachers across the city a year later to determine the popularity of the single salary schedule, the TG and the TU publicly despaired for the unity of the city teachers' corps.[90] Meanwhile, the JCTO argued that the HSTA's maneuver was "prompted solely by the disappointment in personal ambitions of several of the present leaders of the H.S.T.A. to attain membership on the Joint Committee's Executive Board." The HSTA clung to the position that the JCTO had never really been a unified organization and that, moreover, the HSTA's withdrawal from the JCTO provided a great service to the city teachers "by dramatically emphasizing the lack of teacher unity in New York City."[91] The rift between the HSTA and the JCTO made unified action by city teachers impossible for the next decade.

The conflict between the teachers' organizations was put on hold in April 1950 when the HSTA called for a teachers' boycott of voluntary extracurricular activities in the high schools. The HSTA announced the "strike" after Mayor O'Dwyer dropped $13 million from its Board of Education–approved budget for 1950–1951. Cognizant of the teachers' electoral clout, and with an election coming up, the mayor recommended a pay hike of $250 per year for high school teachers and $150 per year for elementary school teachers. But such an offer fell far short of the $600-per-year increase demanded by the HSTA or the $1,200 demanded by the JCTO, TU, and TG. To make matters worse, Governor Dewey signed a bill that gave educational administrators and officials pay increases of up to 30 percent. On April 17, the boycott began and all academic and vocational high schools in the city were participating, as union and guild teachers joined their HSTA colleagues. The JCTO came out against the boycott. Senior proms were canceled, school club activities were suspended, and the coaching of athletic teams was stopped.[92] On April 26, in a maneuver that startled the city administration, thousands of students cut classes to rally and, in some cases, riot in favor of giving teachers the pay hikes that they demanded. For nearly four days, police and truant officers were kept busy, rounding up protesters and sending them home, to school, or in some cases to the police station. Both the HSTA and TG called for calm,[93] although neither organization called off the boycott.

Numerous city organizations came out in favor of the teachers. AFL President William Green pledged his organization's support in a letter to Rebecca Simonson.[94] The support of the United Parents Association (UPA) was especially valuable, given the sensitivity of the strike for the students' parents. When the New York State Board of Mediation appointed a fact-finding committee to recommend a proper salary package for the teachers, the TG's labor connections kicked in. A number of city unions sent messages to Arthur Meyer, chairman of the fact-finding committee, in support of the teachers. Their rationales for such support varied from the belief in the "value and dignity" of teachers' work to the danger of harming teachers' morale, given that teachers help the United States "strengthen the forces of world democracy against the aggression of totalitarian communism."[95]

Efforts to engineer a compromise between the teachers' associations revealed the depth of the split between them. In April 1951, the fact-finding committee pushed its recommendation for a $400 salary adjustment, $200 short of the HSTA's demand. The JCTO was the only organization to accept the proposal, but that organization had, by this time, lost its influence over most of the city's high school teachers, except for some TG members. Later that month, the New York Times reported that "the inflationary tide has worn off some of the luster of 'professionalism,'" such that only the Condin-Wadlin Law, forbidding public-sector employee strikes in the state of New York, stood between the teachers and a full-blown work stoppage.[96] When the teachers rejected the salary compromise, Ruth Farbman, UPA president, said that her organization would reconsider its position on the strike. She also pointed out that the HSTA did not represent the views of all teachers and that the JCTO constitutive organizations favored salary compromise.

The boycott constituted a de facto challenge to the city's Board of Education to regulate the hours and duties of school employees, and it was on those grounds that the city broke the boycott. Extracurricular activities had been a gray area for years, and that gray area was now being exploited. The matter came to a head in May, when the state Education Department ruled on a challenge that the HSTA had made to the Board of Education. The board had ordered teachers to take a Red Cross "refresher" course as part of the city's civil defense program, but the teachers refused, claiming that the course should be voluntary. The board argued that "it had the right to require public school teachers to devote after-school time to related school projects, thus bringing the entire question of extracurricular activities into the picture."[97] The department ruled that while teachers could not be forced to take the refresher course, the Board of Education did, indeed, have the power it claimed to have. The representatives of the teachers' organizations were infuriated, and the TG and the TU both threatened full teachers' strikes if the city tried to enforce the ruling to break the extracurricular strike. An appeal to the New York State Supreme Court was not successful. Finally, the teachers accepted a Board of Estimate salary plan that largely followed the fact-finding committee's proposal.

In terms of the teacher associations' demands, the strike was a modest failure. The teachers won raises, but not the ones that the HSTA and other groups had demanded. But the episode also taught the teachers that the city administration responded to pressure. From April 1950 to August 1951, neither teachers nor administration backed down. Of course, the teachers were aided by a sympathetic superintendent, Jansen, and the backing of the UPA, as well as the children themselves. The teachers were even ready to fight the legal rulings against them. Only the volte-face of the UPA convinced the teachers that the fight was lost. The teachers also realized the difficulty of bargaining with the administration without any institutionalized mechanisms for doing so. That problem would become the target of the subsequent mobilization efforts of the teachers' organizations.

The teachers' organizations were also drawn into the city's assault on the TU. Indeed, the very presence of the TU—now Local 555 of the United Public Workers, CIO—made city teachers, as well as the AFT, guilty by association: "No matter how explicit the AFT was about its past, to the broader public it was the 'teachers' union' that had been nailed as a Communist union, and many conveniently chose not to make the distinctions the AFT would have them make."[98] So they, and the guild in particular, could not be passive.

The TG continued to be at odds with the TU. When the Hartley Subcommittee invited Lefkowitz to offer testimony in 1948, he initially refused. However, when the subcommittee subpoenaed him, he related the story of the TU's Communist history, dating back to the 1920s. His reluctance was clear. "I have not much confidence in committees of a reactionary anti-labor Congress," he said before beginning, "who rely upon guilt by association instead of time-honored legal methods."[99] While the subcommittee was conducting its work, Lefkowitz was also fighting the union in his capacity as principal of Samuel J. Tilden High School. Louis Jaffe was a social studies teacher there, teaching allegedly left-wing versions of recent history, particularly with regard to the recently created United Nations. When his supervisor in the history department, Michael Glassman, had him transferred, the union cried foul, accusing Lefkowitz and Glassman of having a political agenda.[100] The guild struck back, accusing the TU of using the "Jaffe case" as a political tool to "attack Lefkowitz and, through him, the Guild."[101] The escalation of anticommunist sentiment, meanwhile, moved Rebecca Simonson to use her monthly *Guild Bulletin* column to warn against "Fanatical Allegiances . . . witch hunts, and guilt by association, and other undemocratic practices widely exercised by totalitarians."[102] But it refused to countenance a "united front" of teachers, for fear of "strengthening a group to whose means and ends" it took exception.[103] When State Senator Fred G. Morritt of Brooklyn organized a Citizens' Committee against the Feinberg Law, he recruited Simonson and Lefkowitz to be a part of it. But he also added members of the TU, including Rose Russell, and members of the American Labor Party, moving Simonson and Lefkowitz to abandon it only a few days after its foundation. "There are on the committee those who have not proven themselves to be true defenders of democracy," Simonson said.[104]

The other teachers' organizations would not collaborate with the government on what they saw as infringements on academic freedom. The TG objected to the Feinberg Law from the moment it was enacted, noting that its focus on Communists suggested that fascism was no cause for alarm,[105] and objecting to its method of uncovering subversion: guilt by association and informing on other teachers.[106] It did not approve of the Timone Resolution,[107] particularly in light of the diminished power of Local 555. "At this time," a guild executive board member wrote to Charles Bensley, a member of the Board of Education, "when the American Communists have sunk to their lowest point of effectiveness in a generation, hardly a single American is likely to be impressed by anything which may be said at a meeting of a Communist's group, whether in a school building or anywhere else."[108] A decade before, the guild had actively worked to subvert the union. By the early 1950s, with anticommunism at its peak moment of intensity and the TU increasingly isolated in city politics, the guild had other priorities. At the 1954 AFT national convention, Lefkowitz argued that "any teacher who took the Fifth Amendment 'as a cloak to hide membership in the Communist Party' should not be defended by the union."[109] The HSTA, however, endorsed the Feinberg Law. This endorsement, along with their disagreement on the salary schedule, ensured that the guild and the HSTA would continue to be at odds for some time to come.

The anticommunist political movement of the early 1950s destroyed the TU. There was little that teachers summoned before SISS, Jansen, or Moskoff could do to save their jobs. Being summoned before the Board of Education was enough to ruin their careers. Even teachers who could prove their lack of CPUSA affiliation could hope to save their jobs only by informing on other teachers, but this was a solution that few were willing to countenance. By invoking Fifth Amendment privilege, teachers could avoid federal sanctions. But refusing to answer the senators' questions triggered section 903 of the New York City Charter, which declared such refusal insubordinate, thereby enabling Jansen to terminate their employment without any review. Nearly all of the teachers who testified before SISS took the Fifth, and many demanded that the record show that they justified their refusal to answer questions on the basis of the First and Sixth Amendments as well, even though committee members routinely told them that they could recognize refusals only on the basis of the Fifth. One teacher, Irving Adler, invoked his right to due process on the basis of an ongoing lawsuit against Superintendent Jansen concerning his right to interrogate.[110] A college professor, Harry Slochower, launched a legal challenge to SISS after he suffered a "903 dismissal," a challenge that wound up in the Supreme Court. *Slochower v. U.S.* (1956) declared such dismissals unconstitutional on due process grounds. But by then, the damage had been done, with hundreds of teachers dismissed, their teaching careers terminated.

Changing Understandings of Militancy

While the matter of Communism in the city teachers' corps played itself out, other kinds of changes were transpiring in the broader world of teacher organizing. During the postwar years, a wave of teacher work stoppages shook the educational establishment. Table 6.1 shows a clear spike in the number and intensity of strikes between 1946 and 1948. The frequency and intensity of these actions were unprecedented. With a teacher shortage and school budgets flooded with state funding,[111] teachers were more eager than ever to secure salary hikes. The strikes also had a consequence unforeseen by the teachers involved: State legislatures began passing antistrike laws for public employees. While strikes had occasionally been threatened in the past, the fact of their actualization prompted this more emphatic response.

The priorities of the national teachers' organizations were also changing. The NEA began 1947 by issuing a policy statement that "urged teachers to employ 'group action' to obtain salary increases, declaring that 'the former practice where teachers individually bargained with the superintendent of schools or the board of education for their salaries is largely past.'"[112] In fact, one of the strikes of 1946 was an NEA-led strike in Norwalk, Connecticut. Here, the NEA's *Defense Bulletin* denied that the Norwalk teachers were striking, referring instead to "professional group action by professional methods."[113] When the teachers stopped working, they had not yet signed their new contracts;

TABLE 6.1   WORK STOPPAGES INVOLVING TEACHERS, 1940–1952

Year	No. of stoppages	No. of workers involved	Annual man-days idle	Average duration (calendar days)	No. of stoppages for wages/ hours	No. of stoppages for organization	No. of stoppages for other working conditions
1940	2	100	900	9.5			2
1941	1	120	120	2.0	1		
1942	2	170	2,090	28.5			2
1943	2	100	330	3.5	2		
1944	4	1,710	7,960	11.3	3		1
1945	1	15	160	17.0		1	
1946	16	3,060	37,100	13.3	11	4	1
1947	20	4,720	21,100	7.3	16		4
1948	12	4,210	60,300	8.3	4	3	5
1949	9	440	920	3.7	3	2	4
1950	4	90	860	8.3	2	2	
1951	10	4,510	67,000	12.1	4	1	5
1952	7	1,570	7,540	4.4	4		3
Total no.	90	20,815	206,380	9.9	50	13	27
Total %	100				56	14	30

Source: Bernard Yabroff and Lily Mary David, "Collective Bargaining and Work Stoppages Involving Teachers," *Monthly Labor Review* (May 1953): 475–479.

hence, the NEA executive secretary claimed that the Norwalk teachers were not in violation of the NEA's code of ethics.[114] But the NEA came out as antistrike on most other occasions. "The Association . . . believes that the strike is an unsatisfactory method of solving professional problems."[115] For example, the NEA criticized the AFT-backed strike in St. Paul in November and December 1946. In both cases, teachers got what they wanted: higher salaries. The NEA's shift in position was slight but substantial, given that it had already carved out a space as the professional and, hence, politically orthodox teachers' organization. While strikes were still unprofessional behavior, the idea that classroom teachers' collective action was a legitimate way to make claims on city administrations was novel, as far as NEA support was concerned.

The AFT, meanwhile, continued to walk its decades-old tightrope: appearing more militant before its membership while fostering a professional identity in its public performances. After the threat of Communism within the AFT had been eliminated, the organization became more attractive for the masses of teachers. Membership figures climbed during the final years of World War II. While the NEA had obtained a reputation for being nationalistic and a leader in postwar reconstruction, the AFT could now fight for that reputation.[116] The AFT organized the Commission on Reconstruction, led by Floyd Reeves, a favorite of President Roosevelt. However, the AFT also tried to bolster its credentials as the outsider. "The real choice," the commission announced, "is between American imperialism and militarism, versus a program of international cooperation."[117] Domestically, the AFT began to introduce the questions of race and school segregation into its discourse. While *Brown v. Board* was still years away—and the NEA stayed clear of civil rights until the late 1960s—the AFT locals were mostly urban organizations whose members faced the explosiveness of racial conflict on a daily basis.[118] Some of these locals were themselves segregated, and after 1951, "the AFT Executive Council voted not to charter new locals that were segregated."[119] By 1955, the AFT had resolved to take an integrationist stance. That same year, the AFL merged with the CIO, and under Walter Reuther, the new labor juggernaut shared the integrationist position with the AFT. At the same time, the AFT was also dealing with what were then common efforts at undermining the union. For example, as the secretary-treasurer of the AFT, Irvin Kuenzli, reported, "Superintendents and principals in some cities are bringing pressure of classroom teachers . . . to persuade or compel them to join non-union teachers' organizations."[120] There were also many nonunion teachers' organizations across the country trying "to secure the support of organized labor without affiliating with labor," many of which were in cahoots with the National Association of Manufacturers, "which had consistently fought the program of social progress of the labor movement."[121] The AFT thus tried to be progressive on social issues while continuing to eschew the radicalism that had caused such problems during the 1930s.

Competition and Unity in New York City

The ruination of the TU did not instantly create unity among the teachers' organizations. As noted previously, the HSTA withdrew from the JCTO in 1949, the same year that the Smith Act legally forbade radicalism in the New York public services. The TG withdrew from the JCTO in 1954. As far back as 1942, Rebecca Simonson had claimed that the TG "does not take the position that the Joint Committee answers all the needs of all the teachers."[122] New guild president Charles Cogen explained "that the JCTO had ceased to represent the teachers, that it afforded small organizations too much influence, and that its recent salary campaigns had been 'apathetic.'"[123] This was a reference to the JCTO's acceptance of the then-recent 1951 compromise that ended the strike of extracurricular activities. Cogen also knew that the JCTO would never support collective bargaining, which Cogen saw as the future of city teachers' relationship with the administration. While Simonson paid lip service to "teacher unity," she came to see it as a chimera, frustrated as she was by the HSTA's and the TU's divisive tactics and ideas. Cogen, however, put a premium on teacher unity, and he spent much of his TG presidency (1952–1960) fighting for it. The guild's advocacy of the single salary schedule meant something different for Cogen. While Simonson had argued for it on justice grounds, Cogen saw it as a useful tool to bring teachers together. Finally, the JCTO remained aloof, satisfied with regular pay raises and suspicious of both the HSTA's increasing militancy and the guild's unionist pretentions.

In 1954, the TG launched a "minimum participation movement" in response to Mayor Robert Wagner's refusal to grant a $750 across-the-board salary hike—he offered $300, which all teachers' organizations rejected. The HSTA announced that it would embark on an extracurricular activity boycott, similar to the one from 1950. Cogen was eager to find a political opening that would allow the TG to stake out its own identity as a more militant organization that could secure real gains for city teachers. Given that the guild had, since the boycott, come to be seen as relatively soft,[124] that need had never been more pressing. So, in May 1954, the guild's delegate assembly voted in favor of enacting "minimum participation" in school activities. Minimum participation entailed that teachers "report about one minute before scheduled time and leave promptly at the end of the school day."[125] They were expected to avoid taking part in school conferences and committee meetings, class excursions and field days, after-school clubs and student publications, athletics, drama, and dance. Teachers were asked not to devote any of their "personal" time to their jobs, and they "should refuse to use personal materials in classroom activities."

The boycott was the best evidence yet that teachers could apply at least some kinds of extra-institutional pressure without reprisal. The HSTA joined the TG in organizing boycotts, in response to what Cogen branded a "farce" of an offer from the mayor regarding salaries. In the spring of 1956, with popular support of the boycott already dwindling, eight organizations from the JCTO began speaking out against the boycott.[126] In June, the Board of Education authorized Jansen to give a directive forcing teachers to return to their extracurricular activities. Jansen asked principals to enforce the directive and report all teachers who failed to meet their responsibilities.[127] The 1951 ruling by the state Education Department, discussed earlier, verified the board's legal authority to enforce an end to the boycott. But the board did not take action until the beginning of the 1956–1957 school year, after the enthusiasm of the teachers and their supporters, including the UPA, had already begun to fade. By then, the guild had secured an important accomplishment: It had cultivated a reputation for toughness. While the guild's membership figures were slight, it had clout with the new superintendent of schools, Dr. John J. Theobald. In 1958, for example, Theobald made three separate proposals for revising salary scales, each of which the guild rejected.

By this time, the TG had turned its attention to collective bargaining. For Cogen, collective bargaining was a democratic process, the benefits of which ought to be extended to all workers supportive of democracy (a clear swipe at the TU).[128] He also understood that a true collective bargaining agreement with the city, comparable to what organized labor had in private industries, would not be possible with the teachers' corps as fragmented as it was. In April 1958, the TG began to make strike preparations, against the wishes of every other city teachers' association. The strike was called off after TG officers and Superintendent Theobald came to an agreement, but then Theobald proceeded to outflank them. He "invited fourteen teachers' associations to a conference at which he proposed a different settlement, although some of the provisions that had been agreed upon during his discussions with the guild were included."[129] This was precisely the kind of tactic Cogen thought the teachers could preclude by joining forces. He wrote to leaders of the other teachers' organizations to make this point. "We should be fed up with the perennial reply to our demands at the Board of Education, 'We can't give you this because you are not in agreement on what you want.'"[130] Marie O'Doran of the Kindergarten–6B Teachers' Association was pessimistic: "There can be no amalgamation as long as the High School Teachers' Association persists in opposing the Single Salary Schedule."[131] By the 1950s, most women teachers in the city, if they belonged to any teachers' association, belonged to O'Doran's Kindergarten–6B Association, a group that eschewed trade unionism in favor of an apolitical professionalism.

A year prior to the eventual merger, there seemed to be little hope for unity. At the beginning of 1959, an associate of David Selden's told Selden that "it would be something approximating a miracle if the Guild and H.S.T.A. could get together."[132] Both sides dug in their heels over the following months. The HSTA and TG essentially asked each other to give up their most valued positions in order for there to be a chance for a merger.[133] But after the guild's overtures in this direction were rebuffed again in December 1959, a group of HSTA members, frustrated with their organization's inability to compromise with the TG, formed the Committee for Action through Unity (CATU) to negotiate a deal with the guild. "The single salary schedule was supplemented by another principle: equal pay for equal preparation."[134] In this manner, greater compensation would be given to teachers who had more credentials. That was enough to satisfy CATU followers. In May 1960, the guild absorbed a mass of the high school teachers to form the UFT.[135]

Unity between these associations finally emerged out of the escalating stakes of teacher militancy. During January 1959, evening high school teachers, mostly represented by the HSTA, struck for three weeks, avoiding legal sanction by calling their maneuver a "resignation." The guild came out in favor the strike, which helped ease tensions between the two organizations. Guild leaders also publicly stated their support for a merger, thus putting the burden on the HSTA to explain their position, which continued to rest on the single salary schedule. More than two thousand of the city's nearly ten thousand high school teachers signed a petition claiming they would be in favor of a merger. Two weeks later, the HSTA threatened a mass resignation in response to the 1959–1960 school budget, which provided only a $200 raise, instead of the $300 raise teachers were told to expect. The TG called for a one-day strike in mid-April. The JCTO was predictably opposed to this plan, but the HSTA objected, too. The city's last-minute offer to negotiate headed off the strike, as the extra $100 was found in the budget.[136] From the perspective of the city teachers, the city blinked, and guild membership soared as high as six thousand.

By 1962, the UFT had clearly become the singular political voice for organized teachers in the city. In June 1961, teachers won a collective bargaining election by a 3-to-1 margin. Given the resistance from the two national teacher's organizations, the NEA and AFT, to collective bargaining for teachers, this was an impressive victory. Once the vote had been won, however, the AFT moved its entire machine behind the New York City teachers, seeing in them a huge source of power and money waiting to be harnessed. In December of the same year, the UFT defeated an NEA-backed coalition, called the Teachers Bargaining Organization, and the TU in a collective bargaining election. The JCTO opposed collective bargaining in theory and practice, and it did not participate in the election. When contract talks stalled, the UFT members voted to strike, and this time, half the teachers walked out, even in the face of threats of heavy fines and imprisonment. Now UFT leaders were worried. The teachers backed this strike more strongly than they had backed earlier ones, but previous disruptions had been more symbolic than strategic. With a collective bargaining agreement, teachers understood that their first contract would set the stage for subsequent negotiations, so it had to be a good one. The purpose of the strike was to force the Board of Education to make the concessions that the teachers wanted, including "a substantial pay raise, free lunch periods, check-off for union dues, and one hundred and forty-seven other items dealing with work-place conditions."[137] Most important, the teachers wanted an actual written contract that legally bound the city to make good on the agreement. Without such a contract, city teachers might find themselves in the same situation as so many times before: lobbying local and state officials for money that was not there. As it was, the city needed an extra $13 million to give the teachers what they wanted. Mayor Wagner, a gubernatorial hopeful, used the issue of striking teachers as political leverage. He pointed the finger at Governor Nelson Rockefeller, claiming that the state's budget cuts were hurting public education and city teachers. A settlement was reached (only hours after Cogen had urged the teachers to go back to work), according to which the governor would lend the city the necessary funds, "based on anticipated income in the following year."[138] This was an emergency measure, dating back to the 1930s, and it allowed the teachers to go back to work with a contract, their first. The result of the strike, then, was a real structural shift in the way that teachers would do business with the Board of Education that has continued to this day. After this victory, the UFT was inscribed in the education world as the most powerful representative of teachers in New York City.

Conclusion

While there were contextual factors that made the end of the 1950s more amenable to the success of the New York City teachers' drive for collective political power than earlier years—the earlier success of blue-collar labor organizing, legalization of public-sector unionism, and growth of the city education system and teachers' corps—I have emphasized here the crucial significance of divisions within the teachers' corps. Selective engagement in New York City revolved around the simultaneous efforts of city and state governments to contain, if not totally suppress, organized teachers' politics, while non-Communist teachers' organizations marginalized the TU. From the end of World War I until the establishment of the UFT, the stigma of Communism haunted all the teachers' associations. While a relatively small number of teachers actively participated in collective claim making, the very existence of the Communist minority in the teachers' corps became a tool for the city and state governments to sanction politically active teachers. Prior to the fragmentation of the TU in 1935, teachers' organizations were faced with a dilemma. The JCTO organized the mass of teachers' organizations as a single, politically moderate unit. However, it was an open secret that whatever successes the committee enjoyed, it enjoyed because of the talents of Local 5's representatives when politicking in the state legislature. Local 5 worked for the JCTO, but it also worked independently to advance its own agenda in city and state politics, an agenda that was at odds with the political orthodoxy of the time. In particular, the union's robust advocacy of academic freedom and strident socialism kept it at a distance from the JCTO's moderate demands for higher salaries and with the ideological current of the 1920s Red Scare. Meanwhile, city and state governments tolerated the relatively tame politicking of the JCTO. Satisfying some of the JCTO's demands, however dependent they might have been on Local 5's efforts, enabled the JCTO to assert its identity as the legitimate political voice of the teachers.

It also helped to marginalize the union at a time when the number of Communists in that organization was increasing, thereby making the organization less palatable to the rest of the teachers' corps and to the political establishment.

With the foundation of the TG and the ascendancy of the Communists to leadership positions in the TU, the lines of selective engagement shifted. Two organizations of militant radicals, one Communist and the other anticommunist, competed with the JCTO to win the attention of city and state governments. The Rapp-Coudert hearings ensured that within the teachers' corps, the union would bear the stigma of Communism for the remainder of its existence. Communism had its own stigma independent of education politics in New York City, of course, but in a community of workers that typically advocated freedom of thought and political opinion, the TU's identity was unusually polarizing in city politics. The TG leadership, and Henry Linville and Abraham Lefkowitz in particular, were for the most part unsympathetic with the travails of the union, which it worked to marginalize. The guild worked to advanced its agenda through the JCTO up through the end of World War II, even while it acquiesced to more moderate policies to satisfy its committee colleagues. After the Rapp-Coudert hearings, the TU was forever weakened as an organization, although its members continued to do important social work in the city and compiled excellent teaching records. The consolidation of state power in the late 1940s regarding suppression of Communism ensured that the TU would never again be a substantial force in city politics.

While the city, state, and federal governments were extinguishing the TU's political power, the fracture of the JCTO again highlights the dynamism of selective engagement. When the HSTA quit the committee in 1949 over the unified salary schedule, it positioned itself, among the high school teachers, as a radical alternative to the guild. When, in 1954, the guild also left the JCTO, the TG intensified its competition with the HSTA to represent the radical wing of the teachers' movement, a movement that was spearheaded, then as in 1917, by the high school teachers. Both organizations waged these battles under the banners of professionalism, which the HSTA believed meant higher salaries for the better-qualified, better-educated high school teachers and the guild believed meant a single salary schedule for all teachers. The 1960 settlement that created the UFT was a compromise between these positions that ensured that professionalism would be bound up with salary concerns in a way that prior to 1960 had been uncertain and contestable. Under the leadership of Charles Cogen, the teachers of New York City created a single union with formal bargaining power, thereby institutionalizing teachers' collective claim-making activities and setting new standards for moderation in teachers' organized claim making. Against the intentions of all actors involved, the city government's understanding of legitimate collective action among public school teachers shifted toward the acceptance of trade unionism and contained, regularized bargaining. The idea of a teachers' union would change, in New York City as elsewhere, but that is another story.[139]

IV

✳ ✳ ✳

CONCLUSION

7

✳

Marianne and Uncle Sam Revisited

The preceding chapters constitute, among other things, an effort to respond to the lacuna identified by Peter Lindert at the very beginning of
this book: Comparative institutional histories of public education are few
and far between. Today, with their extensive collective bargaining contracts and
unity density the envy of unions in the private sector, teachers' unions are an
important part of the decision-making and administrative structures of public
education in the democracies of North America and Europe, as well as one of
the last bastions of organized labor. The history of teachers' unions is embedded
in broader histories of the expansion of schooling, particularly primary schooling for the masses, along with the struggles of organized labor more generally
and the ideological divisions that split societies during the late nineteenth and
twentieth centuries.

Examining the history of unionization struggles in education means looking at both the crucial role that organized teachers have come to play in the
politics of public education and at changes in the state apparatus. Public school
teachers live and work at the periphery that separates state from society and
mediates relations between them. The legitimation of their political associations constitutes a shift in the structure of state authority. If the argument advanced in this book is correct, then the very effort that states made to secure
central control over primary schooling at the end of the nineteenth century
triggered the contentious activism and subsequent political struggles that
yielded teachers' unions. Just as surely as public school teachers are a part of
the state apparatus, so too are their unions anchored in the state. The study of
teacher unionism, then, is germane to scholarship on the state, as well as social
movements and labor organizing.

Before I return to centralization and selective engagement, the two causal processes of chief importance in this book, the events of 1968 require some elaboration. No book dealing with teachers' collective claim making could neglect a few words on the tumults of that year, particularly a book that that treats centralization as a key causal process.

French and American Education in 1968

It took decades for the centralization struggles detailed in this book to nurture popular discontent intense enough to generate widespread protest during the 1960s. To be sure, the social and political upheavals of 1968 in these countries had myriad causes. The frustration of (and with) organized labor, widespread disillusion with prevailing political forces, animosity toward war in Vietnam (particularly in the United States), fragmentation and polarization in the civil rights community, and intergenerational angst fail to exhaust the causes of the social turmoil that, in 1968, spilled over into the streets. And the fact that the mobilization of youth was so important is not solely an outcome of the nature of the school systems where teens and young adults spent so much of their lives. The perception that the school system was overcentralized and inflexible had become widespread by 1968 among urban city dwellers in the United States and just about everywhere in France.

France

By 1968, the French public education system had become the albatross of the central government. Over half a million students crowded the French universities as the children born in the immediate postwar years entered the higher education system; the number was 180,600 only ten years earlier.[1] For the first time in French history, the children of craftsmen, clerks, shopkeepers, and even farmers attended the universities, alongside the children of businessmen and professionals. But the schools were slow to meet the needs and demands of a more diverse student population. Furthermore, the Education Ministry routinely underfunded the universities, and most of them lacked proper classroom equipment. The professoriat, meanwhile, had not grown nearly as fast as the number of junior professors and assistants: 7,596 teaching assistants for 1,194 university professors in the sciences, and 2,740 for 1,168 in the humanities and social sciences.[2] These discrepancies intensified generational and hierarchical differences. The older generation dominated the highest teaching posts in the academy and held privileged decision-making positions within it. The pedagogical tradition of impersonal professor-pupil relations and the authoritarian mind-set of many professors exacerbated university students' dissatisfaction with their education and the overall scholastic environment, which appeared unhelpful in navigating their transition into the adult world of work

and citizenship. And finally, the centralized structure of the entire system reinforced hierarchies and frustrated reform efforts.[3]

The basic outline of the May–June uprisings is well known, and I offer only
a brief summary here.[4] The previous November, students conducted a ten-day
strike at the new university in Nanterre, several miles outside Paris. The students were protesting against not only the overcrowded classrooms and poor
facilities (and professors) but also the recently enacted Fouchet reforms. The
Fouchet reforms created a bifurcated college degree, with different tracks for
traditional and vocational education, and forced students to choose their academic specialty within the first year of university studies.[5] Two months later,
students at Nanterre clashed with the youth minister, François Missoffe, who
was in town to dedicate a new swimming pool. The brutality of the police repression and the administrative discipline against the students catalyzed latent
dissatisfaction with the university system—its inattentiveness to the needs of a
changing student body; its bureaucratic, hierarchical structure; and the central
government's perennial underfunding of it—and galvanized the intergenerational struggle that the education system had inadvertently been nurturing for
the previous two decades.[6] In March, more than one hundred students occupied
the University of Nanterre, prompting the government to close it for the next
month. For the next two months, incidents of labor unrest throughout provincial France made headlines, as students joined workers in demonstrations in
favor of higher pay and better working conditions, along with the more highly
charged issues of self-management and broader social change. But the center
of activity soon moved to Paris itself. Student radicalism of the left inspired a
group of government sympathizers, calling themselves the Occident, to stage
counterprotests. On May 2, fearing violence, the dean of the Sorbonne closed
the school. The next day, the very violence the dean had feared broke out on the
streets of Paris. Over the course of the next few days, students clashed with police in the Latin Quarter of Paris, resulting in hundreds of arrests and injuries.
For the rest of the month, striking students shut down the entire French school
system, and striking workers took to the streets in an unprecedented display of
institutional subversion.

What was the teachers' role in the student uprising? The Syndicat Nationale
de l'Éducation Supérieur (SNESup), which represented most of the teaching
aides and assistants, along with the more radical members of the university fac-
ulties, was the only organization to support the students unambiguously and
from the very beginning. Not long before, it had, by a small majority, elected
Alain Geismar as secretary general. Geismar put the weight of the SNESup
behind the students' association, in spite of the opposition of its Communist
minority, to protest the closing of the Sorbonne, by sponsoring the street demonstrations of May 6 and making a series of demands on the government: to
reopen the Sorbonne and Nanterre campuses, to order the police to evacu-
ate all universities and their vicinities, and to free all students who had been

taken into custody following the May 3 disturbances. For the rest of May and into June, Geismar and the SNESup were dependable allies of the student movement.

As far as the rest of the teachers' movement was concerned, however, the situation was more complicated. For over half a century, French teachers had been fighting for public respectability, political rights equal to those of their fellow citizens, and professional independence and autonomy. Now many of these hard-earned goals seemed to be under threat from the very population in whose name teachers claimed to serve and within the framework of some of the same leftist ideas that had inspired the teachers' movement in the early part of the century. The work stoppages and labor discontent outside education seemed to echo the dreams of the interwar teachers' unions, as it appeared that proletarians and their children would march side by side first in the streets of the Latin Quarter, then in the rest of Paris, and finally throughout the country. But the generational conflict of the era pitted many of these marchers against the half million "establishment" teachers, more than 50 percent of them *instituteurs* and *institutrices*, largely represented by the FEN. Indeed, the FEN had elected an *instituteur*, James Marangé, to be secretary general of the organization in 1966. The students' protests, of course, were not specifically directed at the elementary schools, but the degrees of separation between the worlds of primary and secondary and higher education were not as pronounced as they had been in years past. Even teachers in the elementary schools felt the heat. Less than two years later, the pedagogical authority that teachers had fought for before the war was placed in jeopardy by the very students in whose service they worked.

However, the FEN and its members had their own reasons to be angry with the government. Not only had the union opposed the Fouchet reforms but de Gaulle's education policies had also routinely antagonized the FEN leadership. The Debré Act of 1959 gave financial assistance to Catholic schools that met the central government's educational standards. The FEN, still bearing the historical residue from the anticlerical struggles of the previous generation, fought against this legislation to no avail.[7] The FEN's initial response to the student demonstrations, and the worker demonstrations that followed, was one of cautious support. Neither Marangé nor SNI leader Jean Daubard desired a revolution, but they certainly saw the student protests as an opportunity to force the government to deal seriously with the problems of the French education system. The FEN demanded repeal of the Fouchet reforms, abrogation of the Debré Act, and more funding for public education. On the evening of May 20, after a day of striking by millions of French workers, the FEN became the only union federation in the country to make a national call for an unlimited general strike, scheduled to begin on May 22.[8] On that day, most of the rest of the teachers joined the SNESup rank and file on the streets, "though in obedience to the instructions of their unions some of them went to school and remained in touch with the pupils."[9]

In regard to working-class solidarity, however, the situation was a bit different. While the teachers and their union leaders spoke out in favor of working-class solidarity during the interwar period, the outbreak of workers' strikes on May 14 aggravated the organizational fissures within the FEN. On the weekend of May 18–19, the SNI and the SNES issued statements of very different tenors about the strikes. The SNES called for an "unlimited" work stoppage and requested the FEN to issue a similar call and organize the unions and leftist parties, in an effort to generate a government response "to the views of the masses populaires."[10] The SNI, meanwhile, made more modest commitments, making reference to only the demands of the teachers, and it did not call on the FEN to do anything; rather, the SNI called on its departmental sections to "reinforce their cohesion."[11] The following evening, after the various segments of the FEN jockeyed for position all day and afternoon, the FEN made its call for a general strike. Across the country, the response rate was greater than 80 percent. But on the morning of May 24, when Prime Minister Georges Pompidou called together representatives of the labor unions and the employers' federation to begin the dialogues to bring the strikes to a conclusion, the FEN was not included. Marangé addressed a formal complaint to the labor unions and to the prime minister, while FEN militants all over the country encouraged the central office, by phone call and by telegram, to demand a place in the negotiations. The following afternoon, the government invited a FEN delegation to join the negotiations. The Grennelle agreements were the result of the meetings, but the administration dealt in bad faith with the FEN. Two days later, the government sent Minister of Public Services Edmond Michelet to discuss education and other matters with the FEN and other labor organizations, including the Force Ouvrière (FO). But Michelet lacked any legal power to negotiate with the teachers. The functionary organizations walked out on the "negotiations," and the teachers' strikes continued.

By the beginning of June, signs of trouble for the striking teachers had begun to appear. The *instituteurs* and *institutrices* encountered problems very familiar to those of their prewar predecessors. Town mayors, councilmen, and parents expressed hostility toward the teachers' work stoppage. Reports arrived at the FEN's central office of heated arguments between teachers and local authorities, property damage and death threats aimed at teachers, store owners refusing to serve strikers, mayors threatening to divest teachers of secretarial responsibilities in their offices, and even some local calls for national unity in the wake of President de Gaulle's call for new elections.[12] The FEN's internal cleavages also created friction. When negotiations between government and teachers began on the morning of June 4, eighteen different FEN representatives were in attendance to represent the various groups within it. After two days of negotiations that yielded nothing, the FEN's national council convened. Marangé, himself a former *instituteur*, was very aware of the pressures to which the primary teachers in particular were being subjected in their communities. He called for a return to work, and Daubard announced that he agreed, after a majority of SNI mandates voted in favor of the return. The SNES and SNESup, however, wanted the strike to continue until all their demands were met. But on June 6, the national congress voted to end the strike. Over the next few days, regional affiliates representing nearly all the FEN's factions complained, but the strike ended.

The actions of the FEN, and the SNI within it, during the May crisis earned the teachers' union an air of respectability. While the orthodoxy of teachers' participation in political affairs had become normalized by 1968, the radicalism of some of the FEN's "tendencies" remained controversial. The events of 1968, however, demonstrated the ability of the federation to internalize political extremism and stave off the possibility of a regime-threatening general strike of one of the most important corps of public servants in the country. By this time, the teachers' federation could no longer rely on the defense of secular schooling to maintain internal solidarity. "The principles that had long nourished the union activity of teachers on all levels—lay control of education and defense of the State against those who hold privileges of money and birth—had long since lost their power."[13] Over the next two decades, the FEN became one of the most important forces in France for maintaining what unity the left could muster in its various political struggles. In 1992, with the collapse of the Soviet Union, the precipitous and ongoing decline of the French Communist Party, and the severing of the left from Communist ideology, the FEN fragmented.[14]

The United States

Although social and political unrest was nationwide in 1968, with episodic protests and street violence transpiring throughout the country, in regard to conflict in the world of public education, New York City was the focal point. *Brown v. Board* had repoliticized race relations in New York City, as had occurred everywhere in the country. In the decade that followed, school integration happened at a snail's pace, as the mayor's office and Board of Education dragged their feet. African American families in Brooklyn, Manhattan, and the Bronx gradually abandoned the expectation of integration and worked instead to improve the public schools in their communities. The drive to decentralize the city school system had escalated in 1961, when the state legislature revived local school boards ostensibly to include community groups into decision-making processes. But the tone of community activism around public schooling shifted in 1964 after the city began to build a new school, Intermediate School 201 in East Harlem. In spite of intense activism from parents, churches, and antipoverty organizations, local school officials would not commit to integrating the new school.[15] In fact, the board appointed a white principal, much to the frustration of the African American and Latino families whose children would be served by the school. In the polarized climate of the mid-1960s, in a diverse city whose teachers' corps was 90 percent white, such an appointment was almost guaranteed to be seen as a slight against communities of color.

The Ocean Hill–Brownsville neighborhood of Brooklyn became the battle-ground for community control.[16] On May 9, 1968, thirteen unionized teachers and six administrators who worked in Ocean Hill–Brownsville received word that they had been fired. The neighborhood's governing board, led by Reverend Herbert Oliver, authorized the dismissals. School Superintendent Bernard Don-ovan ordered the district to let the teachers return to work, claiming that the district had no legal authority to have them fired. Of the 556 unionized teach-ers in Ocean Hill–Brownsville, 350 walked out of their classrooms in a show of solidarity. Over the following summer, the local board hired new teachers, African American and white, to replace the ones who had been dismissed. In addition, the school board hired an African American judge, Francis Rivers, to preside over hearings on each of the dismissed teachers. Judge Rivers ruled that none of the dismissed teachers were guilty of any wrongdoing and should be reinstated. When autumn arrived, however, the local board would not budge.

If the teachers' strike of 1962 announced the arrival of the teachers' move-ment as a legitimate collective actor in New York City politics, the strikes of 1968 entrenched the UFT as a powerful force. About fifty-four thousand of the fifty-seven thousand teachers, nearly 94 percent of the city's entire teach-ers' corps, did not report to work on either the first or second days of school, September 9 and 10, demanding that the district take back the teachers who had been dismissed in May. The Board of Education, Superintendent Dono-van, and Mayor John Lindsay all ordered the district to comply. But when the dismissed teachers returned to their school buildings, crowds of parents, stu-dents, local board members, and activists from Brooklyn's Congress of Racial Equality (CORE) chapter were there to meet them and block them from en-tering. At Junior High School 271, the principal allowed the teachers to enter, only to summon them to the auditorium, where about fifty members of the African American community were waiting to threaten and harass them. On September 12, the teachers struck again, this time for eighteen days. And once again, the Ocean Hill–Brownsville board refused to allow the teachers to re-turn to work. Two weeks later, the UFT led its troops back to the picket lines for a third time. This time, the Ocean Hill–Brownsville board signaled that it was ready to deal in earnest with the union and the municipal administra-tion. But Albert Shanker was now looking beyond the immediate conflict to a greater principle, and it would be five weeks before a settlement brought the teachers back to work. He wanted to demonstrate to the city that the union was there to stay, that the right to due process was worth fighting for, and that civil rights were worth fighting for no matter whose civil rights were under attack. He reached out to allies in the labor community and the academy, and he found plenty of support. Most important, two luminaries of the civil rights move-ment, A. Philip Randolph and Bayard Rustin, sided with the teachers, arguing that the due process that the UFT was fighting for was precisely what had been, and was, at stake in the civil rights movement. Randolph's and Rustin's repu-tations in the African American community never fully recovered from their support of Shanker and the UFT instead of Reverend Oliver and the Ocean Hill–Brownsville board. But their voices in the African American community rendered them particularly influential to Shanker. Just as Rustin's support in particular encouraged Shanker to keep the strike going, Rustin's plea "that the UFT not insist on an all-out victory" helped moderate Shanker's position and bring an eventual end to the strike.[17]

The strike ended in a relative victory for the teachers. The UFT participated in a brokered compromise with civic organizations, the municipal government, and corporate and local business leaders to end the strike. The settlement devolved limited authority over instruction and day-to-day activities to community school districts with locally elected school boards. But the central administration maintained power over financing and, most important to the teachers' union, personnel. All of the teachers who were still out of work after the Ocean Hill–Brownsville board dismissed them were reinstated. The state commissioner, James Allen, created the State Supervisory Committee specifically to protect teachers' rights. And the city suspended the governing board pending compliance with the terms of the agreement. In the meantime, a state trustee would govern the district's schools. Two years later, the state legislature passed a new decentralization law that maintained the power to hire and fire teachers in a central Board of Examiners. The power of organized teachers was affirmed.[18]

In light of the centralization struggles and selective engagement politics that had transpired over the previous three-quarters of a century, the Ocean Hill–Brownsville conflict was laced with irony. The very centralization that teachers decried at the turn of the twentieth century was now the source of teachers' union rights, including due process, and the foundation of their professional autonomy. Beyond that, the UFT's tactics were similar to those that Nicholas Murray Butler and his allies used *against* the teachers during the centralization struggle described in Chapter 4: "A teacher's attachment to community interests and needs had been seen as a sign of unprofessional conduct,"[19] just as the UFT actively discouraged its members from getting too involved in their communities. In addition, the commitment to civil rights that the radical wing of the teachers' movement had pursued with such passion during the 1930s and 1940s was suddenly in question, as the same communities that TU activists had once worked with now fought against the UFT. Indeed, many former TU members sided with the African American community that they had served during the 1940s and 1950s. The UFT's victory in 1968 was, from a public relations perspective, a Pyrrhic victory, with local communities newly hostile to the union, even as the new law forced the union and its newly created community adversaries to work together. That the majority of the city's teachers were white, and the majority of the white teachers were Jewish, only exacerbated the hostilities. The two historically stigmatized, oppressed communities had a history of political alliances in the city, at least within the middle class,[20] but whatever goodwill had been nurtured over the previous half century evaporated during the 1960s, as the Ocean Hill–Brownsville conflict transformed patterns of solidarity within the city's ethnic groups. And the conflict also generated solidarity within the teachers' corps, as the teachers' strikes of May 1968 were characterized by higher participation rates and much greater teacher solidarity than had existed in 1960–1962. Selective engagement was not a viable strategy for the city, partly because of a mayor who was more interested in preserving civic peace than defeating the UFT but also because of how the existence of collective bargaining and the hard-nosed leadership of Albert Shanker engineered solidarities that might not otherwise have been possible. It goes too far to say that "decentralization and community control were never really the issues"[21]— they were very much at stake in 1968—but by the end of November, it is true that, in no small part because of Shanker's vocal leadership of the UFT, these matters had become wrapped up with the matter of due process for teachers.

Historian Diane Ravitch puts the matter mildly, but succinctly: "The union's victory established it as a political power in the city and state, but the price of victory was high."[22]

Centralization and Selective Engagement Revisited

The events of 1968 beg a question that returns us to the beginning of this book: How could teachers have become such firmly established members of the political establishment with such a long history of disunity and repression by the state?

This book has made the case that two causal processes capture the dynamic historical sequence by which teachers' organizations became embedded in the state apparatus. *Centralization of education* shifted the administrative structures within which teachers worked, incentivizing them to mobilize what resources they had (or could develop) to influence central authorities. The process also signaled the increased political value of teachers to centralizing authorities, in the context of both the politics of centralization and the broader political conflicts and social changes to which centralization was supposed to respond. That signal was accompanied by a more or less concerted effort by central authorities to impose a corporate identity on teachers' corps, principally through the development of training institutions: normal schools, pedagogical conferences, teaching institutes, and so forth.

Much of the variation between the effects of centralization on teachers in the French and American cases comes from two sources: the different positions teachers took in the politics of centralization and the different histories of teachers' involvement in public politics when governments engaged in centralization politics. In urban America, public education was organized through wards, in which various ethnic communities decided who would teach, what would be taught, and to whom. Teachers had long-established networks of influence through these wards, so it is not surprising to see them fight education reformers so publicly during this era. New York City was unusual only insofar as it was among the first cities in the United States to centralize its school system. Centralization triggered a wave of teacher organizing, however, as the school system expanded and took on the hallmarks of centralized organization: hierarchy and bureaucracy. The first sign of radicalism in the teachers' corps came in the form of the equal-pay-for-equal-work campaign, which lasted until the city mayor signed equal-pay legislation in 1911, although the principle of equal salaries would be subverted in a number of ways. But it was the New York City TU that created the biggest stir, as its fight for academic freedom and increased teacher influence in the politics of education provoked the mayor's office and the Board of Education, along with the New York state government in the early 1920s. With the growth in numbers and the influence of the conservative NEA, the standards for professional legitimacy were becoming tougher, just as teachers' political assertiveness was becoming more pronounced and the rise of Communism in New York City created a new source of stigma for the city teachers and their collective claim-making activities. In France, however, teachers supported centralization. But their participation in public politics was verboten, and their capacity for collective action was limited by their isolation in communities that identified them as apolitical. When the early Third Republic sought to extract moral from religious education and make the towns subject to centralized, secular regulation, thousands of teachers made their voices heard in their local pedagogical conferences and meetings of former normal school students. They perceived centralization as an attack on the Catholic Church, to which many teachers attributed the cause of their poverty and poor working conditions. But they wanted to play an active role in the defense of their own collective well-being rather than surrender collective control over the occupational destinies to an overbearing central state. Their demand for a union in 1887 was rejected, and the government officially declared unionism in the teachers' corps to be illegal.

Selective engagement was the strategy that governments deployed during the postcentralization years to prevent teachers' contentiousness from threatening public order. Selective engagement meant choosing to engage a particular faction from within a social movement in order to isolate others, particularly when the movement was divided along moderate-radical lines. In the two cases in this book, this mechanism altered relations between the movement factions and governments, but it also altered relations between moderates and radicals within the teachers' movements themselves. Different teachers' associations began bidding for state support in their efforts to secure power in the education system and benefits for their members. Selective engagement unintentionally legitimated the moderates' collective claim-making activities, as a variety of external pressures—religious authorities, different governing units, and so forth—forced governments' hands, encouraging them to deal with moderates in order to contain teachers' involvement in public politics. Such an intervention constituted a crucial step in the direction of establishing the teaching profession in these two countries.

There were three important differences between the dynamics of selective engagement in these two cases. First, teachers' histories of collective claim making at the time of centralization struggles in the two countries were quite different. While rural French teachers lacked both an associational life and any opportunity to participate in collective action, teachers in urban America participated in public politics with relative freedom, both individually and collectively. The governments in these two cases perceived threats from teachers' collective actions in correspondingly differently ways. The French government perceived a threat when, at a critical moment in the politics of centralizing education, teachers attempted to carve out an autonomous political space for their public claim making. It took the reactivation of church-state conflict during the Dreyfus Affair for French governments to begin tolerating teachers' collective action. At this point, the anticlerical identity that the state had unintentionally nurtured in its *instituteurs* prior to the Third Republic became a source of political power for the still-young regime. But New York City teachers' participation in city politics did not constitute a threat to the city government until after the city centralized the education system. Centralization enabled efficiency-minded administrators to become increasingly influential in running city schools, and people like Nicholas Murray Butler had already decided that the women who taught in the city's primary schools were incompetent schemers. The teachers' equal-pay-for-equal-work campaign, in which the majority of an increasingly large and diverse pool of women teachers were active participants, generated tensions between the new administrative regime and the workforce in the public schools. Professionalism and Americanization became the sources of a new categorical identity that male administrators generated to assert power over the largely female teaching force.

A second important difference between the two cases concerns the kinds of divisions within the teachers' corps. Teachers were divided not only by political radicalism but also by a series of professional and social distinctions that sometimes yielded organizational expression. In France, neither regional nor religious difference created important cleavages within the teachers' corps, but gender certainly did. Feminist teachers' organizations emerged in France after the male leaders of the *amicales* and *syndicats* failed to voice their concerns, particularly with regard to unequal salaries and the unwelcome attention to their private lives. In New York City, however, gender was only one of many socially recognized differences to permeate the city teachers' corps. And sometimes gender itself became the source of political action coded as radical from the perspective of the government, as the activities of the IAWT made clear. As in most American cities, teachers' collective identities were cross-cut by religion, ethnicity, professional orientation, and gender. However, during the interwar years, only a small minority of teachers participated in public politics, choosing instead to rely on the JCTO to represent them in public affairs. The more militant male high school teachers of the TU, meanwhile, saw the JCTO as a vehicle to advance the union's own agenda in city and state politics. The existence of the JCTO complicated the responsiveness of the moderates and radicals to each other and to state authorities by forcing radicals to cooperate with moderates in order to effectively access the corridors of power in city and state governments and by forcing moderates to rely on the more politically experienced radicals for their lobbying success. Only after the non-Communist teacher associations isolated the Communist-affiliated TU, thereby demonstrating their loyalties and their professional responsibility, were they able to press for more substantial gains, up to and including collective bargaining.

Finally, the two cases differ in the character of state power. In France, teacher organizing initially sprang from local associations of normal school alumni and pedagogical conference attendees, but education politics was a centralized affair. Certainly in regard to the state's response to unorthodox political behavior, the actions of the central state were most consequential. While the chief executive, the education minister, and the interior minister did not always see eye to eye on the legitimacy of teachers' organizations, including their unions, the French state's image of itself and its teachers' corps was of a unitary body. Selective engagement in New York City, however, involved multiple state agents. While the municipal government was the proximate state actor, teachers' organizations sometimes had to deal with the state or even the federal government. The neutralization of the TU as a politically powerful organization in city politics happened only when a relatively unified state apparatus exerted its energies toward that goal. The accomplishment of that goal, however, generated another shift in the dynamics of selective engagement, whereby different groups of teachers came to represent radicalism and moderation from the perspective of state authorities. Although neither the TG nor any other teachers' organization represented a threat to public order in the way that rioters or insurgents would, the teachers' extracurricular "strikes" of 1950–1951 and 1954 were disruptive enough to make the municipal government perceive the guild and HSTA as radical and the JCTO as moderate.

This overview of the differences between the two cases suggests at least two avenues for further investigation. First, there is the matter of the feminization of primary teaching. While centralization precipitated the feminization of the rural teachers' corps in France, urban primary education was already feminized in the United States. Indeed, as Table 7.1 shows, women already constituted a majority of elementary school teachers in the United States at the dawn of the centralization era. Centralization in both cases probably intensified this process, as the central governments' control of primary education generated unprecedented pressures to make schooling the masses cost effective, and governments routinely paid women teachers less than their male counterparts.[23] Grace Strachan's equal-pay-for-equal-work movement in New York City was a response to this injustice and clearly served to intensify the citywide stigmatization of teachers' collective claim-making activities. I did not pursue the significance of gender in any systematic way in my discussion of the drive for collective bargaining in the 1950s, but there was surely a gendered dimension

TABLE 7.1   TEACHERS IN PUBLIC ELEMENTARY SCHOOLS
IN THE UNITED STATES

Year	No. of men	No. of women	Total no. of teachers	Percentage of women
1890	121,877	232,925	354,802	65.6
1900	116,416	286,274	402,690	71.1
1910	91,591	389,952	481,543	81.0
1920	63,024	513,222	576,246	89.1
1930	67,239	573,718	640,957	89.5

Source: Biennial Survey of Education, 1928–1930 (Washington, DC: U.S. Government Printing Office, 1932), 2:8.

to the conflict.[24] The disproportionate number of male high school teachers in the HSTA and TG and female elementary school teachers in the JCTO did not go unnoticed when it was time to unify the associations and fight for collective bargaining. The UFT has, until relatively recently, been a male-dominated association. In France, meanwhile, women teachers' political position was quite different; their private lives were certainly under scrutiny, but their "maternal" identities wound up being the source of some collective power. It was precisely through deploying this identity that they were able, through both their union affiliation and other associations, to publicly fight for pacifism and a greater political voice for women in international affairs more generally.

Finally, there is the question of my theory's portability. The unionization of teachers is, of course, not unique either to the advanced industrialized democracies or, within the United States, to New York City. However, the argument that centralization, followed by selective engagement, best explains the recognition of public school teachers as legitimate collective claim makers is limited to the regimes of Europe and the United States. The reason is that countries with histories of early transitions to industrial capitalism, long-lasting institutions of local governance, the dominance of Christian churches, and colonial expansion have, as the state-building literature suggests, distinct trajectories of state expansion. The traditions of public service and professional ethos in these countries will, broadly speaking, be comparable. In regard to the emergence of teachers as collective political actors, I expect that centralization will be the catalytic event in a country's history, as some combination of domestic social or political upheaval, nationalist responses to external threat, and drive to create an industrial workforce propel central governments to infiltrate peripheries to seize control over local schooling practices. Teachers' efforts at becoming legitimate collective claim makers emerged out of their desire for autonomous power in the newly centralized educational apparatus of the state. The status of teacher organizing at the time of centralization conflict and the degree of support that teachers have for centralizing education should dictate how governments responded to teachers' contentiousness and what kinds of teachers' organizations eventually emerge. A gloss on one other case, Russia, where teacher organizing was unusually vibrant during the interwar years, will help reveal the strengths and limitations of the causal argument of this book while also suggesting avenues for further research across all of these cases.

The Case of Russia, 1861–1905

Centralizing primary education in Russia was advanced in 1864 through two statutory innovations: the law of July 14 and the creation of self-governing representative assemblies, the *zemstvos*. The July 14 law created a centralized administrative structure for education in which every district and regional government had a school board, and a classification system was established to distinguish schools run by the Ministry of Public Instruction, by other ministries, and by ecclesiastical authorities and those run jointly by a government and private individuals. The law also standardized the curriculum for religion, reading, writing, arithmetic, and the singing of religious songs.[25] The law did not, however, render education obligatory or force towns to maintain schools, although the following year, the central government began giving grants to parishes that wanted to found schools. The other innovation of 1864 had a much greater immediate impact. The czarist government created the *zemstvos* to mediate relations between the central government and the villages, a task that the freeing of the serfs in 1861 made necessary for the sake of social order. *Zemstvos* were charged with responsibility for the provision of social services, and public schooling was the one mission that all district and provincial deputies had in common. Over the next four decades, the schools created by the *zemstvos* emerged as competitors with the religious schools, which were backed by the Holy Synod and inspired by the short-lived Sunday school movement that had, coterminously with the 1861 reforms, generated enormous demand for schooling, especially in the South and Southwest.[26] But the lack of competent teachers was a problem, just as it was in France in the 1830s, and the central government was reluctant to supply them until the 1890s, when the Russian intelligentsia interpreted the famine and cholera of 1891–1892 as a symbol of rural deprivation and ignorance that popular schooling could help to mitigate.

While the French *instituteur* of 1900 was en route to becoming the prestigious *hussard noir* in the popular imagination, the Russian elementary school teacher was already being denigrated as the "*zemstvos* rabbit." The reluctance of the central administration to devote material resources, particularly books and training schools, to assist teachers in their modernizing mission combined with the generation and dissemination of an image of the schoolteachers as a modernizing crusader, part of the "democratic intelligentsia" that would bring Russian culture to the countryside. In addition, many peasant families were not happy with the pedagogical trends of the later nineteenth century, which repudiated corporal punishment and other forms of harsh treatment of children as vestiges of the barbarism that teachers were ostensibly supposed to be eliminating as part of the state's broader modernization project.[27] The isolation of Russian schoolmasters was as much geographic as social; with towns and villages scattered across an immense territory, divided by rivers and mountains, the task of schooling a peasant population fell to men (the feminization of the teaching force had only just begun in the 1890s) who worked, by necessity, in isolation from one another. They fled their jobs whenever new opportunities arose, such as openings in law enforcement, and turnover rates were high. Many *zemstvos* desired more from their teachers. In 1873, more than sixty of these assemblies had organized periodic meetings with local teachers to discuss pedagogical issues. "Police officials pointed out the ease with which an innocent gathering of rural pedagogues could be converted into an anti-government meeting, and in 1874 rules were issued prohibiting general convocations but permitting specialized gatherings to discuss strictly technical pedagogical questions."[28] With only an inconsistent and half-hearted enthusiasm for normal schooling, teachers remained uneducated and lacking in professional ethos until the end of the 1890s.

An associational movement began during the late 1860s and early 1870s, but the political orthodoxy of schoolteachers became highly questionable after a segment of them became involved in the revolutionary Progressive movement in the 1870s. Beginning in the 1860s, provincial *zemstvos* organized summer courses, emphasizing pedagogy, and local teachers' congresses, emphasizing school administration and the teacher's proper role in society, in order to try to improve the quality of teachers.[29] Between 1867 and 1874, no fewer than two hundred locally organized gatherings of teachers took place in provincial and district towns. But during the 1870s, teachers had become active participants in the Populist movement, which aroused suspicion in both the *zemstvos* and in the central government that teachers were fomenting rebellion. Although some teachers were revolutionary agitators, just as some teachers in Second Republic France had been rabble-rousing socialists, the government's response to the teachers' role in the Populist movement was out of proportion to the number of teachers involved, which probably did not exceed several hundred (from a total of more than twenty-four thousand according to the census of 1880).[30] A new school statute in 1874 granted the school inspectorate more power, vis-à-vis *zemstvos* and school boards, and the following year, the government put *zemstvos* summer courses under the direct supervision of the inspection corps.[31] The government's commitments to rural modernization and rural stability were in clear tension with one another, and from 1874 until the early 1890s, this tension was never resolved save to privilege stability over reform. "Attempting to achieve two essentially irreconcilable aims—spreading basic literacy among peasants while seeking to cordon the village off from outside influences—state policy toward teachers alternated between concessions and repression."[32]

Durable teachers' organizations emerged in the final few years of the nineteenth century in response to a renewed interest in peasant schooling bred from the shock of the 1891–1892 famine. Teachers had never stopped demanding summer courses and lectures, but their petitions had been refused more often than not. Their congresses had been banned by an 1885 statute. But in the mid-1890s, *zemstvo* began to tolerate mutual-aid societies, which could help alleviate the poverty in which most teachers lived. The government would not devote more money to increase teachers' salaries or fund more normal schools but did relax restrictions against summer courses and congresses, as the potential benefits of such institutions for teachers' competence became clearer. Beginning in 1897, provincial *zemstvos* began sponsoring summer courses in increasing numbers—eleven in 1898, twelve in 1899, eighteen in 1900, and twenty-two in 1901—while district *zemstvos* held no fewer than twenty courses during the same period.[33] Attendance was routinely greater than what authorities anticipated. These summer courses stimulated a collective professional consciousness among teachers for essentially the first time in Russian history, even as they enabled teachers to create a more sustained organizational presence in the country.[34] By 1903, an illegal Union of Teachers was in existence in Moscow, and its representatives used the district and provincial teacher congresses to distribute political literature. On the eve of the 1905 Revolution, Russian teachers, especially in urban centers like Moscow and Saint Petersburg, had become a collective actor primed to take part in the struggles on the horizon.

Space does not permit a more thorough discussion of the Russian teachers' movement, but some important themes stand out. As in France, the central government expected Russian teachers to fulfill irreconcilable missions and to do so with insufficient material and organizational resources. "In contrast to French teachers under the Third Republic, Russian teachers did not have the unqualified support of the state."[35] The only resources that teachers had to create associations with any degree of autonomy were those supplied by local governments and authorized by the central one; in other words, they were not autonomous at all. But in the spring of 1905, teachers played a greater role in the political upheavals of that year than French teachers did in 1848 or 1870–1871. All along, the Russian central government refused to grant teachers the professional freedoms they had demanded. This brings up an important subject for further research: the relationship between regime change and public education. How and why do social revolutions, civil wars, and transitions from one regime type to another impact the legitimacy of teachers' collective claim making and their role in national politics more generally? Beginning in 1848, democratizing trends emerged in many continental European countries, and this book has not thematized their importance for understanding teachers' politics. In theory, the consolidation of power in new or drastically reformed regimes could require the large-scale restructuring of the institutions of national unity, including the school system. Whether and how the Russian and French cases of revolution and social upheaval lend credence to this theory is a subject for another book.

Final Thoughts

Finally, we return to the United States. As I suggested earlier in this book, the relationship between centralization and teacher mobilization is more complicated in the United States than it is in France. The active participation of teachers in centralization politics had effects that differed across cases, in relation to specific circumstances: the power of organized labor and socialist ideas (as in Milwaukee), the activation of ethnic and religious organizations (as in San Francisco and Atlanta), and the history of teacher activism (as in Chicago).[36] New York City is unusual, as mentioned earlier, for its diversity, size, and status as an "early riser" regarding centralization. But the representativeness of New York City as a case of Progressive Era urban reform is less important than the particular role that Communist teachers played in splitting the teachers' movement. With the possible exception of Philadelphia, no city teachers' corps was as damaged by a linkage with the Communist Party in its efforts to secure public power than that of New York City. Socialist movements and other radical tendencies existed in the teachers' corps of other major American cities, but the Communist movement in New York City was unusually large and influential. A more careful comparison between urban teachers' union movements in the era after the one covered by Wayne Urban in his book *Why Teachers Organized* is required to understand exactly how important this difference was. Suffice it to say, however, that the politics of selective engagement were overdetermined in New York, where, until the early 1950s, non-Communist teachers bore the stigma of their TU colleagues. Not all union members were Communists, of course—far from it.[37] But the TU's history shaped the left-leaning city teachers' interest in academic freedom and the freedom of political voice for decades after the 1935 split in the movement.

Uncle Sam and Marianne have now been in school for more than a century. Uncle Sam shows every sign of wanting more involvement in public education; Marianne is more ambivalent. In both countries, decisions regarding the quality and quantity of school reform cannot be taken without the voice of the teachers' unions being heard. Whatever the desirability of such a situation, it exists for a simple reason. Decades ago, the efforts by central governments to assert greater control over local schooling practices, whether in countries with traditions of relatively centralized administration or in countries with more fragmented structures, triggered a reaction from those who did the practice in question—the teachers—and their struggles with governments yielded an institutional settlement through which teachers' unions have come to represent teachers' interests. Although different circumstances across times and places suggest different kinds and magnitudes of reaction, teachers and their organizations have always sought to influence the structures of political control over their labor, particularly when central governments intervene. There is no reason to believe that today is any different, and, indeed, there is no shortage of public commentary in the United States, almost all of it negative, about the influence of teachers' unions in public education. They have stood in the way of important reform initiatives, such as charter schools and vouchers, both of which seem to threaten the power of the unions. But for those of us who believe that the construction of markets in education, no less than the construction of unions, is a political enterprise, there is every reason to believe that teachers and their organizations will continue to be on the front lines of battles for control over public education well into the future.

NOTES

CHAPTER 1

1. Max Ferré, *Histoire du mouvement syndicaliste révolutionnaire chez les institu-teurs des origines à 1922* (Paris: Société Universitaire d'Éditions et de Librairie, 1955), 21–29.

2. The French administrative structure, from the bottom up, runs as follows: *commune, canton, arrondissement, département*.

3. Judith Wishnia, *The Proletarianizing of the Fonctionnaires: Civil Service Workers and the Labor Movement under the Third Republic* (Baton Rouge: Louisiana State University Press, 1990), 46–47.

4. Tammany Hall refers to the Democratic Party's political apparatus in New York during the late nineteenth and early twentieth centuries.

5. "Mob of Teachers Besieges City Hall," *New York Times*, March 28, 1900; "Mayor Disapproves Mayor's Teachers Bill," *New York Times*, March 31, 1900; "A Thousand Teachers at Davis Bill Hearings," *Brooklyn Eagle*, March 28, 1900.

6. "Teachers' Bill Repassed," *New York Times*, April 5, 1900.

7. "Teachers' Bill Hearing," *New York Times*, April 14, 1900.

8. "Davis School Bill Signed," *New York Times*, May 4, 1900.

9. Marjorie Murphy, *Blackboard Unions: The AFT and the NEA, 1900–1980* (Ithaca, NY: Cornell University Press, 1990), 97.

10. See the Education International website at http://www.ei-ie.org.

11. Andy Green, *Education and State Formation: The Rise of Education Systems in England, France, and the USA* (London: Macmillan, 1990), 310.

12. Ferré, *Histoire*; Wishnia, *Proletarianizing*; Francis McCollum Feeley, *Rebels with Causes: A Study of Revolutionary Syndicalist Culture among the French Primary School Teachers between 1880 and 1919* (New York: Peter Lang, 1989).

13. Raymond Callahan, *Education and the Cult of Efficiency: A Study of the Social Forces That Have Shaped the Administration of the Public Schools* (Chicago: University

of Chicago Press, 1962); Sol Cohen, *Progressives and Urban School Reform: The Public Education Association of New York City, 1895–1954* (New York: Teachers College, 1964).

14. Raymond A. Mohl, "Schools, Politics, and Riots: The Gary Plan in New York City, 1914–1917," *Paedagogica Historica* 15 (1972): 39–72.

15. James M. Clark, *Teachers and Politics in France: A Pressure Group Study of the Fédération de l'Éducation Nationale* (Syracuse, NY: Syracuse University Press, 1967); Paul Peterson, *The Politics of School Reform, 1870–1940* (Chicago: University of Chicago Press, 1985). While Peterson does not address his book to interest group theorists, he clearly advances a pluralist understanding of education reform during the Progressive Era.

16. Albert A. Blum, ed., *Teacher Unions and Associations: A Comparative Study* (Urbana: University of Illinois Press, 1969); Bruce S. Cooper, ed., *Labor Relations in Education: An International Perspective* (Westport, CT: Greenwood Press, 1992); Martin Lawn, ed., *The Politics of Teacher Unionism: International Perspectives* (London: Croom Helm, 1985); Susan Robertson and Harry Smaller, eds., *Teacher Activism in the 1990s* (Toronto: James Lorimer, 1996).

17. Green, *Education and State Formation*; Ira Katznelson and Margaret Weir, *Schooling for All: Class, Race, and the Decline of the Democratic Ideal* (New York: Basic Books, 1985); Abram de Swaan, *In Care of the State: Health Care, Education, and Welfare in Europe and the USA in the Modern Era* (Cambridge, UK: Polity Press, 1988).

18. To their credit, in *Schooling for All* Ira Katznelson and Margaret Weir do account for the Catholic Church's hostility to popular primary education. Their account of teachers' role in education politics, however, is limited to teachers' relationship with the working class. My focus is on teachers' relationship with the state.

19. Murphy, *Blackboard Unions*, 24–34; Wayne Urban, *Why Teachers Organized* (Detroit: Wayne State University Press, 1982), 36–40.

20. Michael Lipsky, *Street-Level Bureaucracy: Dilemmas of the Individual in Public Services* (New York: Russell Sage, 1980). Lipsky focuses on city workers, but nothing in his analysis prevents consideration of rural teachers as well. While rural and urban teachers have some different concerns, everything that pertains to street-level bureaucrats pertains to both rural and urban teachers.

21. Ibid., xi.

22. Margaret Levi, *Bureaucratic Insurgency: The Case of Police Unions* (Lexington, MA: D. C. Heath, 1977).

23. Gianfranco Poggi, *The Development of the Modern State: A Sociological Introduction* (Stanford, CA: Stanford University Press, 1978); Thomas Ertman, *Birth of the Leviathan: Building States and Regimes in Medieval and Early Modern Europe* (New York: Cambridge University Press, 1997).

24. R. W. Connell, "Transformative Labour: Theorizing the Politics of Teachers' Work," in *The Politics of Educators' Work and Lives*, ed. Mark B. Ginsburg (New York: Garland, 1995), 97, 99.

25. Maria Lorena Cook, *Organizing Dissent: Unions, the State, and the Democratic Teachers' Movement in Mexico* (University Park: Pennsylvania State University Press, 1996), 21.

26. Ernest Gellner, *Nations and Nationalism* (Ithaca, NY: Cornell University Press, 1983), 35–38; Stephen Harp, *Learning to Be Loyal: Primary Schooling as Nation Building in Alsace and Lorraine, 1850–1940* (Dekalb: Northern Illinois University Press, 1998).

27. This is an abbreviated version of the story. In fact, the relationship between economic considerations and sexual discrimination in salaries and benefits was rarely a straightforward one. See James Albisetti, "The Feminization of Teaching in the Nineteenth Century: A Comparative Perspective," *History of Education* 22, no. 3 (1993):

253–263; Sandra Acker, "Gender and Teachers' Work," *Review of Research in Education* 21 (1995–1996): 99–162.

28. Rick Fantasia, *Cultures of Solidarity: Consciousness, Action, and Contemporary American Workers* (Berkeley: University of California Press, 1988); Sidney Tarrow, *Power in Movement: Social Movements and Contentious Politics* (New York: Cambridge University Press, 1998); Chris Ansell, *Schism and Solidarity in Social Movements: The Politics of Labor in the French Third Republic* (New York: Cambridge University Press, 2001).

29. Theda Skocpol, *States and Social Revolutions: A Comparative Analysis of France, Russia, and China* (New York: Cambridge University Press, 1979); Jeff Goodwin, *No Way Out: States and Revolutionary Movements, 1945–1991* (New York: Cambridge University Press, 2001); Atul Kohli, "State, Society, and Development," in *Political Science: The State of the Discipline, Centennial Edition*, ed. Ira Katznelson and Helen V. Milner (W. W. Norton, 2002), 84–117.

30. Timothy Mitchell, "The Limits of the State: Beyond Statist Approaches and Their Critics," *American Political Science Review* 85 (1991): 77–96; Joel Migdal, *State in Society: Studying How States and Societies Transform and Constitute One Another* (New York: Cambridge University Press, 2001); Mara Loveman, "The Modern State and the Primitive Accumulation of Symbolic Power," *American Journal of Sociology* 110, no. 6 (2005): 1651–1683.

31. Charles Tilly, "Power—Top Down and Bottom Up," *Journal of Political Philosophy* 7 (1999): 330–352; James Scott, *Seeing like a State: How Certain Schemes to Improve the Human Condition Have Failed* (New Haven, CT: Yale University Press, 1998).

32. I write this in 2011, in the midst of an extended period of federal involvement in public education, dating back to the Elementary and Secondary Education Act of 1965. For useful discussions of increasing federal involvement in public education, see Patrick McGuinn, *No Child Left Behind and the Transformation of Federal Education Policy, 1965–2005* (Lawrence: University Press of Kansas, 2006); and Paul Manna, *School's In: Federalism and the National Education Agenda* (Washington, DC: Georgetown University Press, 2006).

33. Stein Rokkan and Derek W. Urwin, "Introduction: Centres and Peripheries in Western Europe," in *The Politics of Territorial Identity: Studies in European Regionalism* (London: Sage, 1982), 4.

34. Mark Kesselman, "Research Choices in Comparative Local Politics," *New Atlantis* 1, no. 2 (Winter 1970): 48–64.

35. One small exception to this is the importation of the Gary school model from Gary, Indiana, to New York. I discuss this matter in Chapter 4.

36. This is the explanatory approach put forward by the Dynamics of Contention project. See Douglas McAdam, Sidney Tarrow, and Charles Tilly, *Dynamics of Contention* (New York: Cambridge University Press, 2001); Sidney Tarrow and Charles Tilly, *Contentious Politics* (Boulder, CO: Paradigm Press, 2007).

37. Sonia Chabot, "Éducation civique, instruction publique, et liberté de l'enseignement dans l'oeuvre d'Alexis de Tocqueville," *Tocqueville Review/La revue de Tocqueville* 17, no. 1 (1996): 211–249; Nicholas Toloudis, "Tocqueville's Guizot Moment," *French Politics, Culture and Society* 28, no. 3 (2010): 1–22.

CHAPTER 2

1. I draw this distinction between members and challengers from Douglas McAdam, Sidney Tarrow, and Charles Tilly, *Dynamics of Contention* (New York: Cambridge University Press, 2001).

2. Peter B. Evans, Dietrich Rueschemeyer, and Theda Skocpol, eds., *Bringing the State Back In* (New York: Cambridge University Press, 1985).

3. Margaret Levi, "The State of the Study of the State," in *Political Science: The State of the Discipline, Centennial Edition*, ed. Ira Katznelson and Helen Milner (New York: W. W. Norton, 2002), 33–55. See also Adam Sheingate, "Why Can't Americans See the State?" *The Forum* 7, no. 4 (2009): 1–14.

4. As Charles Tilly provocatively notes, the assumption that social movements have "continuous, self-contained life histories in somewhat the same sense that individuals and organizations have life histories" does not correspond to the reality of social movements as clusters of sustained public performances. I mean to suggest here only that social movement scholarship typically inquires into some facet of such a life cycle: movement origin, development, and/or demise. See Charles Tilly, "From Interactions to Outcomes in Social Movements," in *How Social Movements Matter*, ed. Marco Giugni, Doug McAdam, and Charles Tilly (Minneapolis: University of Minnesota Press, 1999), 256.

5. Sidney Tarrow, "States and Opportunities: The Political Structuring of Social Movements," in *Comparative Perspectives on Social Movements: Political Opportunities, Mobilizing Structures, and Cultural Framings*, ed. Doug McAdam, John D. McCarthy, and Mayer N. Zald (New York: Cambridge University Press, 1996), 41–61; Sidney Tarrow, *Power in Movement: Social Movements and Contentious Politics* (New York: Cambridge University Press, 1998).

6. James Jasper, *The Art of Moral Protest: Culture, Biography, and Creativity in Social Movements* (Chicago: University of Chicago Press, 1997); Jeff Goodwin and James M. Jasper, "Caught in a Winding, Snarling Vine: The Structural Bias of Political Process Theory," *Sociological Forum* 14, no. 1 (1999): 27–54; Barbara Hobson, ed., *Recognition Struggles and Social Movements* (New York: Cambridge University Press, 2003); David S. Meyer, "Protest and Political Opportunities," *Annual Review of Sociology* 30 (2004): 125–145.

7. Russel Hardin, *One for All: The Logic of Group Conflict* (Princeton, NJ: Princeton University Press, 1995); Mark Lichbach, *The Rebel's Dilemma* (Ann Arbor: University of Michigan Press, 1995).

8. McAdam, Tarrow, and Tilly, *Dynamics of Contention*; Sidney Tarrow and Charles Tilly, *Contentious Politics* (Boulder, CO: Paradigm Press, 2007); Charles Tilly, *Regimes and Repertoires* (Chicago: University of Chicago Press, 2006).

9. The best example is Hanspeter Kriesi, Ruud Koopmans, Jan Willem Duyvendak, and Marco G. Giugni, *New Social Movements in Western Europe: A Comparative Analysis* (Minneapolis: University of Minnesota Press, 1995).

10. McAdam, Tarrow, and Tilly, *Dynamics of Contention*, 315–317.

11. Ibid., 47–48.

12. Stein Rokkan and Derek W. Urwin, "Introduction: Centres and Peripheries in Western Europe," in *The Politics of Territorial Identity: Studies in European Regionalism* (London: Sage, 1982), 5.

13. T. Dunbar Moodie, "Mobilization on the South African Gold Mines," in *Social Movements: Identity, Culture, and the State*, ed. David S. Meyer, Nancy Whittier, and Belinda Robnett (New York: Oxford University Press, 2002), 48. See also William A. Gamson and David S. Meyer, "Framing Political Opportunity," in McAdam, McCarthy, and Zald, *Comparative Perspectives on Social Movements*, 275–290; Goodwin and Jasper, "Caught in a Winding, Snarling Vine."

14. Charles Tilly, *Stories, Identities, and Political Change* (Lanham, MD: Rowman and Littlefield, 2002), 199.

15. See Pierre Bourdieu and Jean-Claude Passeron, *Reproduction in Education, Society, and Culture* (London: Sage, 1977).

16. For more on the concept of "gendered opportunity structure," see Holly J. McCammon, Karen E. Campbell, Ellen M. Granberg, and Christine Mowery, "How Movements Win: Gendered Opportunity Structures and U.S. Women's Suffrage Movements, 1866 to 1919," *American Sociological Review* 66, no. 1 (2001): 49–70.

17. Matthew Lange, "Embedding the Colonial State: A Comparative-Historical Analysis of State-Building and Broad Based Development in Mauritius," *Social Science History* 27, no. 3 (2003): 400.

18. Raymond Grew and Patrick Harrigan, *School, State, and Society: The Growth of Elementary Schooling in Nineteenth-Century France—A Quantitative Analysis* (Ann Arbor: University of Michigan Press, 1991), 155–156.

19. Wayne Urban, *Gender, Race, and the National Education Association: Professionalism and Its Limitations* (New York: Routledge Falmer, 2000), 4–5, 64–65.

20. B. A. Hinsdale, *The Training of Teachers*, Monographs on Education in the United States, ed. Nicholas Murray Butler (Albany, NY: J. B. Lyon, 1904); Mark B. Ginsburg, *Contradictions in Teacher Education and Society: A Critical Analysis* (London: Falmer Press, 1988), 1–37; Christine Ogren, *The American Normal School: "An Instrument of Great Good"* (New York: Palgrave Macmillan, 2005).

21. Chris Tilly and Charles Tilly, *Work under Capitalism* (Boulder, CO: Westview Press, 1998), 29.

22. Devashree Gupta, "Selective Engagement and Its Consequences for Social Movement Organizations," *Comparative Politics* (October 2007): 331.

23. Ibid., 332.

24. For more on the concept of inscription as it pertains to social boundaries, see Charles Tilly, "Social Boundary Mechanisms," *Philosophy of Social Sciences* (June 2004): 222–223.

25. Quoted in Max Ferré, *Histoire du mouvement syndicaliste révolutionnaire chez les instituteurs des origines à 1922* (Paris: Société Universitaire d'Éditions et de Librairie, 1955), 39.

26. Maurice Gontard, *L'oeuvre scolaire de la Troisième République: L'enseignement primaire en France de 1876 à 1914* (Toulouse, France: Institut Pédagogique National, 1976), 120.

27. Georges Duveau, *Les instituteurs* (Paris: Seuil, 1957).

28. Andrew Abbot, *The System of Professions: An Essay on the Expert Division of Labor* (Chicago: University of Chicago Press, 1988), 8–9.

29. Tarrow and Tilly, *Contentious Politics*, 33.

30. Michael P. Hanagan, Leslie Page Moch, and Wayne te Brake, eds., *Challenging Authority: The Historical Study of Contentious Politics* (Minneapolis: University of Minnesota Press, 1998), xviii.

31. Tilly, *Stories, Identities, and Political Change*, 49.

32. French historians will note that I do not trace school centralization back to the French Revolution. While the Revolution did create an unprecedented political and ideological concern with schooling the masses, efforts to consolidate central control over the popular education were relatively meager until the July Monarchy. The Lakanal Law of 1794 was the greatest of the Revolutionary efforts to create a primary school system, but its implementation foundered because of the economic disaster that beset the country in the months following its passage. See R. R. Palmer, *The Improvement of Humanity: Education and the French Revolution* (Princeton, NJ: Princeton University Press, 1985);

Isser Woloch, *The New Regime: Transformations of the French Civic Order, 1789–1820s* (New York: W. W. Norton), 173–207.

CHAPTER 3

1. François Guizot, *Mémoires pour servir à l'histoire de mon temps* (Paris: Michel Lévy Frères, 1862), 3:345.

2. Ibid., 350. The Napoleonic "University" refers to the educational bureaucracy and teaching corps that served the secondary schools and other forms of higher education during the nineteenth century. Those who worked for the University were the *universitaires*, with the term *professeurs* referring specifically to the University teachers.

3. Quoted in Liliane Maury, *Les origines de l'école laïque en France* (Paris: Presses Universitaires de France, 1996), 3:21–22.

4. The French Revolution dealt a massive blow to the Catholic Church. For a discussion of education reform during the Revolutionary era, see R. R. Palmer, *The Improvement of Humanity: Education and the French Revolution* (Princeton, NJ: Princeton University Press, 1985).

5. "You believe that man can be man without God. . . . [M]an without God, I have seen him at work since 1793. That man, one does not rule him, one shoots him. I have had enough of that type of man." Quoted in Michalina Vaughn and Margaret Archer, *Social Conflict and Educational Change in England and France* (Cambridge: Cambridge University Press, 1971), 184. Jews and Protestants were not included in this task. Until the Third Republic, successive French governments endorsed separate education systems for religious minorities.

6. Antoine Prost, *Histoire de l'enseignement en France, 1800–1967* (Paris: Armand Colin, 1968), 90–91.

7. Quoted in Isser Woloch, *The New Regime: Transformations of the French Civic Order, 1789–1820s* (New York: W. W. Norton), 217.

8. Ibid., 220.

9. Ibid., 217–224. The mutual method refers to the pedagogical practice of delegating teaching duties in particularly large classes to a few advanced pupils who would cover lessons to subsets of the entire class.

10. Prost, *Histoire de l'enseignement en France*, 165–167.

11. Guizot, *Mémoires*, 3:344.

12. In practice, this distinction between public and primary elementary schools would remain hazy for at least another generation. The public-private distinction also calls into question the relationship between education and family. Throughout this chapter, except if otherwise noted, I am concerned with education as formalized schooling, what would have been called *instruction*, as opposed to the broader process of learning and socialization, usually referred to as *éducation*. Although I do not pursue here the significance of this difference, historians of eighteenth- and nineteenth-century France have shown that the embedding of *éducation* in the family has had profound consequences for the discourse and practice of both *éducation* and *instruction* in regard to "schooling the daughters of Marianne." For sustained reflections on these matters, see Linda L. Clark, *Schooling the Daughters of Marianne: Textbooks and the Socialization of Girls in Modern French Primary Schools* (Albany: State University of New York Press, 1984); Jo Burr Margadant, *Madame le Professeur: Women Educators in the Third Republic* (Princeton, NJ: Princeton University Press, 1990); Rebecca Rogers, *From the Salon to the Schoolroom: Educating Bourgeois Girls in Nineteenth-Century France* (University Park:

Pennsylvania State University Press, 2005); Jennifer J. Popiel, *Rousseau's Daughters: Domesticity, Education, and Autonomy in Modern France* (Durham: University of New Hampshire Press, 2008).

13. The complete law is available at http://www.inrp.fr/she/guizot.

14. For further explanation of the specific differences between Montalivet's and Guizot's laws, see Jean-Philippe David, *L'établissement de l'enseignement primaire au XIXe siècle dans le département de Maine-et-Loire, 1816–1879* (Angers, France: L'Imprimerie d'Anjou, 1967), 141–144.

15. Katherine Alaimo, "Adolescence, Gender, and Class in Education Reform in France: The Development of *Enseignement Primaire Supérieur*, 1880–1910," *French Historical Studies* 18, no. 4 (1994): 1025–1055.

16. Raymond Grew and Patrick Harrigan, *School, State, and Society: The Growth of Elementary Schooling in Nineteenth-Century France—A Quantitative Analysis* (Ann Arbor: University of Michigan Press), 251.

17. Jean-François Chanet, *L'école républicaine et les petites patries* (Paris: Aubier, 1996).

18. Guizot, *Mémoires*, 3:71.

19. Ibid., 3:60. See also Woloch, *The New Regime*, 231.

20. David, *L'établissement*, 148; René Lemoine, *La loi Guizot: Son application dans le département de la Somme* (Abbeville, France: Imprimerie F. Paillart, 1933), 53–54.

21. Lemoine, *La loi Guizot*, 55–56.

22. Mary Jo Maynes, *Schooling for the People: Comparative Local Studies of Schooling History in France and Germany, 1750–1850* (Teaneck, NJ: Holmes and Meier, 1985), 93–96; David, *L'établissement*, 148–151; Lemoine, *La loi Guizot*, 74–77.

23. David, *L'établissement*, 157–158.

24. Guizot, *Mémoires*, 3:78–79.

25. Joseph N. Moody, "The French Catholic Press in the Educational Conflict of the 1840s," *French Historical Studies* 7, no. 3 (1972): 394–415.

26. M. Patricia Dougherty, "The Rise and Fall of 'L'Ami de la Religion': History, Purpose, and Readership of a French Catholic Newspaper," *Catholic Historical Review* 77, no. 1 (January 1991): 21–41; Pierre Pierrard, *Louis Veuillot* (Paris: Beauchesne, 1998), 96–99.

27. Peter V. Meyers, "Professionalization and Societal Change: Rural Teachers in Nineteenth Century France," *Journal of Social History* 9, no. 4 (1976): 543.

28. Peter V. Meyers, "Primary Schoolteachers in Nineteenth-Century France: A Study of Professionalization through Conflict," *History of Education Quarterly* 25, no. 1–2 (Spring–Summer, 1985): 26–27.

29. Pierre Caspard and Pénélope Caspard-Karydis, "Presse pédagogique et formation continue des instituteurs (1815–1940)," *Récherche et formation* 23 (1996): 105–117.

30. Meyers, "Professionalization and Societal Change," 544.

31. C. R. Day, "The Rustic Man: The Rural Schoolmaster in Nineteenth-Century France," *Comparative Studies in Society and History* 25, no. 1 (1983): 29.

32. Chanet, *L'école républicaine*; Marcel Grandière, *La formation des maîtres en France, 1792–1914* (Lyon, France: Institut National de Recherche Pédagogique, 2006).

33. David, *L'établissement*, 246.

34. Gilbert Nicolas, *Instituteurs entre politique et religion: La première generation de normaliens en Bretagne au 19e siècle* (Rennes, France: Editions Apogee, 1993), 68–69.

35. For the complete text of the ordinance, see Octave Gréard, *La législation de l'instruction primaire en France depuis 1789 jusqu'à nos jours recueil des lois, décrets, ordonnances, arrêtés, règlements, décisions, avis, projets de loi* (Paris: Delalain Frères,

1891), 301–304. For a more thorough discussion of the religious component of the pedagogical conferences, see Nicholas Toloudis, "Pedagogical Conferences and Stillborn Professionalism among 19th Century *Instituteurs*, 1830–1848," *Paedagogica Historica* 46, no. 5 (October 2010): 585–599.

36. See, for example, letter from the *comité supérieur* to the mayors and *instituteurs* of the arrondissement of Rochefort, 1835, Charente-Inférieure, Archives Nationales (hereafter AN) F17/11621, Paris, France; letter from the rector of the Rennes academy to the minister, October 7, 1839, Finistère, AN F17/11621.

37. M. R. Aubert, "Les conférences pédagogiques," in *Recueil des monographies pédagogiques publiées à l'occasion de l'éxposition universelle de 1889* (Paris: Imprimerie Nationale, 1889), 3:580.

38. Louis-Pierre Sardella, "Des conférences d'instituteurs aux demi-journées péda-gogiques: Une institution détournée," *Recherche et formation* 3 (1998): 24.

39. Jean Ferrier, *Les inspecteurs des écoles primaires*, vol. 2 (Paris: Éditions l'Harmattan, 1997).

40. Correspondence between J. B. Lorquempot and the minister, November 1834, Pas-de-Calais, AN F17/11622; conference statutes from Tarn-et-Garonne and Yonne, AN F17/11622.

41. Letter from J. B. Lorquempot to the minister, November 1834, Pas-de-Calais, AN F17/11622.

42. Statutes of the "Society of *instituteurs* of the canton of St. Florentin," January 7, 1836, Yonne, AN F17/11622; Statutes for the "Association of *instituteurs* of the arrondisse-ment of Castelsarrasin," July 1834, Tarn-et-Garonne, AN F17/11622.

43. Conference statutes, October 10, 1833, Aube, AN F17/11621.

44. Sharif Gemie, "'A Danger to Society?' Teachers and Authority in France, 1833–1850," *French History* 2 (1988): 278–279. The *instituteurs* received both a steady salary (*traitement fixe*) and a monthly payment given on a per-student basis (*rétribution mensuelle*). Hence, the fewer the students who attended a teacher's class, the less money the teacher took home.

45. Maynes, *Schooling for the People*, 94–96.

46. Letters from the underprefect to the prefect, May 4, 1834, Bas Rhin, AN F17/11622; letters from the prefect to the minister, May 6, 1834, Bas Rhin, AN F17/11622.

47. Letter from ten teachers, December 6, 1840, Ardèche, AN F17/11621; letter from the rector to the minister, January 15, 1841, Ardèche, AN F17/11621; letter from the min-ister to the rector, February 12, 1841, Ardèche, AN F17/11621.

48. Louis Trénard, "Les instituteurs en France à la veille de 1848," in *Actes du quatre-vingt-dixième congrès national des sociétés savants, Nice 1965, section d'histoire et contemporaine* (Paris: Bibliothèque Nationale, 1966), 3:194–205.

49. For more on Meunier, see Henri Dubief, "Arsène Meunier: Instituteur et militant républicain," *Bibliothèque de la Revolution de 1848* 16 (1954): 17–42.

50. *Echo des instituteurs*, no. 1 (January 1845).

51. Max Ferré, *Histoire du mouvement syndicaliste révolutionnaire chez les institu-teurs des origines à 1922* (Paris: Société Universitaire d'Éditions et de Librairie, 1955), 12–16.

52. *Echo des instituteurs*, no. 36 (December 1847).

53. *Echo des instituteurs*, no. 2 (February 1845).

54. Trénard, "Les instituteurs," 206–207; Gontard, *Les écoles primaires de la France bourgeoisie (1833–1875)* (Toulouse, France: Centre Régionale de Documentation Pédagogique, 1964), 50.

55. See letters from the *"voeux"* section of the *Echo des instituteurs*, no. 32 (August 1847); *Echo des instituteurs*, no. 34 (October 1847); *Echo des instituteurs*, no. 35 (November 1847).

56. Dedicated readers of the *Echo* might have recognized this name. In the May 1845 issue, Vaccon was reported to have petitioned the Chamber of Deputies for an increase in teachers' salaries. The petition, like several others of its kind submitted during the mid-1840s, failed.

57. J. Stephen Hazlett, "A French Conception of Republican Education: The Carnot Ministry, 1848," *Paedagogica Historica* 12 (1972): 363–364.

58. Alfred Cobban, "The Influence of the Clergy and the '*Instituteurs Primaires*' in the Election of the French Constituent Assembly," *English Historical Review* 57, no. 227 (1942): 341.

59. Ibid., 341. See also *L'ami de la religion* 137 (1848): 95–96.

60. Chanoine Georges Chenesseau, *La Commission Extraparlementaire de 1849: Texte intégral inédit des procès-verbaux* (Paris: J. de Gigord, 1937), 30–31.

61. Ibid., 316–317.

62. Gontard, *Les écoles primaires de la France bourgeoisie*, 89–91.

63. Along with Cobban, "The Influence of the Clergy," see Paul Lévêque, "Sur quelques instituteurs 'rouges' de la Seconde République," *Annales de Bourgogne* 37 (1965): 289–300; Maurice Gontard, "Le comportement politique des instituteurs des Basses-Alpes sous la Seconde République," *Provence historique* (1977): 171–196; Pierre Pierrard, "La 'petite loi' Falloux du 11 janvier 1850 et les révocations d'instituteurs communaux en 1850," *Revue du Nord* 67, no. 266 (September 1985): 687–702. See also AN F17/11578–11580 for assorted correspondence regarding official sanctions of teachers in 1849–1851.

64. Anne Quartararo, *Women Teachers and Popular Education in Nineteenth-Century France: Social Values and Corporate Identity at the Normal School Institution* (Newark: University of Delaware Press, 1995), 55–56.

65. Ibid., 58–59.

66. Day, "The Rustic Man," 30.

67. Aubert, "Les conférences pédagogiques," 583–584.

68. Ibid.

69. Quoted in Gontard, *Les écoles primaires de la France bourgeoisie*, 143.

70. Ibid., 145–146.

71. The most sophisticated treatment of these essays is Gilbert Nicolas, *Le grand débat de l'école au XIXe siècle: Les instituteurs du Second Empire* (Paris: Belin, 2004). See also Francis Bailleul, "Les instituteurs du Nord d'après le concours de Rouland de 1860," *Revue du Nord* 67, no. 266 (July–September 1985): 703–713; Gilbert Nicolas, "Les instituteurs sous le Second Empire: Pour une approche régionale des mémoires de 1861: L'exemple de l'académie de Rennes," *Histoire de l'éducation* 93 (January 2002): 3–36; François Jacquet-Francillon, *Instituteurs avant la république* (Lille, France: Presses Universitaires du Septentrion, 1999), 123–261, 287–304; Day, "The Rustic Man," 36–47.

72. Nicolas, *Le grand débat*, 173–181.

73. Quoted in Day, "The Rustic Man," 40.

74. Quoted in Jacquet-Francillon, *Instituteurs avant la république*, 181.

75. Bailleul, "Les instituteurs du Nord," 706; Day, "The Rustic Man," 39–40.

76. Susan Trouvé-Finding, "French State Primary Teachers during the First World War and the 1920s: Their Evolving Role in the Third Republic" (Ph.D. diss.: University of Sussex, 1986), 22.

77. Nicolas, *Le grand débat*, 66–71.

78. Guy Chapman, *The Third Republic of France: The First Phase, 1871–1894* (New York: St. Martin's Press, 1962), 156. The strength of Catholicism during the 1870s was most pronounced in the western *départements*. See ibid., 158–159.

79. Frederick Brown, *For the Soul of France: Culture Wars in the Age of Dreyfus* (New York: Anchor Books, 2010), 27–28.

80. Ibid., 51; Chapman, *The Third Republic*, 170–171.

81. Norman Rich, *The Age of Nationalism and Reform, 1850–1890*, 2nd ed. (New York: W. W. Norton, 1977), 193.

82. This is *not* to suggest that there was a strong, consistent connection between popular support for monarchy and Catholicism. Indeed, there were plenty of reasons for rural peasants to oppose the restoration of the crown. See Brown, *For the Soul of France*, 44–45.

83. Anthony LaVopa, *Prussian Schoolteachers, Profession and Office, 1763–1848* (Chapel Hill: University of North Carolina Press, 1980).

84. Mona Ozouf, *L'école, l'église, et la république* (1963; repr., Paris: Seuil, 1982), 62–65.

85. Maurice Agulhon, *La république I: L'élan fondateur et la grande blesseure (1880–1932)* (Paris: Hachette, 1990), 43–45.

86. Judith Stone, "Anticlericals and *Bonnes Soeurs*: The Rhetoric of the 1901 Law of Associations," *French Historical Studies* 23, no. 1 (Winter 2000): 113–114.

87. Quoted in Maury, *Les origines de l'école laïque*, 20.

88. For more on the subtleties of Ferry's thinking on the matter of *laïcité* and the political compromises he and his colleagues made in designing the schooling legislation, see Jean-Marie Mayeur, "Jules Ferry et la laïcité," and Antoine Prost, "Jules Ferry, ministre de l'instruction publique," in *Jules Ferry, fondateur de la république: Actes du colloque*, ed. François Furet (Paris: Éditions de l'École des Hautes Études en Sciences Sociales, 1985).

89. Quartararo, *Women Teachers*, 110.

90. This is not to suggest that the Catholic teaching orders had not changed since the first half of the nineteenth century. Groups like the Christian Brothers had slowly but surely modernized their curricula and methods. But the female orders moved more slowly. With reference to the academy of the Loire, see Sarah Curtis, *Educating the Faithful: Religion, Schooling, and Society in Nineteenth-Century France* (Dekalb: Northern Illinois University Press, 2000).

91. Aubert, "Les conférences pédagogiques," 586–589.

92. M. Hien, "Voyages des instituteurs à l'Exposition Universelle," 1878, AN F17/11624.

93. *Révue pédagogique* 9, no. 5 (1882): 576–580.

94. Quoted in Quartararo, *Women Teachers*, 159.

95. Ibid., 159–160.

96. Ibid., 159.

97. *Conférences pédagogiques de Paris en 1880* (Paris: Hachette, 1880).

98. "Rapport sur les conférences pédagogiques départementales faites à l'École Normale de Toulouse au mois d'août, 1879," AN F17/11624.

99. The first pedagogical congress took place in 1878 but was conceived of two years earlier. However, this congress was not devoted solely to *instituteurs* but also to politicians, members of education societies, and other concerned citizens. In 1880, a congress was held at the Sorbonne for normal school directors and primary school inspectors. See Émile Courturier, "Les congrès pédagogiques d'instituteurs," in *Recueil des monographies pédagogiques publiées*, 3:628.

100. The task at hand "had little chance of success without the certainty of harmony between the creative spirits who conceived of the progressive measures and the most humble workers who had to execute them." See ibid., 632.

101. *Congrès pédagogique des instituteurs et institutrices publics de France, 1881* (Paris: Hachette, 1881), 101.

102. Courturier, "Les congrès pédagogiques," 648–650.

103. "Congrès pédagogique, à Paris, en 1881. 1re Question: Des moyens d'assurer la fréquentation scolaire. 7e section. Procès-verbal," AN F17/11625.

104. "Congrès départementalle de 1881, Rapport général sur les travaux du Congrès des instituteurs de l'Aveyron, presenté par M. Gay, instituteur public à Sainte-Eulalie-du-Larzac," AN F17/11624, 14. In Aveyron, the 100 teachers who gathered for the Rodez conference in 1879 grew to 300 in 1880 and 500 (including about 150 *institutrices*) by 1881.

105. Ibid., 15.

106. Ibid.

107. AN F17/11614, folders, divided by *département*, with rectors' reports on administrative sanctions of teachers during the *seize mai* (May 16) crisis. In a circular dated December 20, 1877, Bardoux had requested that each rector report on "the political question" and the role it played in punishing the *instituteurs* and compensate the ones who were unjustly punished.

108. Francis McCollum Feeley, *Rebels with Causes: A Study of Revolutionary Syndicalist Culture among the French Primary School Teachers between 1880 and 1919* (New York: Peter Lang, 1989), 114.

109. Quartararo, *Women Teachers*, 160; Courturier, "Les congrès pédagogiques," 647–650.

110. Quoted in Prost, *Histoire de l'enseignement en France*, 387.

111. Quoted in Feeley, *Rebels*, 115.

112. Buisson and Spuller are both quoted in Feeley, *Rebels*, 115.

113. Ferré, *Histoire*, 39.

114. Maurice Gontard, *L'oeuvre scolaire de la Troisième République: L'enseignement primaire en France de 1876 à 1914* (Toulouse, France: Centre Régionale de Documentation Pédagogique, 1976), 120.

115. Ibid.

CHAPTER 4

1. "Why Teachers Protest," *New York Times*, April 21, 1895.

2. For more on the Progressive model of education, see Charles Taylor Kerchner, David Menefee-Libey, and Laura Steen Mulfinger, "Comparing the Progressive Model and Contemporary Formative Ideas and Trends," in *The Transformation of Great American School Districts: How Big Cities Are Reshaping Public Education*, ed. William Lowe Boyd, Charles Taylor Kerchner, and Mark Blyth (Cambridge, MA: Harvard Education Press, 2008).

3. Kate Rousmaniere, *City Teachers: Teaching and School Reform in Historical Perspective* (New York: Teachers College Press, 1997).

4. Robert E. Doherty, "Tempest on the Hudson: The Struggle for 'Equal Pay for Equal Work' in the New York City Public Schools, 1907–1911," *History of Education Quarterly* 19, no. 4 (Winter 1979): 413–434; Patricia Carter, "Becoming the 'New Women': The Equal Rights Campaigns of New York City Schoolteachers, 1900–1920," in *The Teacher's Voice: A Social History of Teaching in Twentieth-Century America*, ed.

Richard J. Altenbaugh (Bristol, PA: Falmer Press, 1992); Sandra Adickes, *To Be Young Was Very Heaven: Women in New York before the First World War* (New York: St. Martin's Press, 1997).

5. Sherry Gorelick, *City College and the Jewish Poor: Education in New York, 1880–1924* (New Brunswick, NJ: Rutgers University Press, 1981), 123. See also Selma Cantor Berrol, "Immigrants at School: New York City, 1898–1910" (Ph.D. diss.: Yeshiva University, 1968), 63–64.

6. Robert W. Iversen, *The Communists and the Schools* (New York: Harcourt Brace, 1959); Marjorie Murphy, *Blackboard Unions* (Ithaca, NY: Cornell University Press, 1990), 150–195.

7. David Nasaw, *Schooled to Order: A Social History of Public Schooling in the United States* (New York: Oxford University Press, 1978), 105–113.

8. Diane Ravitch, *The Great School Wars: A History of New York City Schools* (Baltimore, MD: Johns Hopkins University Press, 1974), 83.

9. "Opposition Not Genuine," *New York Times*, April 22, 1895. See also "Teachers and the School Bill," *New York Times*, April 21, 1895; *Educational Review* (May 1895): 98; Ravitch, *The Great School Wars*, 146–149.

10. Raymond Callahan, *Education and the Cult of Efficiency: A Study of the Social Forces That Have Shaped the Administration of the Public Schools* (Chicago: University of Chicago Press, 1962); Denise Gelberg, *The "Business" of Reforming American Schools* (Albany: State University of New York Press, 1997); Kenneth Fox, *Better City Government: Innovation in American Urban Politics, 1850–1937* (Philadelphia: Temple University Press, 1977).

11. Richard Skolnik, "The Crystallization of Reform in New York, 1890–1917" (Ph.D. diss.: Yale University, 1964), 82–88.

12. Felix Adler, *The Moral Instruction of Children* (New York: D. Appleton, 1892), 30.

13. Jacob Riis, *The Children of the Poor* (New York: Charles Scribner's Sons, 1902), 181.

14. Sol Cohen, *Progressives and Urban School Reform: The Public Education Association of New York City, 1895–1954* (New York: Teachers College, 1964).

15. Michael Rosenthal, *Nicholas Miraculous: The Amazing Career of the Redoubtable Dr. Nicholas Murray Butler* (New York: Farrar, Straus and Giroux, 2006), 99.

16. Ibid., 99–100.

17. Ibid., 95–96.

18. Ravitch, *The Great School Wars*, 143.

19. Rosenthal, *Nicholas Miraculous*, 101–103.

20. Ravitch, *The Great School Wars*, 163.

21. *School*, September 26, 1889, 29.

22. *School*, September 12, 1889, 3.

23. *School*, February 13, 1890, 179; *School*, December 25, 1890, 131.

24. *School*, November 14, 1889, 75–76; *School*, January 23, 1890, 155; *School*, June 12, 1890, 313–314; *School*, June 22, 1893, 399.

25. *School*, March 13, 1890, 215; *School*, February 5, 1891, 179.

26. *School*, October 31, 1889, 63; *School*, November 7, 1899, 67–68.

27. *School*, October 24, 1889, 51.

28. *School*, September 12, 1890, 6.

29. *School*, March 13, 1890, 215.

30. *School*, November 14, 1889, 77.

31. *School*, June 11, 1891, 323.

32. *School*, December 25, 1890, 131.

33. *School*, February 5, 1891, 179.

34. *School*, April 17, 1890, 255.

35. *School*, September 26, 1889, 19.

36. Ibid., 21.

37. *School*, January 30, 1890, 163; *School*, February 6, 1890, 171.

38. *School*, December 11, 1890, 115.

39. David Conrad Hammack, "The Centralization of New York City's Public School System, 1896: A Social Analysis of a Decision" (Master's thesis: Columbia University, 1970), 23–24; David Tyack, *The One Best System: A History of American Urban Education* (Cambridge, MA: Harvard University Press, 1974), 102.

40. "Besieged by Teachers," *New York Times*, April 19, 1896. See also "Mrs. Morton Criticized," *New York Times*, April 16, 1896.

41. *School*, February 20, 1896, 202.

42. Rosenthal, *Nicholas Miraculous*, 105.

43. Murphy, *Blackboard Unions*, 27.

44. Quoted in Cohen, *Progressives*, 40.

45. Katherina Kroo Grunfeld, "Purpose and Ambiguity: The Feminine World of Hunter College, 1869–1945" (Ph.D. diss.: Teachers College, Columbia University, 1991), 47.

46. Ibid., 49–61.

47. *School*, February 20, 1896, 206.

48. Rousmaniere, *City Teachers*, 17.

49. Ibid., 21.

50. Ibid., 50.

51. Department of the Interior, "Status of Voluntary Teachers' Associations," *Bulletin* 1930, no. 36 (Washington, DC: U.S. Government Printing Office, 1931), 6.

52. "Teachers Avoid Politics," *New York Times*, October 21, 1900.

53. The case of Chicago is a notable exception to the aversion to unionism among the teachers by 1900. See Murphy, *Blackboard Unions*.

54. Ravitch, *The Great School Wars*, 165.

55. Murphy, *Blackboard Unions*, 51.

56. Ibid., 50.

57. Wayne J. Urban, *Why Teachers Organized* (Detroit: Wayne State University Press, 1982), 93–94.

58. Ibid., 94.

59. Ira Katznelson and Margaret Weir, *Schooling for All: Class, Race, and the Decline of the Democratic Ideal* (New York: Basic Books, 1985), 87; see also Grace C. Strachan, *Equal Pay for Equal Work: The Story of the Struggle for Justice Being Made by the Women Teachers of the City of New York* (New York: B. F. Buck, 1910), 284–285. Twenty of the forty-six board members voted for the measure, and sixteen voted against it.

60. Strachan, *Equal Pay*, 277–278, 292–294.

61. Michael R. Olneck, "Americanization and the Education of Immigrants, 1900–1925: An Analysis of Symbolic Action," *American Journal of Education* 97, no. 4 (August 1989): 398–423.

62. Cohen, *Progressives*, 10–13, 48–49.

63. Department of the Interior, "Americanization as a War Measure: Report of a Conference Called by the Secretary of the Interior, and Held in Washington, April 3, 1918," *Bulletin* 1918, no. 18 (Washington, DC: U.S. Government Printing Office, 1918).

64. Department of the Interior, "Training Teachers for Americanization: A Course of Study for Normal Schools and Teachers' Institutes," *Bulletin* 1920, no. 12 (Washington, DC: U.S. Government Printing Office, 1920), 8.

65. Ibid., 11.

66. Department of the Interior, *Report of the Commissioner of Education for the Year Ended June 30, 1919* (Washington DC: U.S. Government Printing Office, 1919), 190–191.

67. "Make Americans on July 4," *New York Times*, May 26, 1915.

68. *School*, October 24, 1895, 61; *School*, October 31, 1895; *School*, November 7, 1895, 77–78; *School*, November 14, 1895, 87; *School*, November 21, 1895, 93–94.

69. "Schoolma'ams Want Men Teachers' Pay," *New York Times*, April 30, 1905.

70. Carter, "Becoming the 'New Women,'" 45.

71. Doherty, "Tempest on the Hudson."

72. "Women Teachers Angry," *New York Times*, October 11, 1905.

73. Doherty, "Tempest on the Hudson," 380–381.

74. Adickes, *To Be Young*, 120; Carter, "Becoming the 'New Women,'" 97.

75. "Henrietta Rodman Loses on Appeal," *New York Times*, June 9, 1915.

76. Strachan, *Equal Pay*, 277–278, 308–320.

77. Ravitch, *The Great School Wars*, 195.

78. Quoted in "Teachers Assailed by the Controller," *New York Times*, June 9, 1915.

79. "Fights City Hall Control of Schools," *New York Times*, June 18, 1915.

80. Raymond A. Mohl, "Schools, Politics, and Riots: The Gary Plan in New York City, 1914–1917," *Paedagogica Historica* 15 (1972): 45.

81. "Teachers to Reply to Mayor Mitchell," *New York Times*, June 16, 1915.

82. Students at several city high schools had recently struck in protest against a ninety-minute lengthening of the school day. See "Teachers Now Join Long-Day Protest," *New York Times*, October 12, 1917.

83. "German Teacher on Trial for Disloyalty," *New York Times*, May 18, 1918.

84. *School*, March 16, 1916, 371–372.

85. Murphy, *Blackboard Unions*, 103–110.

86. For a particularly striking one, see "Teachers Who Are Not Loyal," *New York Times*, November 18, 1917.

87. Quoted in "The Disloyal Teacher Problem," *New York Times*, November 25, 1917.

88. "Charges Out in Case of Ousted Teachers," *New York Times*, November 20, 1917; "Disloyal Teachers Must Go, Says Wade," *New York Times*, November 21, 1917; "Attack Disloyalty at Teachers' Rally," *New York Times*, November 28, 1817.

89. Quoted in "Consider Teacher's Views," *New York Times*, December 24, 1917.

90. *Department Reports of the State of New York* (Albany, NY: J. B. Lyon, 1919), 18:407–408.

91. "Wants Loyal Teachers," *New York Times*, March 23, 1917; Urban, *Why Teachers Organized*, 98.

92. Urban, *Why Teachers Organized*, 106–107.

93. Harvey Klehr, John Earl Haynes, and Fridrikh Igorevich Firsov, *The Secret World of American Communism* (New Haven, CT: Yale University Press, 1995), 5–6.

94. Quoted in Todd J. Pfannestiel, *Rethinking the Red Scare: The Lusk Committee and New York's Crusade against Radicalism* (New York: Routledge, 2003), 19–20.

95. *Report of the Joint Legislative Committee Investigating Seditious Activities, Filed April 24, 1920, in the State of New York*, 4 vols. (Albany, NY: J. B. Lyon, 1920); see, especially, vol. 1, *General Introduction*, 7–36.

96. Pfannestiel, *Rethinking the Red Scare*. See also "Governor Approves Two Loyalty Bills," *New York Times*, May 10, 1921.

97. Quoted in Pfannestiel, *Rethinking the Red Scare*, 114.

98. Ibid., 115.

99. "Demands Justice for Two Teachers," *New York Times*, October 18, 1922.

100. Hammack, "Centralization," 9–10.

CHAPTER 5

1. The CGT was France's major trade union for blue-collar workers.

2. AN F7/13743. Along with the police report, see the selection of newspaper articles from *Populaire, Bataille, Petit parisien, Radical, Homme libre*, and *Victoire*, August 3–4, 1918.

3. Max Ferré, *Histoire du mouvement syndicaliste révolutionnaire chez les instituteurs des origines à 1922* (Paris: Société Universitaire d'Éditions et de Librairie, 1955), 182–183.

4. Réné Mouriaux, *Le syndicalisme enseignant en France* (Paris: Presses Universitaires de France, 1996), 30–35.

5. For a description of the debates leading up to this strike and an explanation for why the Seine teachers found themselves isolated from teachers elsewhere, see Guy Brucy, *Histoire de la FEN* (Paris: Belin, 2004), 97–110.

6. Along with the authentic *amicales*, the *cercles pédagogiques*, the *réunions pédagogiques*, and others all proliferated by 1900. During the 1900s, these groups appeared to congeal, many of them changed their names to *amicale*, and the *Bulletin général des amicales* listed these other groups as members of the *amicale* federation.

7. *Bulletin générale des amicales d'instituteurs d'institutrices publics de France et des colonies* (July 1903): 82.

8. *Bulletin générale des amicales* (March 1904): 141–142.

9. This is a conservative estimate of the extent of "amicalization." Wishnia cites statistics showing 90,000 of 111,000 teachers (about 82 percent) organized in *amicales* "within a few years" of Emile Combes's 1903 statement of support to the national federation. The national Fédération des Amicales claimed that there were 90,000 dues-paying members in 1909, out of a total teacher corps of 115,000. See Judith Wishnia, *The Proletarianizing of the Fonctionnaires: Civil Service Workers and the Labor Movement under the Third Republic* (Baton Rouge: Louisiana State University Press, 1990), 46–47; Francis McCollum Feeley, *Rebels with Causes: A Study of Revolutionary Syndicalist Culture among the French Primary School Teachers between 1880 and 1919* (New York: Peter Lang, 1989), 308.

10. Jacques Girault, *Instituteurs, professeurs: Une culture syndicale dans la société française (fin XIXe–XXe siècle)* (Paris: Sorbonne, 1996), 102.

11. Suzanne Baudard, *Le mouvement syndicaliste dans le corps des instituteurs* (Ph.D. diss.: Faculté de Droit de Dijon, 1920), 28.

12. Jacques Ozouf, "Les instituteurs de la Manche et leurs associations au début du XXᵉ siècle," *Revue d'histoire moderne et contemporaine* 13, no. 1 (1966): 102–103.

13. René Crozet, *Les instituteurs de Seine-et-Oise vers 1900* (Saint-Ouen-l'Aumône, France: Musée Départemental de l'Education, 1991), 529.

14. Jacques Ozouf, "Une jeune fille rangée," in *Nous les maîtres: Autobiographies d'instituteurs de la Belle Époque* (Paris: Gallimard, 1973), 55.

15. Girault, *Instituteurs, professeurs*, 100.

16. Quoted in ibid., 101.

17. In this way, the *amicales* absorbed many of the mutual-aid societies for teachers, some of which dated back to the Second Empire. In the case of the Seine-et-Oise, the *amicale* seemed to spur on the teachers' mutual-aid society. In 1895, the society comprised less than half of the *instituteurs* and less than a fifth of the *institutrices*, but after the 1900 founding of the *amicale*, the mutual-aid society grew considerably. See ibid., 105.

18. *Bulletin général des amicales* (April 1901): 4–8.

19. *Bulletin général des amicales* (May 1902): 8–9.

20. Ferré, *Histoire*, 67.

21. This is one of the main theses of Mona Ozouf in *L'école, l'église, et la république* (1963; repr., Paris: Seuil, 1982). Joseph Moody also notes that there is some truth to Harold Laski's exaggerated claim in *Authority in the Modern State* that the struggle between church and state over control of the schools is "the central thread in the history of France since the Revolution." Quoted in Joseph N. Moody, "The French Catholic Press in the Educational Conflict of the 1840s," *French Historical Studies* 7, no. 3 (1972): 402.

22. Antoine Prost, *Histoire de l'enseignement en France, 1800–1967* (Paris: Armand Colin 1968), 203–206; Roger Henry Soltau, *French Political Thought* (New York: Russell and Russell, 1931), 322–325.

23. M. Ozouf, *L'école*, 149.

24. Feeley, *Rebels*, 32–35. As previously noted, Ferry was not a friend to syndicalism among the teachers.

25. Soltau, *French Political Thought*, 326–328.

26. Ibid., 346–347.

27. Charles Tilly, *Contention and Democracy in Europe, 1650–2000* (New York: Cambridge University Press, 2004), 130. See also Charles Tilly, *The Contentious French: Four Centuries of Popular Struggle* (Cambridge, MA: Harvard University Press, 1986), 303.

28. Paul Gerbod, "Associations et syndicalismes universitaires de 1828 à 1928," *Mouvement social* 55 (1966): 21–23.

29. D. R. Watson, "The Politics of Educational Reform in France during the Third Republic, 1900–1940," *Past and Present* 34 (July 1966): 86.

30. Feeley, *Rebels*, 119.

31. Jacques Ozouf, *Nous les maîtres: Autobiographies d'instituteurs de la Belle Époque* (Paris: Gallimard, 1973), 264.

32. M. Ozouf, *L'école*, 133.

33. Quoted in Thierry Flammant, *École emancipée: Une contre-culture de la Belle Époque* (Treignac, France: Les Monédières, 1982), 43.

34. Quoted in Ferré, *Histoire*, 61–62.

35. Ibid., 180.

36. The 1884 law legalizing trade unions in the private sector bears the name of Waldeck-Rousseau.

37. Soltau, *French Political Thought*, 359–360.

38. Wishnia, *Proletarianizing*, 23. See also Judith Stone, "Anticlericals and *Bonnes Soeurs*: The Rhetoric of the 1901 Law of Associations," *French Historical Studies* 23, no. 1 (Winter 2000): 103–128.

39. Brucy, *Histoire*, 33. See also Jean Jeanneney, *Associations et syndicats de fonctionnaires: Étude legislative* (Paris: Librairie Hachette, 1908), 296.

40. Quoted in Ferré, *Histoire*, 43.

41. *Bulletin général des amicales* 2, no. 1 (April 1901): 9–13; Ferré, *Histoire*, 28–29.

42. Feeley, *Rebels*, 120.

43. Ferré, *Histoire*, 31.

44. Wishnia, *Proletarianizing*, 46.

45. Quoted in Ferré, *Histoire*, 56.

46. Feeley, *Rebels*, 120.

47. Ibid.

48. See, for example, the first issue of the *Bulletin général des amicales*, no. 2 (April 1901): 18–32 (about the *pourcentage*), and 33–50 (about pensions), as well as *Bulletin général des amicales*, no. 4 (April 1903): 66–71.

49. Feeley, *Rebels*, 17.

50. Wishnia, *Proletarianizing*, 50.

51. Flammant, *École émancipée*, 175–176.

52. Ibid., 177–178.

53. Combes was a former professor of theology and, since abandoning the church, had become fiercely anticlerical.

54. Thierry Flammant reported on the sixty-eight teachers who were most important to the pre-1914 *syndicalist* teachers' movement, including their years of birth, the professions of their fathers, their political affiliations (SFIO or anarchist), and their home *département*. The three best-represented *départements* were the Seine (with ten leaders), the Bouches-du-Rhône (six), and Maine-et-Loire (five), all regions known for being either bastions of socialist mobilization or "rural regions where clerical oppression was sovereign." Many of the leaders of the socialist teachers' movement came from Marseille and Angers, and the FNSI headquarters was moved from Paris to Marseille in 1908. See Flammant, *École émancipée*, 266–267, 46.

55. Feeley, *Rebels*, 125.

56. Ibid., 236.

57. While the former principle was near and dear to most schoolteachers, the latter, at this point, was quite unusual, its part in the 1901 *amicale* federation meeting notwithstanding. Pacifism in the teachers' corps did not become popular until the 1920s. See Mona Siegel, *The Moral Disarmament of France: Education, Pacifism, and Patriotism* (Cambridge: Cambridge University Press, 2004).

58. Flammant, *École émancipée*, 46–47.

59. Ferré, *Histoire*, 80.

60. Quoted in Feeley, *Rebels*, 155.

61. *L'émancipation de l'instituteur*, no. 67 (November 1911).

62. Feeley, *Rebels*, 154–156.

63. Ibid., 23.

64. Quoted in Wishnia, *Proletarianizing*, 81.

65. Ibid., 76–77.

66. Quoted in ibid., 55.

67. For a copy of the letter in its entirety, see Ferré, *Histoire*, 104–105.

68. The FNSI congress pledged its support to the dockers. See Flammant, *École émancipée*, 50–51.

69. Wishnia, *Proletarianizing*, 78.

70. For a distillation of this image, see Barnett Singer, *Village Notables in Nineteenth-Century France: Priests, Mayors, Schoolmasters* (Albany: State University of New York Press, 1983).

71. Jean-François Chanet, *L'école républicaine et les petites patries* (Paris: Aubier, 1996), 94–97.

72. Wishnia, *Proletarianizing*, 57.

73. Ferré, *Histoire*, 110.

74. While Nègre himself was long lauded as one of the early architects of the radical teachers' movement, he was also criticized for his insistence that teachers were comparable to industrial workers. During World War I, he drifted away from the autonomous teachers' organizations and became more deeply involved in the activities of the Section Française de l'Internationale Ouvrière. See Feeley, *Rebels*, 239–244.

75. Fortunately for the teachers' movement, these two *départements*—the Maine-et-Loire and the Bouches-du-Rhône—were the home of many teachers who were not only dedicated to the cause but also charismatic and popular, including Gabrielle and Louis Bouët, both of whom came to play an important role in the interwar period. "The admirable Marseille team" of Antoine Ripert, Adolphe Bezot, and Ismael Audoye proved themselves more than capable of managing the FNSI. Flammant, *École émancipée*, 75–76, 281.

76. Wishnia, *Proletarianizing*, 56.

77. Ibid., 147–149.

78. Ferré, *Histoire*, 163–168.

79. Quoted in ibid., 169.

80. Ibid.

81. Ibid., 171–172.

82. Quoted in ibid., 173.

83. Ibid., 173–174.

84. Feeley, *Rebels*, 220.

85. Ibid., 170.

86. Wishnia, *Proletarianizing*, 183.

87. Feeley, *Rebels* , 179.

88. Quoted in ibid., 195.

89. Ibid., 195–196.

90. Ferré, *Histoire*, 180–181.

91. AN F7/13743. The folder for the year 1918 contains numerous newspaper clippings and police reports on meetings in which teachers, both individually and as a group, expressed outrage at the treatment of their colleagues and comrades. For example, the prefect of Maine-et-Loire received a request from the FNSI to grant amnesty to a dozen other teachers, along with Brion and the Mayoux (undated document, numbered 166).

92. Feeley, *Rebels*, 248.

93. Ibid., 285–286. As Feeley notes, besides the fifty-four teachers he lists were many other provincial teachers who were the subjects of administrative investigations without being the subjects of disciplinary action. AN F7/13743–13748 contain dozens more police reports on the activities of unionist teachers between 1918 and 1935.

94. Wishnia, *Proletarianizing*, 194–196.

95. Quoted in Girault, *Instituteurs, professeurs*, 148.

96. Feeley, *Rebels*, 172.

97. Quoted in ibid., 173.

98. Ibid., 174.

99. Ferré, *Histoire*, 173.

100. Feeley, *Rebels*, 246.

101. Quoted in Ferré, *Histoire*, 176.

102. Quoted in Feeley, *Rebels*, 246. Brion spoke these words at the second wartime congress of unionist teachers in Paris on Bastille Day, 1916.

103. Feeley, *Rebels*, 174–177.

104. For examples, see ibid., 187–193.

105. Ibid., 181.

106. Ibid., 178–179.

107. Ibid., 182.

108. Siegel, *Moral Disarmament*, 97.

109. Ibid., 98.

110. Ibid., 99.

111. Paul Gerbod, "Associations et syndicalismes universitaires de 1929 à 1937 dans l'enseignement secondaire public," *Le mouvement social* 73 (October–December 1970): 79–110.

112. Siegel, *Moral Disarmament*, 99.

113. Some teachers actually advocated the complete elimination of history from the education curriculum. See Mona Siegel, "'History Is the Opposite of Forgetting': The Limits of Memory and the Lessons of History in Interwar France," *Journal of Modern History* 74 (December 2002): 770–800; Brucy, *Histoire*, 53–56.

114. Feeley, *Rebels*, 222–223.

115. Articles from *La bataille*, April 11, 1919, and *Le populaire*, April 16, 1919, AN F7/13743.

116. Feeley, *Rebels*, 219.

117. Ibid., 225.

118. Article from *Vie ouvrière*, July 23, 1919, AN F7/13743. Here, Loriot writes, "An unrepentant Bolshevik, I am for revolutionary violence. . . . I am, in short, emphatically against parliamentarism." Loriot later joined the Third International and worked for the French Communist Party in 1921–1922. For a brief biographical sketch of Loriot, see Flammant, *École émancipée*, 390. See also Feeley, *Rebels*, 277–279, for a revealing letter that Bouët wrote to a school inspector.

119. *Humanité* article, September 23, 1919, AN F7/13743.

120. *Le journal* article, September 5, 1919, AN F7/13743; Ferré, *Histoire*, 223.

121. *La bataille* article, September 25, 1919, AN F7/13743. The vote, however, did not precipitate CGT affiliation.

122. Ibid.

123. Article from *Information sociale*, October 9, 1921, AN F7/13744. The figures for the FMEL are dubious. Other sources put FMEL membership level at 8,000 in the spring of 1921, and given the repressiveness of the regime, it is not likely that this figure had increased by the autumn. What is certain is that the SNI greatly outnumbered the FMEL for the remainder of the Third Republic. The SNI membership grew to 58,000 in 1922 and 78,000 in 1925. After remaining near this number for a few years, the SNI experienced another period of rapid growth in the 1930s, from 80,000 members in 1931 to 112,000 in 1938. See Wishnia, *Proletarianizing*, 231; Girault, *Instituteurs, professeurs*, 195.

124. Quoted in Feeley, *Rebels*, 267. See also Roger Martin, *Idéologie et action syndicale: Les instituteurs de l'entre-deux guerres* (Lyon, France: Presses Universitaires de Lyon, 1982), 51–52.

125. Quoted in Martin, *Idéologie*, 58.

126. Article from *Populaire*, October 20, 1919, AN F7/13743.

127. Brucy, *Histoire*, 44.

128. Article from *Éclair*, January 19, 1920, AN F7/13744.

129. Brucy, *Histoire*, 45.

130. Wishnia, *Proletarianizing*, 232.

131. AN F7/13744. See, in particular, the correspondence between the prefects and the Interior Ministry during the autumn of 1920 and the first two weeks of July 1921.

132. AN F7/13744 contains many of the dossiers on these teachers, organized by region.

133. Ferré, *Histoire*, 234.

134. Letters of March 30, 1918, and April 3, 1918, from the prefect of the Rhône, AN F7/13743.

135. Martin, *Idéologie*, 58–59.

136. Announcement from La Section Syndicale des Instituteurs du Var, July 3, 1918, AN F7/13743. See also Jacques Girault, "Aux origines du syndicalisme enseignant: Un example: Le Var," in *Mélanges d'histoire sociale offerts à Jean Maitron* (Paris: Les Éditions Ouvrières, 1976), 113–126.

137. Report from the prefect of the Var, May 19, 1920, AN F7/13744.

138. Letter from the minister of the interior to the prefect of the Finistère, July 23, 1918, AN F7/13743. The minister was also concerned that Gueran was in touch with two known radicals, Loriot and Audoye.

139. February 1920, AN F7/13744. Like the other far-left teachers' organizations, the syndicate also demanded that all control of public education be passed to the teachers, "together with the workers' organizations."

140. Quoted in Ferré, *Histoire*, 260–261.

141. *Internationale* article from January 6, 1922, AN F7/13745.

142. AN F7/13745, various documents from March and April 1922. Sennelier and his "professional" association had a history of campaigning against the *bolcheviste* teachers in these local elections. See *Le peuple* article from March 10, 1922, AN F7/13745; *Humanité* article from April 12, 1920, AN F7/13744; and *Populaire* article from April 8, 1920, AN F7/13744.

143. Article from November 10, 1922, AN F7/13745.

144. Mona Siegel, "'To the Unknown Mother of the Unknown Soldier': Pacifism, Feminism, and the Politics of Sexual Difference among French *Institutrices* between the Wars," *French Historical Studies* 22, no. 3 (1999): 423.

145. Leslie Page Moch, "Government Policy and Women's Experience: The Case of Teachers in France," *Feminist Studies* 14, no. 2 (Summer 1988): 301–324.

146. See Siegel, "'To the Unknown Mother,'" 421–451 passim.

147. Anne-Marie Sohn, "Exemplarité et limites de la participation feminine à la vie syndicale: Les institutrices de la C.G.T.U.," *Revue d'histoire moderne et contemporaine* 24 (July–September 1977): 393–394.

148. Siegel, "'To the Unknown Mother,'" 437–440. The rest of this article explains in more detail the ideological differences between the associations' advocacy of pacifism.

149. Wishnia, *Proletarianizing*, 242.

150. Articles from *Internationale*, March 28, 1922, and March 30, 1922, AN F7/13745. Penancier, a senator and member of the departmental council of Seine-et-Marne, was reportedly unconcerned that the parents of Semeur were upset that Laguesse had been fired.

151. Several articles from local newspapers in the Yonne, March 9, 1923, AN F7/13746.

152. As John Talbott points out, "The demands of war seem to highlight in an especially harsh and intensive way the inadequacies of an educational system. Indeed, there is a tendency to fix upon formal education more blame for deficiencies in military conduct than seems fairly its share." See John Talbott, *The Politics of Educational Reform in France, 1918–1940* (Princeton, NJ: Princeton University Press, 1969), 35.

153. Ibid., 180.

154. Wishnia, *Proletarianizing*, 245.

155. Talbott, *Politics of Educational Reform*, 97–98.

156. Wishnia, *Proletarianizing*, 289.

157. As Talbott points out, "Léon Blum was a Socialist; Edouard Herriot a Radical; both were *Normaliens*." See John Talbott, "The Politics of Educational Reform in France during the Third Republic, 1900–1940," *Past and Present* 36 (1967): 126–130.

158. Talbott, *Politics of Educational Reform*, 101.

159. Watson, "Politics of Educational Reform," 90.

160. Anne Quartararo, *Women Teachers and Popular Education in Nineteenth-Century France: Social Values and Corporate Identity at the Normal School Institution* (Newark: University of Delaware Press, 1995). In 1935, against strong opposition from the teachers' federations, the Laval government enacted a reform of the normal schools that eliminated the academic rigor of their curricula, as well as their boarding facilities. See André Bianconi, *L'idéologie du syndicat national des instituteurs de 1920 à 1939: Politique et enseignement* (Toulouse, France: Presses de l'Institut d'Etudes Politiques de Toulouse, 1985), 59–61.

161. Article from *Internationale*, October 10, 1922, AN F7/13745. See also Marc Riglet, "L'école et la Révolution: Aspects du discours révolutionnaire sur l'école pendant l'entre-deux-guerres," *Revue française de science politique* 28, no. 3 (June 1978): 488–507.

162. Talbott, *Politics of Educational Reform*, 137.

163. Ibid., 138. "The union always took care to distinguish nationalization from state control." See Bianconi, *Idéologie*, 65.

164. Quoted in Bianconi, *Idéologie*, 65.

165. For more on the Cartel's electoral strategy of 1924, see Serge Berstein, *Édouard Herriot ou la république en personne* (Paris: Presses de la Fondation Nationale des Sciences Politiques, 1985), 96–105.

166. Wishnia, *Proletarianizing*, 236.

167. Ibid., 237.

168. Ferré, *Histoire*, 295.

169. Brucy, *Histoire*, 47.

170. Ferré, *Histoire*, 296.

171. Ibid., 296–297.

172. Wishnia, *Proletarianizing*, 286–287. Although membership statistics suggest a huge numerical advantage of the SNI over the FMEL, the numerical superiority is offset, in political terms, by the FMEL's more activist membership. See ibid., 293–295.

173. Laurent Frajerman, "L'engagement des enseignants (1918-1968)," *Histoire de l'éducation* 117 (January–March 2008), 64.

174. Ibid., 73–74; Wishnia, *Proletarianizing*, 242–243. For an earlier example of teachers organizing youth, see Ted W. Margadant, "Primary Schools and Youth Groups in Pre-war Paris: Les 'Petites A's," *Journal of Contemporary History* 13, no. 2 (April 1978): 323–336.

175. Jacques Girault, "Le syndicat des instituteurs," in *La France et les Français en 1938 et 1939*, ed. Réné Rémond and Janine Bourdin (Paris: Presses de la Fondation Nationale des Sciences Politiques, 1978), 189.

176. Frajerman, "L'engagement des enseignants," 65.

177. Wishnia, *Proletarianizing*, 292.

178. Brucy, *Histoire*, 61.

179. Ibid., 61–62.

180. Ibid., 63–69.

181. Ibid., 78–79.

182. Mouriaux, *Le syndicalisme enseignant*, 33.

183. Ibid., 80.

184. Laurent Frajerman, "Le syndicalisme enseignant français et la grève: Normes et normalization d'une pratique (1948–1959)," *Paedagogica Historica* 44, no. 5 (2008): 543–554.

185. Among recent works of scholarship that delve into the difference between the popularized images of Third Republic elementary school teachers and the reality "on the ground," see Chanet, *L'école républicaine*; Marcel Grandière, *La formation des maîtres en France, 1792–1914* (Lyon, France: Institut National de Recherche Pédagogique, 2006).

186. Wishnia, *Proletarianizing*.

187. Such an allowance constitutes "engagement" in the context of turn-of-the-century France. The formation of autonomous, professional associations among primary school teachers was politically unorthodox for nearly all of the nineteenth century. As I have shown, the power of the Catholic Church, the pressures of provincial life, and an onerous legal regime circumscribed teachers' role in public politics. Allowing the teachers' associations to meet during the early years of the twentieth century constituted a shift in the civic life of teachers that they had not previously known. See, in particular, Christopher Ansell, *Schism and Solidarity in Social Movements: The Politics of Labor in the French Third Republic* (New York: Cambridge University Press, 2001), and, for an earlier era, William Sewell, *Work and Revolution: The Language of Labor from the Old Regime to 1848* (New York: Cambridge University Press, 1980).

CHAPTER 6

1. Kate Rousmaniere, *City Teachers: Teaching and School Reform in Historical Perspective* (New York: Teachers College Press, 1997); Kate Rousmaniere, "Losing Patience and Staying Professional: Women Teachers and the Problem of Classroom Discipline in New York City Schools in the 1920s," *History of Education Quarterly* 34, no. 1 (Spring 1994): 49–68.

2. Rousmaniere, "Losing Patience," 67.

3. "Ettinger Reminds Principals of Duty," *New York Times*, September 18, 1920.

4. Stephen Cole, *The Unionization of Teachers: A Case Study of the UFT* (New York: Praeger, 1969), 19.

5. Marjorie Murphy, *Blackboard Unions* (Ithaca, NY: Cornell University Press, 1990), 277.

6. Ibid., 104.

7. Ibid., 106.

8. Belle Zeller, *Pressure Politics in New York: A Study of Group Representation before the Legislature* (New York: Prentice Hall, 1937), 170–171, 176.

9. "Governor Smith Vetoes Teachers' Pay Rise and 17 City Bills," *New York Times*, April 24, 1925.

10. Zeller, *Pressure Politics*, 178.

11. Robert W. Iversen, *The Communists and the Schools* (New York: Harcourt Brace, 1959), 13.

12. Quoted in "Teachers Union Head Answers Dr. O'Shea," *New York Times*, November 5, 1926. See also Philip Taft, *United They Teach: The Story of the United Federation of Teachers* (Los Angeles: Nash, 1974), 23, 84.

13. "Insists Lefkowitz Is Misrepresented," *New York Times*, November 15, 1926.

14. Zeller, *Pressure Politics*, 175.

15. "Walker Plan to Cut Subway Cost Ready," *New York Times*, July 25, 1932.

16. Iversen, *The Communists and the Schools*, 17.

17. Murphy, *Blackboard Unions*, 153.

18. Andrew Feffer, "The Presence of Democracy: Deweyan Exceptionalism and Communist Teachers in the 1930s," *Journal of the History of Ideas* 66, no. 1 (2005): 83.

19. Ibid., 83.

20. *Union Teacher*, June 1932, 6.

21. *Union Teacher*, May 1933, 2–4.

22. Taft, *United They Teach*, 34.

23. Iversen, *The Communists and the Schools*, 43.

24. Quoted in ibid., 40.

25. Quoted in Murphy, *Blackboard Unions*, 153.

26. For more details about the Dewey report and the showdown within the union, see Feffer, "The Presence of Democracy."

27. Letter from Clara Naftolowitz, secretary of Local 5, to William Green, January 14, 1935, Robert F. Wagner Labor Archives, UFT series (hereafter WA/UFT), Box 10, Folder 54, Bobst Library, New York.

28. Letter from William Green to Clara Naftolowitz, January 21, 1935, WA/UFT, Box 10, Folder 54.

29. Iversen, *The Communists and the Schools*, 50.

30. Letter from Henry Linville to John Dewey, December 19, 1935, WA/UFT, Box 3, Folder 55.

31. Letter from Henry Linville to Helen Taggart, July 24, 1936, WA/UFT, Box 3, Folder 38. "There may never be another political movement as malevolent as the Communists are," Linville goes on to write, "but they may make more trouble than we can handle, teachers being as slow of comprehension as they are, before the real criminality of these devils becomes generally known. . . . It would be better that there be no local in New York than one of the kind existing at present. The present deluded members do not know it, but time will tell the certain story of failure."

32. Letter from Selma Borchardt to Henry Linville, February 4, 1936, WA/UFT, Box 3, Folder 38.

33. Letter from Selma Borchardt to Henry Linville, February 10, 1936, WA/UFT, Box 3, Folder 38.

34. Jack Schierenbeck, "Class Struggles: The UFT Story, Part 3," available at www.uft.org/your-union-then-now/class-struggles-uft-story-part-3.

35. "Candidates to Get Teachers' Queries," *New York Times*, October 9, 1936.

36. JCTO Constitution, February 18, 1937, WA/UFT, Box 5, Folder 63.

37. *Union Teacher*, October 1932, 5–6.

38. "Teachers' Fight on Pay Cut Wanes," *New York Times*, December 7, 1932; *Union Teacher*, January 1933, 4.

39. "Notes of the New York Schools," *New York Times*, January 20, 1935. The JCTO supported the Feld-McGrath Bill, designed to protect teachers' tenure. The state legislature passed the bill in March, but the governor vetoed it, explaining in a memorandum that he vetoed because of the opposition to the bill by La Guardia and Controller Frank J. Taylor, on account of the city's finances.

40. "36,000 Teachers Get United Voice," *New York Times*, February 28, 1937.

41. *New York Teacher*, November 1936, 17.

42. Diane Ravitch, *The Great School Wars: A History of New York City Schools* (Baltimore, MD: Johns Hopkins University Press, 1974), 236.

43. Diane Ravitch, *Left Behind: A Century of Battles over School Reform* (New York: Touchstone, 2000), 243.

44. Larry Cuban, *How Teachers Taught: Constancy and Change in American Classrooms: 1890–1990* (New York: Teachers College Press, 1984), 66–69.

45. Murphy, *Blackboard Unions*, 162.

46. Ibid., 158–159.

47. Wayne J. Urban, *Why Teachers Organized* (Detroit: Wayne State University Press, 1982), 139.

48. "Reaction Rides High at City College," *New York Teacher*, May 1936, 133; "Schappes Fight Goes On," *New York Teacher*, June 1936, 157; *Teacher News*, May 11, 1936.

49. For more on the Schappes case, see Celia Lewis Zitron, *The New York City Teachers Union, 1916–1964* (New York: Humanities, 1968), 183–184; *Clarion: Newspaper of the Professional Staff Congress of the College of the City of New York*, November 2004.

50. American Federation of Teachers, *The Jerome Davis Case: Final Report of an Investigation Conducted by the American Federation of Teachers into the Proposed Dismissal of Professor Jerome Davis from the Stark Chair of Practical Philanthropy at the Yale Divinity School* (Chicago: American Federation of Teachers, 1937).

51. *New York Teacher*, January 1937, 3–4.

52. Lauri Johnson, "Making Democracy Real: Teacher Union and Community Activism to Promote Diversity in the New York City Public Schools, 1935–1950," *Urban Education* 37, no. 5 (November 2002): 575.

53. Ibid., 575–576.

54. *New York Teacher*, November 1939, 6–7; *New York Teacher*, January 1940, 10–11. The union had been affiliated with the American League for Peace and Democracy, an antiwar organization created after Hitler's rise to power in 1933, until October 1939. The league, which dissolved in December 1939, was later decried by HUAC as one of the largest Communist front organizations in the United States.

55. *New York Teacher*, April 1940, 5.

56. *New York Teacher News*, January 3, 1942.

57. The full name of the committee was the Joint Legislative Committee to Investigate Procedures and Methods of Allocating State Moneys for Public School Purposes in Subversive Activities of the State of New York. The fourth chapter of the committee's report deals entirely with the TU.

58. "Bishop Manning Makes Protest against Russell's Appointment," *New York Times*, March 1, 1940.

59. "K. of C. Protests Russell Selection," *New York Times*, March 4, 1940.

60. "Russell Keeps Post by Vote of 11 to 7," *New York Times*, March 19, 1940.

61. "Text of the Court Decision Voiding Bertrand Russell's Appointment to the Faculty of City College," *New York Times*, March 31, 1940.

62. State of New York, *Report of the Subcommittee Relative to the Public Educational System of the City of New York* (New York: State of New York, 1942), 7. The committee report also investigated Nazi and fascist activities in the schools, interviewing 234 people, interrogating 63 witnesses, and compiling 1,610 pages of testimony in private hearings. However, it reports to have found no evidence of fascism or Nazism in the schools.

63. This is also a conclusion of both the McCarran Commission and HUAC, discussed later.

64. State of New York, *Report of the Subcommittee*, 22.

65. Bella Dodd, *School of Darkness* (New York: P. J. Kennedy and Sons, 1958), chap. 9.

66. *New York Teacher*, December 1940, 22; *New York Teacher*, February 1941, 18.

67. *New York Teacher*, January 1941, 23.

68. *New York Teacher News*, December 14, 1941; *New York Teacher News*, December 21, 1941, 1.

69. *New York Teacher*, May 1940, 6–7.

70. "Teaching Group Backs Defense," *New York Times*, June 17, 1940.

71. "City Acts to Oust Unfit Teachers," *New York Times*, November 29, 1940.

72. "Lyons Demands Loyal Teachers," *New York Times*, January 26, 1941.

73. State of New York, *Report of the Subcommittee*, 178–179. See also *New York Teacher News*, December 1940, 15.

74. *Guild Bulletin*, April 12, 1943, 3.

75. *Guild Bulletin*, October 22, 1943, 2.

76. Hearings before the Subcommittee to Investigate the Administration of the Internal Security Act and Other Internal Security Laws United States Senate, 1952, I, 313.

77. Ibid., 305.

78. *New York Teacher*, March 1941, 10.

79. Ibid.

80. *New York Teacher*, March 1941, 13–14, 28.

81. Michal R. Belknap, *Cold War Political Justice: The Smith Act, the Communist Party, and American Civil Liberties* (Westport, CT: Greenwood Press, 1977), 51.

82. Christopher M. Finan, *From the Palmer Raids to the Patriot Act: A History of the Fight for Free Speech in America* (Boston: Beacon Press, 2007), 154–155. For a thorough discussion of the politics of the Internal Security Act and the SISS, see Michael J. Ybarra, *Washington Gone Crazy: Senator Pat McCarran and the Great American Communist Hunt* (Hanover, NH: Steerforth Press, 2004), 485–539.

83. Taft, *United They Teach*, 92.

84. *New York Teacher News*, January 8, 1949; "Teacher's Suicide Is Laid to Inquiry," *New York Times*, December 25, 1948.

85. Clarence Taylor, *Reds at the Blackboard: Communism, Civil Rights, and the New York City Teachers Union* (New York: Columbia University Press, 2011), 163–165.

86. Ybarra, *Washington Gone Crazy*, 547.

87. State of New York, *Public Papers of Governor Thomas E. Dewey, Fifty-First Governor of the State of New York, 1947* (Albany, NY: Williams Press), 336–338.

88. *Guild Bulletin*, February 1949, 2.

89. "High School Teacher Unit Secedes from Joint Group in Rift over Pay," *New York Times*, November 18, 1949.

90. *Guild Bulletin*, October 1948, 2; *New York Teacher News*, October 16, 1948, 2.

91. "Notice from the High School Teachers Association," December 2, 1949, WA/UFT, Box 5, Folder 65; "Teachers Accuse High School Unit," *New York Times*, November 28, 1949.

92. Taft, *United They Teach*, 70–71. See also "Extra-Job 'Strike' Voted by Teachers," *New York Times*, April 19, 1950.

93. "10,000 Pupils Defy Police in 'Strikes' Backing Teachers," *New York Times*, April 28, 1950; *Guild Bulletin*, June 1950, 1.

94. *Guild Bulletin*, June 1950, 1.

95. Letters from numerous city labor groups, WA/UFT, Box 8, Folder 18.

96. "School Morale Hit as Teacher 'Strike' Enters Its 2nd Year," *New York Times*, April 15, 1951.

97. "City Teachers Lose Extra-Work Fight," *New York Times*, May 16, 1951.

98. Murphy, *Blackboard Unions*, 185.

99. *Guild Bulletin*, October 1948, 1.

100. *New York Times*, October 14, 1948; *Teacher News*, September 18, 1948, 1–2; "The Case of Mr. Louis Jaffe: From Appeal to Inquisition," from the Teachers Union, Local 555, UPW-CIO, February 28, 1949, WA/UFT, Box 5, Folder 13. The *New York Teacher News* continued to run at least one column per issue devoted to the Jaffe case.

101. *Guild Bulletin*, October 1948, 4.

102. *Guild Bulletin*, November 1948, 2.

103. *Guild Bulletin*, October 1949, 3.

104. *New York Times,* October 8, 1949; *Guild Bulletin*, October 1949, 4.

105. *Guild Bulletin*, April 1949, 1; *Guild Bulletin*, May 1949, 1, 3.

106. *Guild Bulletin*, September 1949, 2.

107. *Guild Bulletin*, May 1950, 2.

108. Letter from a guild executive board member to Charles Bensley, July 2, 1951, Box 2, Folder 27, Municipal Archives Series 315, New York. Bensley was the only member of the Board of Education to vote against the Timone Resolution.

109. Murphy, *Blackboard Unions*, 192.

110. Adler had already been an appellant in a lawsuit challenging the constitutionality of the Feinberg Law, *Adler et al. v. Board of Education* (1952), which failed. Only in 1967, with *Keyishian v. Board of Regents of the University of the State of New York*, did the Supreme Court strike down Feinberg.

111. Although the federal government had helped alleviate the budgetary crisis of the Depression, the war put new pressures on school districts across the country. During the 1940s, states began to supply the help that the federal government used to provide.

112. Bernard Yabroff and Lily Mary David, "Collective Bargaining and Work Stoppages Involving Teachers," *Monthly Labor Review*, May 1953, 476.

113. Quoted in Murphy, *Blackboard Unions*, 183.

114. Yabroff and David, "Collective Bargaining," 479.

115. Quoted in ibid., 477. See also "Group Unity Urged to Aid Teacher Pay," *New York Times*, January 2, 1947.

116. Murphy, *Blackboard Unions*, 176.

117. Quoted in ibid., 182.

118. Only during the late 1940s and 1950s did the issue of race become salient in New York City school politics. The African American population increased sharply during the 1940s, and after 1946, there was a large wave of Puerto Rican immigrants as well. "Thus, by 1950, the new black and Puerto Rican immigration constituted one million people in a city which only ten years before imagined it had successfully absorbed and assimilated the last of the great migrations." See Ravitch, *The Great School Wars*, 242; Zitron, *The New York City Teachers Union*, 85–86.

119. Murphy, *Blackboard Unions*, 197.

120. Letter from Irvin R. Kuenzli to the officers of AFT locals, September 15, 1944, WA/UFT, Box 7, Folder 4.

121. Letter from Irvin R. Kuenzli to the officers of State Federations of Labor and Central Labor Unions, December 8, 1944, WA/UFT, Box 7, Folder 4.

122. Letter from Rebecca Simonson to Philip Shorr, August 6, 1942, WA/UFT, Box 5, Folder 62.

123. Taft, *United They Teach*, 74.

124. Looking back on their experiences in the history of teacher unionism, many teachers and organizers recall the guild's lack of political sharpness. Albert Shanker,

who would go on to fame as UFT and AFT president, remembered listening to brilliant speeches at guild meetings. "After three hours you'd leave edified with nothing done." Rubin Maloff, a convert from the TU, recalls the guild's "aristocratic" bearing and claimed that "you could sense the patrician in the Guild leadership." In 1986, Roger Parente of the rival HSTA claimed that his group had "pictured them as a debating society rather than a group ready to take action," although he also noted that "in retrospect it wasn't fear but caution." See Schierenbeck, "Class Struggles: The UFT Story, Part 4," available at http://www.uft.org/your-union-then-now/class-struggles-uft-story-part-4.

125. "The Guild Minimum Service Program, 1954," WA/UFT, Box 10, Folder 54.

126. JCTO press release, March 27, 1956, WA/UFT, Box 5, Folder 61. See also "8 Teacher Groups Condemn Boycott," *New York Times*, April 21, 1956.

127. "Jansen Outlaws Teacher Boycott," *New York Times*, June 6, 1956.

128. "The Right to Organize," statement of views of the New York Teachers' Guild, AFL, in regard to questions raised at the Mayor's Public Hearing on Collective Bargaining, held at City Hall, March 25, 1955, WA/UFT, Box 3, Folder 4. See also Taft, *United They Teach*, 77–78.

129. Taft, *United They Teach*, 79.

130. Separate but nearly identical letters from Charles Cogen to Emil Tron, president of the HSTA; to John Towers, member of the JHS Teachers' Association; and to Marie O'Doran, president of the Kindergarten–6B Association, May 28, 1958, WA/UFT, Box 7, Folder 35.

131. Letter from Marie O'Doran to Charles Cogen, July 14, 1958, WA/UFT, Folder 35.

132. Letter from Solomon Feingold, Special Representative, New York City Teachers' Guild, to David Selden, January 2, 1959, WA/UFT, Box 7, Folder 35.

133. "Compromise, Not Surrender, Key to Teacher Unity," Teachers' Guild press release, June 18, 1959, WA/UFT, Box 7, Folder 9.

134. Taft, *United They Teach*, 80.

135. "Guild Executive Board Reaches Agreement with Committee for Action through Unity to Change Name, Organizational Structure, and Salary Policy," press release, February 23, 1960, WA/UFT, Box 7, Folder 9.

136. Prior to the announcement of the budget, David Selden recalls, there was not much support for the work stoppage. "In order to reassure [Cogen], I drew up a 'pledge of support,' a petition-like sign-up sheet, so that I could estimate the amount of teacher support for the stoppage. Copies of the sheet were sent to the school chapter chairpersons, who were asked to report to the Guild office each week. But response to the pledge call was so poor that I had to pad the totals or risk cancellation of the walkout." Only after the revelation of the budget made teachers feel cheated did they start to sign up in large numbers. See David Selden, *The Teacher Rebellion* (Washington, DC: Howard University Press, 1985), 26.

137. Murphy, *Blackboard Unions*, 216.

138. Ibid., 217.

139. Charles Taylor Kerchner and Douglas E. Mitchell, *The Changing Idea of a Teachers Union* (Philadelphia: Falmer Press, 1988).

CHAPTER 7

1. Guy Brucy, *Histoire de la FEN* (Paris: Belin, 2004), 310.

2. Ibid.

3. But see Michael Duclaud-Williams, "Centralization and Incremental Change in France: The Case of the Haby Educational Reform," *British Journal of Political Science*

13 (1984): 71–91; Michael Duclaud-Williams, "Local Politics in Centralized Systems: The Case of French Education," *European Journal of Political Research* 13 (1985): 167–186.

4. The literature on the "May crisis" is immense. For useful perspectives on these events, see Daniel Singer, *From Prelude to Revolution: France in May 1968* (Cambridge, MA: South End Press, 1970); Alain Touraine, *The May Movement: Revolt and Reform*, trans. Leonard F. X. Mayhew (New York: Random House, 1971); Adrien Dansette, *Mai 1968* (Paris: Librairie Plon, 1971); Bernard E. Brown, "The French Revolt: May 1968" (New York: McCaleb-Seiler, 1970).

5. Dansette, *Mai 1968*, 39–40.

6. In fact, the disturbances at Nanterre dated back to 1966, when students had protested against the prohibition of opposite-sex visitors in the dormitories.

7. De Gaulle's year-old government dominated the legislature at this time, as evinced by the 427 to 71 victory of the Debré Law in the Chamber of Deputies. For more on the Debré legislation, see Aline Coutrot, "La loi scolaire de 1959," *Revue française de science politique* 13, no. 2 (1963): 352–388; Robert M. Healey, "The Year of the Debré Law," *Journal of Church and State* 12, no. 2 (Spring 1970): 213–235; James M. Clark, *Teachers and Politics in France: A Pressure Group Study of the Fédération de l'Éducation Nationale* (Syracuse, NY: Syracuse University Press, 1967), 141–163.

8. Brucy, *Histoire*, 322.

9. Singer, *Prelude*, 158.

10. Brucy, *Histoire*, 320.

11. Ibid., 321.

12. Ibid., 336.

13. Touraine, *The May Movement*, 106.

14. For summaries of these events, see Brucy, *Histoire*, 518–547; Frances Fowler, "The French FEN: Resistance to Economic Restructuring through Power Politics," in *Teacher Activism in the 1990s*, ed. Susan Robertson and Harry Smaller (Toronto: Lorimer, 1996), 191–204.

15. For more on the dispute over Intermediate School 201, see Naomi Levine, *Ocean Hill–Brownsville: A Case History of Schools in Crisis* (New York: Popular Library, 1969), 11–16; Barbara Carter, *Pickets, Parents, and Power: The Story behind the New York City Teachers' Strike* (New York: Citation Press, 1971), 6–15; Miriam Wasserman, *The School Fix, NYC, USA* (New York: Outerbridge and Dienstfrey, 1970), 211–306; and Diane Ravitch, *The Great School Wars: A History of New York City Schools* (Baltimore, MD: Johns Hopkins University Press, 1974), 292–311.

16. Beyond the works just cited, see Jerald E. Podair, *The Strike That Changed New York: Blacks, Whites, and the Ocean Hill–Brownsville Crisis* (New Haven, CT: Yale University Press, 2004); Jane Anna Gordon, *Why They Couldn't Wait: A Critique of the Black-Jewish Conflict over Community Control in Ocean-Hill–Brownsville,1967–1971* (New York: Routledge, 2001); Richard D. Kahlenberg, *Tough Liberal: Albert Shanker and the Battles over Schools, Unions, Race, and Democracy* (New York: Columbia University Press, 2007).

17. Kahlenberg, *Tough Liberal*, 110.

18. The importance of race and the politics of integration in the context of the teachers' collective bargaining revolution of the 1960s is an important story that has not received the attention it deserves. For the case of Philadelphia, see René Luis Alvarez, "'There's No Such Thing as an Unqualified Teacher': Unionization and Integration in the Philadelphia Public Schools," *The Historian* 65, no. 4 (2003): 837–865.

19. Marjorie Murphy, *Blackboard Unions* (Ithaca, NY: Cornell University Press, 1990), 242.

20. The African American–Jewish alliance in New York City, as elsewhere in the United States, did not always cross-cut class differences. For more on this topic, see Cheryl Lynn Greenberg, *Troubling the Waters: Black-Jewish Relations in the American Century* (Princeton, NJ: Princeton University Press, 2006).

21. Philip Taft, *United They Teach: The Story of the United Federation of Teachers* (Los Angeles: Nash, 1974), 217.

22. Ravitch, *The Great School Wars*, 378.

23. This reality attests to the long-term relationship between state formation and the patterning of gender inequalities in the workplace. For more reflections on this matter, see Alice Kessler-Harris, "In the Nation's Image: The Gendered Limits of Social Citizenship in the Depression Era," *Journal of American History* 86, no. 3 (1999): 1251–1279; Alice Kessler-Harris, "Reframing the History of Women's Wage Labor: Challenges of a Global Perspective," *Journal of Women's History* 15, no. 4 (2004): 186–206.

24. There was certainly a gendered dimension to the conflict over community control in the 1960s. Most of the strident advocates for community control in New York City were mothers in the African American communities of Brooklyn and Harlem. See Nancy A. Naples, "Materialist Feminist Discourse Analysis and Social Movement Research: Mapping the Changing Context for 'Community Control,'" in *Social Movements: Identity, Culture, and the State*, ed. David S. Meyer, Nancy Whittier, and Belinda Robnett (New York: Oxford University Press, 2002), 226–246.

25. For more on the particular importance of religious singing in Russian elementary schools, see Lynn M. Sargeant, "Singing the Nation into Being: Teaching Identity and Culture at the Turn of the Twentieth Century," *History of Education Quarterly* 49, no. 3 (2009): 291–322; Lynn M. Sargeant, "Whoever Can Speak Can Sing," *Paedagogica Historica* 46, no. 5 (2010): 601–622.

26. Patrick L. Alston, *Education and the State in Tsarist Russia* (Stanford, CA: Stanford University Press, 1969), 57–58.

27. Ben Eklof, "Worlds in Conflict: Patriarchal Authority, Discipline, and the Russian School, 1861–1914," in *School and Society in Tsarist and Soviet Russia*, ed. Ben Eklof (London: St. Martin's Press, 1992), 95–120.

28. Ibid., 240.

29. Scott Joseph Seregny, *Russian Teachers and Peasant Revolution: The Politics of Education in 1905* (Bloomington: Indiana University Press, 1989), 39–40.

30. Ibid., 41.

31. Ibid., 40–41.

32. Ibid., 7.

33. Ibid., 43–44.

34. Ibid., 54.

35. Scott J. Seregny, "Teachers, Politics, and the Peasant Community in Russia, 1895–1918," in Eklof, *School and Society*, 129. As previous chapters have suggested, Seregny's observation is an overstatement. The French government's support of its teachers had its limits.

36. William J. Reese, "'Partisans of the Proletariat': The Socialist Working Class and the Milwaukee Schools, 1890–1920," *History of Education Quarterly* 21, no. 1 (Spring 1981): 3–50; Victor L. Shradar, "Ethnicity, Religion, and Class: Progressive School Reform in San Francisco," *History of Education Quarterly* 20, no. 4 (Winter 1980): 385–401; David N. Plank and Paul E. Peterson, "Does Urban Reform Imply Class Conflict? The Case of Atlanta's Schools," *History of Education Quarterly* 23, no. 2 (Summer 1983): 151–173; William J. Reese, *Power and the Promise of School Reform: Grassroots Movements*

during the Progressive Era (New York: Teachers College Press, 2002); David Levine, "The Milwaukee Platoon School Battle: Lessons for Activist Teachers," *Urban Review* 34, no. 1 (March 2002): 47–69; Wayne J. Urban, *Why Teachers' Organized* (Detroit: Wayne State University Press, 1982).

37. For a thorough, nuanced evaluation of the role of Communism in the rise and fall of the TU, see Clarence Taylor, *Reds at the Blackboard: Communism, Civil Rights, and the New York City Teachers Union* (New York: Columbia University Press, 2011).

INDEX